ECONOMIC ACTIVITY

ECONOMIC ACTIVITY

BY

G. C. HARCOURT
Reader in Economics, University of Adelaide
Sometime Fellow of Trinity Hall, Cambridge

P. H. KARMEL
The Vice-Chancellor, The Flinders University of South Australia
Formerly George Gollan Professor of Economics
University of Adelaide

R. H. WALLACE
Reader in Economics
The Flinders University of South Australia

CAMBRIDGE
AT THE UNIVERSITY PRESS
1967

Published by the Syndics of the Cambridge University Press
Bentley House, 200 Euston Road, London, N.W. 1
American Branch: 32 East 57th Street, New York, N.Y. 10022

© Cambridge University Press 1967

Library of Congress Catalogue Card Number: 67–11521

Printed in Great Britain
at the University Printing House, Cambridge
(Brooke Crutchley, University Printer)

PREFACE

Economic Activity has its origins in a course of lectures given since 1950 to first-year undergraduates at the University of Adelaide. That course was originally given by P. H. Karmel; in later years the other two co-authors inherited it. Little attention was paid to financial factors in the first-year course. A second-year course of macro-economics (given on several occasions by R. H. Wallace) was built upon the first course, and in this the inter-relationships between the financial and production sectors of the economy were considered in detail. The second-year course was set in the context of the particular institutional framework of the Australian economy, and students were introduced to the relevant statistical material. The book draws upon material from both courses, but the discussion of the financial sector is essentially theoretical.

The book is Keynesian in spirit, and designed to give a simplified but rounded exposition of the workings of a modern mixed economy. Final drafts of the book were used for this purpose by G. C. Harcourt in a course of lectures given in the Lent and Michaelmas Terms, 1966, to undergraduates taking Part I of the Economics Tripos at the University of Cambridge. However, the book is designed so that it can be used in courses where the financial system is not considered in detail, and in that case chapters 6, 7 and 13 would be omitted. Chapters 4 to 7 and 10 could be used to cover the macroeconomic sections in an introductory survey course of economics.

The book is written in the belief that economists are best trained by an early introduction to economic theory. Once the student attains a certain level of skill in the manipulation of theoretical models, he can proceed to the real work of an economist—the examination of new problems with the aid of a theoretical model developed specifically for the purpose. Students at the University of Adelaide were encouraged to regard economic theory as a 'do-it-yourself construction kit'; for this purpose, simple quantitative problems which could be solved by the use of variants of the basic models presented in lectures proved to be a suitable basis for tutorial work.

While the book draws upon Australian experience for illustrations of the argument, it is a text-book of economic theory. The choice of the assumptions to be used was influenced by the nature of the

Australian economy. For example, the assumption that the level of production in the export sector is independent of the level of national income would not be appropriate to the British economy. Again, the Hicks–Hansen LM-IS analysis which is widely used in British and American text-books is not specifically used because, among other reasons, the assumptions which it implies about the capital market are not sufficiently applicable to the Australian situation.[1] It is inevitable that an introduction to Keynesian economics must be in terms of a highly simplified model; the authors consider it extremely important that students should be aware of the assumptions underlying the argument, and they have tried to make their own assumptions explicit, and also to define clearly the terms and concepts used. It is hoped that the book will prove a useful foundation for more advanced theoretical, and for applied, work in macroeconomics.

The authors have been greatly assisted by comments from many colleagues. In acknowledging specifically their gratitude to R. R. Hirst, H. F. Lydall and E. A. Russell of the University of Adelaide, M. J. Artis and K. J. Hancock of The Flinders University of South Australia, and C. A. E. Goodhart and G. Whittington of the University of Cambridge, it should not be thought that they are unaware of their indebtedness to many other economists. And they are most appreciative of the assistance given by their long-suffering, but cheerful, typists.

G. C. H.
P. H. K.
R. H. W.

---

[1] This is not meant to suggest that any particular originality is claimed for the alternative brief treatment of the interaction between the financial and production sectors. The argument of chapter 13 is obviously rooted in the Hicksian general equilibrium analysis.

CONTENTS

1

INTRODUCTION

Mass unemployment and year-to-year fluctuations in the level of economic activity were the major economic problems of the interwar years in advanced industrial economies. In the United Kingdom, unemployment did not fall below one million wage-earners for the whole of the interwar period; in Australia, for the same period, it was never less than $5\frac{1}{2}$ per cent of the work force, and for several years in the 1930s it exceeded 25 per cent. It is not surprising, therefore, that the main preoccupation of policy-makers and academic economists alike was to discover the causes of mass unemployment and fluctuations in economic activity, and to devise economic policies which would provide full employment. Pre-eminent among the economists analysing the causes of unemployment was John Maynard Keynes, the great Cambridge economist.[1] His book, *The General Theory of Employment, Interest and Money*, published in 1936, was the first systematic explanation of the forces which determine the level of economic activity and its associated level of employment; it provided the theoretical backing for subsequent economic policies designed to rid these economies of unemployment with its attendant human misery and waste.

In the post-war period discussions of economic policy have been concerned with other problems and other objectives of economic policy, as well as with the avoidance of mass unemployment. The problems include inflation, disequilibrium in the balance of payments, and continued, if less violent, fluctuations in the level of economic activity. Some idea of the extent of these fluctuations in Australia in the post-war period can be gauged from figures 1.1 and 1.2, which show respectively, GNP and GNP per head in average 1959–60 prices, from 1948–49 to 1962–63, and the principal economic indicators

---

[1] John Maynard Keynes (1883–1946), Fellow of King's College, Cambridge, and, among many other attainments in a relatively short but incredibly full life, confidential economic adviser to the Chancellor of the Exchequer in the Second World War. For a full account of Keynes's life and work, see R. F. Harrod, *The Life of John Maynard Keynes* (London: Macmillan, 1951) and E. A. G. Robinson, 'John Maynard Keynes, 1883–1946', *Economic Journal*, (March 1947).

for the same period. The rate of economic growth has also emerged as a vital concern of policy-makers. Economists are studying anew the factors underlying the rate of growth as well as those underlying the level of, and fluctuations in, economic activity.

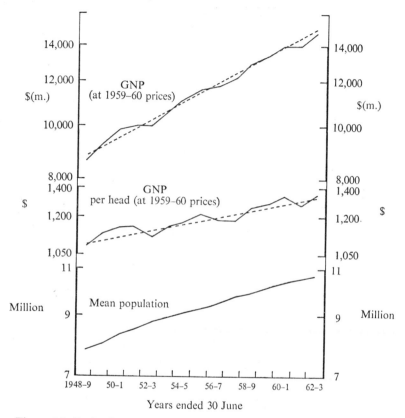

Figure 1.1. Ratio chart showing population, gross national product and gross national product per head at average 1959–60 prices, 1948–49 to 1962–63. [*Source*: Commonwealth Statistician: *Demography Bulletin*, no. 80, 1962; *Australian National Accounts 1948–49 to 1962–63*. (GNP at average 1959–60 prices has been linked to GNP at average 1953–54 prices.)]

The scheme of analysis developed by Keynes in *The General Theory* has been adapted to provide the basic mode of thought about this wider range of problems, and the appropriate economic policies with which to tackle them. This book is an introduction to the modern Keynesian theory of income-determination. Keynes's work not only involved major theoretical advances; it also led to a great improvement in the collection and publication of statistics. In particular, developments in the field of national (or social) accounting stem directly from the theoretical framework of *The General Theory*. It is

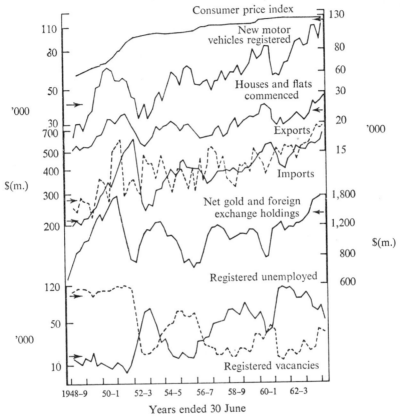

Figure 1.2. Ratio chart showing principal economic indicators, quarters 1948–49 to 1962–63. [*Source*: Consumer price index, new motor vehicles registered, houses and flats commenced, and imports and exports—Commonwealth Statistician; net gold and foreign exchange holdings—Reserve Bank; registered unemployed and registered vacancies—Department of Labour and National Service.]

not possible to understand the modern theory of income-determination until the relationships summarized in the national accounts have been mastered. Accordingly, chapter 2 of the book contains outlines of the principles which underly the construction of the national accounts, the major concepts involved in the accounts, and

3

the relationships between the concepts. The national product is shown to be a measure of economic activity. The discussion is based on current Australian practice and the illustrations are taken from Australian sources. But the same principles of national accounting are used in other advanced economies.

For most of the analysis in the later chapters, the interest lies chiefly in real quantities, that is, in the levels of real expenditure and production and the accompanying employment offered to the labour force. In the last section of chapter 3 there is a discussion of the procedure by which the influence of changes in the price level can be removed in order to measure the changes in the real national product.

The following chapters are primarily concerned with the forces which determine the level of economic activity in the short run, as measured by real national product. The short run is a period of time in which the aggregate stock of capital can be taken as given. In chapter 4, the basic idea that the level of economic activity is determined by the level of planned expenditure is presented. In the simplified economy postulated in chapter 4 the equilibrium level of activity is shown to be the outcome of the interplay of the planned real expenditure on consumption and investment goods and services (aggregate demand), with the production of goods and services (aggregate supply). It is shown that output tends to settle at the level where planned expenditures match output, and that this need not be the full employment level of output. Chapter 5 contains a discussion of the concept of full employment, and of the various types of unemployment. The concepts of the inflationary and deflationary gap, which measure the extent to which the actual level of aggregate demand differs from that necessary to give full employment without inflation, are introduced. In the final section of the chapter it is demonstrated that there is no reason to believe that full employment could be achieved by reducing money-wage rates in situations of unemployment.

Chapters 8 and 9 contain detailed discussions of the factors which determine the levels of planned consumption and investment expenditures respectively. The planned consumption expenditures of individual persons, of different income and occupational groups, and of the community as a whole, are considered. It is explained that there is a close relationship between consumption expenditure and personal real disposable income, but that other factors also influence expenditure decisions. In chapter 9, actual investment expenditure is shown to depend upon expected future sales and operating costs, the cost and availability of finance, the capacity of the existing capital stock and especially the capacity of the investment goods industries. Reasons are given for the instability of planned investment expenditure in the short period.

The influence of the quantity of money and the cost and availability of finance upon expenditure plans is discussed in chapters 6 and 7. The role of the central bank and of the trading banks is explained, and the various techniques whereby monetary policy can be implemented are also discussed.

In chapter 10 the consequences for the level of production and employment of changes in the expenditure plans of households and firms are explained. The important concept of the multiplier is introduced; it is shown that, in conditions of unemployment, an increase in the level of planned expenditure gives rise to an increment of output in excess of that produced to meet the initial increment of expenditure. The additional output is in response to the induced increment in consumption expenditure and its amount is shown to be dependent upon the magnitude of the leakage of income to personal saving.

The modifications to the analysis made necessary by the introduction of the government and oversea sectors are discussed in chapters 11 and 12. It is shown that changes in government expenditure and in the proceeds from export sales have impacts on the equilibrium level of economic activity which are analogous to those associated with changes in planned investment and consumption expenditures. Taxation and imports are shown to be analogous to saving, in that they represent leakages from the production–income–expenditure circuit. Three types of taxation, viz. lump sum, income and sales taxes, are discussed in chapter 11 and the multiplier analysis is extended to show the effects of changes in the level of government expenditure and the structure of taxation. In chapter 12, the multiplier analysis is applied to the open economy. The concepts of the balance of trade and the balance of payments and the relationships between the level of economic activity, the level of imports, and the balance of trade are explained.

To simplify the exposition, the argument to chapter 12 proceeds usually upon the assumption that the cost and availability of finance, and the general level of prices are unchanged. In chapter 13, the assumption that the cost and availability of finance, and the level of national product (valued at market prices) are determined independently is discarded, and the interaction between the financial and production sectors is considered.

The relationship between the general level of prices and the level of economic activity is discussed in chapter 14. It is shown that, while it may be possible in principle to distinguish elements of demand-pull and cost-push pressures as causes of inflation, in practice the two are usually inextricably intermingled. The chapter also considers the question as to whether once prices begin to rise they will continue to do so.

The final chapter is concerned with the objectives and making of economic policy. The arguments of the other chapters are drawn together, and used to show how the authorities in a modern mixed economy can attempt to achieve their objectives. It is explained why the various objectives of economic policy cannot all be simultaneously achieved. Consequently, the final decision as to the particular economic policy to be implemented must be made at the political level—the economist's task being to clarify the possible alternative courses of action open to society.

2

THE NATIONAL ACCOUNTS AND THE INCOME-CREATION PROCESS

This chapter differs from the others of this book in that it is designed, first, to explain a method of looking at the economy and, secondly, to define the basic concepts and measures—in particular, *national product, national income* and *domestic expenditure*—which are used below in the analysis of the determination of the level of economic activity. As economic activity is measurable it is important to understand exactly what each concept and measure means. It is also necessary to construct the national accounting framework, for the relationships between the economic aggregates of the later chapters are fitted into this framework. The following discussion is based upon two publications of the Commonwealth Statistician, the White Paper *National Income and Expenditure* which is published with the Budget Papers each August, and a recent publication, *Australian National Accounts.*[1] It should be noted that three terms used in the text, viz. *gross national income* (GNI), *gross market expenditure* (GME), and *gross domestic expenditure* (GDE), are not used in these official publications. However, the terms are applied to aggregates of items, details of which are given in these publications.

1. Entities and sectors

Reduced to the simplest terms the economic process consists of the production of goods and services, the rationale of which is their use either for consumption or for the production of additional goods and services. In modern economies, the producer of a good is not usually its consumer: goods must be transferred from producers to consumers. This is mainly done through transactions between buyers and sellers, although some services do not involve monetary exchanges, for example, the provision of government services such as law and order. Generally goods and services are sold for money, which consumers have acquired as incomes received from the sale of

---

[1] Commonwealth Bureau of Census and Statistics, *Australian National Accounts. National Income and Expenditure 1948–49 to 1963–64* (Government Printer, Canberra, 1965).

their services, for example, wages earned by the sale of labour to firms.

The entities which are responsible for organizing the production of goods and services are called *trading enterprises* and, in aggregate, they comprise the *trading enterprises sector* of the economy. The term 'trading enterprises' includes all forms of productive entities, manufacturing firms and trading organizations as well as entities selling services to the community. It covers incorporated businesses such as public and private companies, for example, Broken Hill Proprietary Company Ltd., and G. J. Coles and Company Ltd.; state-owned business undertakings, for example, Trans Australia Airlines and the Postmaster-General's Department; and unincorporated businesses such as partnerships and sole proprietorships, for example, medical partnerships, plumbing businesses and farms. The distinguishing feature of trading enterprises is that they organize the factors of production—labour, capital equipment, natural resources—in order to produce goods and services for sale.

A second sector of the economy is the *personal sector* (or *households sector*). It comprises the whole population viewed as the aggregate of economic entities, which, as consumers, enjoy the fruits of the production organized by the trading enterprises. Production results in incomes being paid in the form of wages and profits to the owners of the factors of production. In the case of labour, the productive factors are 'owned' directly by persons. Other factors may be legally owned by private enterprises, but, as these are legal fictions, all income flowing from privately owned trading enterprises can be regarded as accruing to individuals. These incomes enable persons to consume part of the production of trading enterprises.

The distinction between trading enterprises and persons is clear: the former organize production, usually in order to make profits; the latter purchase goods and services in order to satisfy their wants. One individual may be both a trading enterprise and a person, for example, a farmer who owns an unincorporated business. When he buys seed wheat, the farmer is acting as a trading enterprise; when he buys bread, he is acting as a consumer.

The distinction between the trading enterprises sector and the personal sector can be made in even the simplest type of economy. However, in a modern complex economy such as Australia, there are entities involved in economic transactions which do not fit into either of the above categories, so that other sectors must be distinguished.

The first of these is the *financial enterprises sector*. It consists of the trading and savings banks, hire purchase, insurance and assurance companies and other financial intermediaries which engage in borrowing and lending. Their function is to provide finance for the activities of the other sectors. Their assets are largely financial and they do not own equipment for the production of goods. Their role in the economy is sometimes likened to that of a lubricant in a machine.

A fourth sector is the *public authority* (or *government*) *sector*. In Australia the government sector comprises the non-trading activities of the Commonwealth, State and local governments and the semi-governmental authorities.[1] The non-trading economic activities of governments are mainly concerned with the provision of services for the collective consumption or use by the community. Examples are law and order, defence, public health and education. These are provided to the community as a whole, and are financed from taxation and loans. *Public enterprises*, that is, business undertakings owned by public authorities, are not included in the public authority sector but in the trading or financial enterprises sectors. This follows from the basic approach of dividing economic entities according to their economic function, not their legal form; thus, the trading enterprises sector includes both TAA and Ansett-ANA, and the financial enterprises sector includes both the Commonwealth Trading Bank and the privately owned trading banks. However, the net income of public enterprises is treated as being transferred to the government sector.

The provision of communal goods and services by governments affects the redistribution of *real* resources—the decision to build a road rather than a school involves a conscious, non-market, decision to provide benefits for road-users rather than school-users. Governments also redistribute *money* income through taxation and cash social service payments. In brief, the government sector uses non-

---

[1] Semi-governmental authorities are bodies established by legislation, or which governments have taken over, and which carry out defined activities on behalf of governments. Examples are the Reserve Bank of Australia, the State Electricity Commission of Victoria, the Snowy Mountains Hydro-electric Authority, the Australian Atomic Energy Commission, and the universities. If the authority is primarily concerned with operating a business it is not included in the government sector, but in one or other of the enterprise sectors. The Reserve Bank of Australia, for example, is a (publicly owned) financial enterprise, and the State Electricity Commission of Victoria, a (publicly owned) trading enterprise.

market techniques to alter the allocation of real resources and the distribution of money income.

The fifth sector, the *rest of the world* (or *oversea*) *sector*, contains those entities which are not resident in the domestic economy; that is, the entities to which exports are sold and those from which goods and services are imported.

The entities which undertake economic transactions can, then, be classified into five sectors, as follows:

Sector	Function
Trading enterprises	Organize production of marketed goods and services; seek profits*
Personal	Consume goods and services; seek satisfaction
Financial enterprises	Provide finance for activities of other sectors; seek profits
Government	Organize production of collective goods and services and redistribute money incomes; seek welfare of the community
Rest of the world	Takes account of economic relationships between the domestic economy and the rest of the world

* Publicly owned enterprises frequently aim to cover their costs, rather than to make surpluses.

The sector classification is useful because the different sectors have different functions, their economic activities are governed by different motives, and they respond in different ways to changes in economic circumstances or policy measures.

2. The concepts of national product, national income and domestic expenditure

(a) National product

The level of economic activity is reflected in the aggregate (or total) production of goods and services. The value of the aggregate production of final goods and services for a period in a particular economy is called the *national product*. The first estimates of the Australian national product were for annual periods. A year is a convenient period because most entities measure their annual income for taxation and accounting purposes. It should be noted, however, that the choice of a period is arbitrary, and since 1960 the Commonwealth Statistician has published quarterly as well as annual estimates of national product. These estimates are an important indicator of economic performance, and are basic information for policymaking.

The concept of national product can best be understood by considering the contribution of an individual trading enterprise to the production of goods and services over a particular year. Clearly this contribution is not the value of the physical output of the enterprise, because this includes the value of goods and services used in the production process which have been produced by other trading enterprises. The contribution to production of a particular enterprise is not great just because it uses expensive raw materials, the value of which is reflected in the value of its output. Rather, the productive contribution of an enterprise reflects *the work done within* the enterprise itself; accordingly, its contribution is defined as the value of its output over the year, less the value of inputs used up in the course of production, which were obtained from other enterprises. The latter are called *intermediate goods*. Examples are raw materials and legal services, both of which enter into the final products of the enterprise concerned. The intermediate goods of an enterprise are the finished outputs of other enterprises which supplied them.

The national product is produced by combining the services of labour with the stock of land and the capital stock of the economy. The capital stock at the beginning of any period consists of the goods and equipment which can be used in the productive process. It comprises the *stocks of goods* which can be used as intermediate goods during the period, together with the community's *productive equipment* (or *capital equipment*). This latter comprises those physical assets which can be used repeatedly in the process of producing *a stream of output*. Productive equipment may be owned by trading enterprises (both public and private) or it may be part of the stock of *social capital*. In the former case the capital equipment will be used either to aid the production of some good sold by the firm, for example, the buildings and machines owned by a biscuit manufacturer; or its services will be sold to other enterprises, for example, commercial buildings rented to tenants. The social capital is the stock of equipment which is owned by the government sector and is either made available to other users without charge, for example, roads, bridges, and museums; or is used within the government sector, for example, the buildings used for public administration. That part of the output of any period which is devoted either to additions to the capital stock or to replacing existing items in the stock is the gross investment expenditure of the period; it comprises investment in stocks and gross fixed capital expenditure.

It should be noted that in this book, unless the contrary is explicitly stated, the words 'capital' and 'investment' refer to real quantities, viz. to the stock, and increments to the stock of certain physical assets, respectively, valued at certain prices. In everyday usage both words are also used to refer to financial quantities, for example, the shareholders' equity in an enterprise may be referred to as the firm's 'capital'; the financial markets (stock exchange, banking system and so on) are sometimes referred to as the 'capital market'; the purchase, of land, shares, existing physical assets and many other financial transactions associated with changes in ownership are commonly referred to as 'investments'. In the main, in this book other terms are used for these financial quantities; the term 'capital market' is however, used to describe financial markets.

The value which an enterprise adds in the production process to its purchases of intermediate goods is the *value of production* or *value added* of the enterprise. Purchases of capital equipment are not regarded as purchases of intermediate goods because the capital equipment of an enterprise wears out only slowly. Nevertheless, capital equipment is partially used up in the production of any period. This using-up, or *depreciation*, is measured by the decline in the value of the capital stock over the period. Conceptually, depreciation is as much an input into current production as are intermediate goods, but in practice it is extremely difficult to estimate.[1] For national accounting purposes, value added is calculated *gross of depreciation*, that is, before allowing for depreciation.

The value of the annual output of an enterprise is the sum of its annual sales to other enterprises together with the change over the year in the value of its stocks of finished or semi-finished goods. This change represents the enterprise's investment expenditure upon stocks and it may be positive or negative. The value of the annual inputs used up in the production of the annual output is the sum of the annual purchases by the enterprise from other enterprises and the

---

[1] There is no generally agreed definition of depreciation. Economists and accountants tend to disagree on the question, which is discussed further in chapter 3 (see pp. 28–29).

change over the year in the value of stocks of inputs. It follows that the annual value added of an enterprise is:

(i) sales of output during the year
and (ii) additions to stocks of finished or semi-finished goods during the year

less

(iii) purchases of intermediate goods and services during the year
and (iv) depletions of stocks of intermediate goods during the year.

When all types of stocks are combined, value added is:

(i) sales of output during the year
and (ii–iv) *net* additions to stocks *of all kinds* during the year

less

(iii) purchases of intermediate goods during the year.

All quantities referred to are expressed in money terms by valuing goods and services at their current market prices.

The following example illustrates the concept of value added. Suppose that a firm starts the year with stocks of finished and semi-finished goods of $1,000 and stocks of intermediate goods of $500. During the year it buys intermediate goods of $2,000 and makes sales of $4,000. Suppose that it finishes the year with stocks of finished goods of $1,100 and intermediate goods of $450. Its value added (in $) therefore is

sales (4,000) + net change in stocks of all kinds ([1,100–1,000] + [450–500]) – purchases (2,000) = value added (2,050).

Governments purchase certain goods and services from trading enterprises, employ public servants and, as a result, provide collective goods and services to the community. They do this without making direct charges. By analogy with the value added of a trading enterprise, the value added of the government sector is defined as the value of collective goods and services provided *less* the value of the goods purchased from trading enterprises (these are intermediate goods from the viewpoint of the government). As the collective goods and services are not sold, they have no market prices. By convention, they are valued at cost, that is, at the cost of the purchases entering into them *plus* the wages and salaries of public servants. It follows that the value added of the government sector is equal to the wages and salaries paid to public servants.

The income of financial enterprises is obtained mainly from the excess of their interest receipts over their interest payments—the income from the sale of their services is usually relatively small. But it is the provision of these services which most nearly corresponds to the outputs of the trading enterprises and government sectors. The interest receipts arise from the ownership of financial assets and not from the provision of current services. Accordingly, the output of financial enterprises may be defined in terms of the value of the services that they provide. However, the charges made by financial enterprises for their services are frequently much less than the cost of providing them (and in some cases no direct charges are made). For national accounting purposes these services are valued at cost; that is, the value of the output of financial enterprises equals the sum of their current purchases of goods and services from trading enterprises and the wages and salaries that they pay to their employees. It follows that the value added by financial enterprises also equals the wages and salaries paid to their employees.

All production in an economy occurs in these three sectors. It is valued at market prices, directly in the case of trading enterprises, and indirectly in the case of the other two sectors. The sum of the values added of the three sectors is the *Gross National Product at Market Prices* or *GNP*. Defining GNP in this way is equivalent to saying that it is the value of the output of all goods and services produced over the year, *less* the value of intermediate goods (that part of this total which is used up in the production of the year, whether produced during the year or drawn from stocks). The deduction of these two items is necessary in order to avoid including the value of any good more than once in the total, that is, to avoid *double-counting*.

This definition of GNP is equivalent to saying that the GNP is a measure of the volume of goods and services produced over the year valued at current market prices, such goods and services being in their *final* form as far as the year under consideration is concerned. Final goods and services are those which are produced in the year and are subject to no further production processes in the year. The inclusion of the qualification, 'final', ensures that no goods which enter into the production of others are counted separately in GNP; for example, meat which has been used to produce sausages is counted in the value of the sausages and it is only meat which has been sold in an unprocessed form to domestic consumers or oversea purchasers, or which has been added to stocks, that is included separately as a component of GNP.[1]

(b) National income

Another aspect of the economic process is the *distribution* of the values added in the three productive sectors as the GNP is created. The values added are divided between:

(1) *Depreciation allowances*: funds retained in trading and financial enterprises as a result of allowing for the using-up of capital equipment in the process of production.

(2) *Company income and the surplus of public enterprises*: the surpluses of trading enterprises (after meeting all their costs) which are available to pay interest, dividends and company income tax, or to be retained in companies as undistributed company income; in the case of public enterprises, the surplus is transferred to the government sector.

(3) *Personal income*: wages and salaries earned by persons together with the profits of unincorporated businesses.

(4) *Indirect taxes less subsidies*: indirect taxes are those assessed on bases other than income.[2] Examples are sales taxes, import duties, motor registration fees and dog licences.

The total of the above items is called the *Gross National Income* or *GNI*. As they are a classification of value added (or GNP), GNI must equal GNP. Except for depreciation and indirect taxes, these items accrue as income receipts to the owners of the factors of production. Indirect taxes are assumed to raise prices. In some instances government subsidies are paid to producers; these allow products to be sold at lower prices than would otherwise be the case and the incomes of the factors of production concerned are then derived from the subsidies received, as well as from the sale of the products. The value of production which is distributed to the private sector is then the market value of production *plus* the subsidies

---

[1] The discussion in the text is concerned with the concept of GNP. The measurement of GNP gives rise to many practical difficulties; for example: Should the value of illegal activities enjoyed by consumers be included? Should the services of owner-occupied houses or only those of rented houses, be included? These practical difficulties are 'solved' by the adoption of arbitrary conventions.

[2] In the *Australian National Accounts* estate and gift duties are treated as direct taxes.

received and *less* the indirect taxes. The net surplus of indirect taxes over subsidies is the *initial* distribution of value added to the government sector. GNI *less* depreciation and *net* indirect taxes (that is, indirect taxes less subsidies) is called *Net National Product at Factor Cost*. In the case of Australia, this item *less* net income payable overseas is called *National Income*. This is the sum of the incomes earned by factors of production resident in the domestic economy and producing the national product.

The previous paragraph described the *initial distribution* of gross national income, that is, the distribution to the factors which are responsible for producing the national product, together with net indirect taxes and depreciation. However, various transfers of income take place *between* the sectors before the incomes actually available to each sector for disposal are arrived at. The latter is referred to as the *final distribution of income*. Thus, companies pay interest to financial enterprises, dividends to persons and company income taxes to the government. The net surpluses of public enterprises are paid to the government. Persons pay taxes to governments, and governments pay pensions, child endowment, and other cash allowances to persons; in the Australian case income taxes are greater than these other transfer payments so that there is a net transfer from persons to governments. Financial enterprises receive interest and dividends on their loans and property holdings; some of this is paid as company income taxes and another portion represents dividends paid to shareholders. A further portion may be regarded as used to finance the financial enterprises' current expenditure on goods and services, and their wage and salary payments; the residual amount may be regarded as allocated to depreciation allowances and retained company income.[1]

Hence the *final distribution* of gross national income[2] takes the following form:

(1) Depreciation allowances—retained by trading and financial enterprises.

---

[1] This is a simplified account of the treatment of financial enterprises in the *Australian National Accounts*.

[2] 'Initial' and 'final' do not denote a time sequence; rather, they reflect the fact that the same contemporaneous flow of production, income and expenditure can be looked at from different viewpoints. For example, if households are regarded as providing labour services, all wages are viewed as flowing to them; if they are regarded as taxpayers, wages split into two streams, direct taxation flowing to the government and the residual flowing to households.

(2) Undistributed company income (the balance of company income after transfers to the personal, financial enterprises, and government sectors)—retained by trading enterprises.

(3) *Personal disposable income*—personal income after the payment of direct taxation and the receipt of transfer payments from governments and enterprises (other than non-incorporated businesses).

(4) Net taxation or the current revenue of the government sector— that is, the taxation collected, both indirect (net of subsidies paid) and direct, and the net surplus of public enterprises, *less* cash social service benefits.

(5) Property income of financial enterprises received from the trading enterprises sector, *less* taxation paid, dividends and interest redistributed to the personal sector and depreciation allowances and retained income transferred to the trading enterprises sector.

From the definitions used, GNI must be of identical value to GNP.

(c) Domestic expenditure

The expenditure on goods and services by the five sectors can be classified as follows:

(1) *Consumption expenditure*: the goods and services purchased by persons to satisfy their current consumption wants.

(2) *Gross investment expenditure* (by the non-government sectors): the goods purchased by trading and financial enterprises to replace and augment their capital equipment and the goods retained by trading enterprises to add to their stocks, together with the value of new dwelling construction.[1]

(3) *Government expenditure*: the goods and services purchased by the government sector for collective current consumption and capital formation.

(4) *Financial enterprises expenditure*: the goods and services purchased by the financial enterprises sector.

(5) *Exports*: the expenditure of the rest of the world on the goods and services of the domestic economy.

The expenditures made in these five categories include the goods and services imported from overseas, which are not part of the production of the domestic economy. In order to determine the

---

[1] The majority of new houses are purchased by owner-occupiers. Conceptually, owner-occupiers are trading enterprises which sell house-services to themselves. The Commonwealth Statistician includes in GNP an estimate of the value of these services; in 1964–65 this item was approximately 4 per cent of GNP.

expenditures which stimulate domestic economic *activity*, as distinct from expenditures on goods and services passing through the Australian market, *imports* must be deducted from the total of the above five categories. As far as the domestic economy is concerned imports are *intermediate goods*.

It should be noted that the term, *gross investment expenditure*, refers to the gross capital formation of the entities in the market (or non-government) sector. These are the entities, the investment decisions of which are made in the light of a comparison of the net revenues expected as a result of the proposed investment, the initial outlay on the investment project, and the cost of investment funds.[1] This sector includes all trading enterprises (including public or government-owned enterprises) and financial enterprises. Strictly, the term 'gross investment expenditure by the non-government sector' should be used, but for brevity the shorter term, 'gross investment expenditure', is used.

Some part of government expenditure is also in the nature of investment expenditure, that is, it is expenditure on items not completely consumed during the year. Such investment, for example, road construction, and the building of public libraries and museums adds to the stock of *social capital*. All government (or public authority) expenditure involves political, not market-determined, decisions. Both capital and current government expenditures are made by the same decision-making entities, and from the viewpoint of their short-run impact upon production, employment and income, the distinction is not relevant. The basis for distinguishing the components of *final* expenditure is the motives of the entities making the expenditures (see p. 10, above). For this reason government expenditure, including expenditure on social capital, is considered as one component item of final expenditure.

The *Australian National Accounts* uses the term *gross national expenditure* (GNE) for the sum of consumption, gross private investment, financial enterprises and government expenditures (all gross of their import content). That is, GNE is the total expenditure by domestic entities on goods and services. For the purpose of this book it is useful to distinguish two other aggregates. First, *gross market expenditure* (GME) describes the total expenditure on goods

---

[1] In the case of investment in private houses, non-monetary considerations such as the pride of ownership and opportunity costs, for example, rental payments escaped, take the place of expected net revenues in these comparisons.

and services (gross of imports) made by all entities whether domestic or oversea. GME is equal then to GNE *plus* exports. The other aggregate distinguished is *gross domestic expenditure* (GDE). This comprises all forms of expenditure *net* of their import contents. That is, GDE is equal to GME *less* expenditure upon imports.

The basic argument of this book is that the level of domestic economic activity in the short run is primarily determined by the level of aggregate expenditure. The level of imports is influenced by the level of GME, but as imports are an intermediate good from the viewpoint of the domestic economy, it is expenditure net of imports, that is, GDE, which is directly relevant to a discussion of the level of domestic economic activity. It will now be shown that when GNP is defined as the sum of the values added of each sector, it is also equal to the GDE. This can be seen from the following:

GNP ≡ value added by trading enterprises
　　　+ values added by financial enterprises
　　　+ value added by governments.

Reference to the definitions of value added given on pp. 12–15 shows that these can be written:

sales to persons	(i)
+ sales to governments	(ii)
+ sales to financial enterprises	(iii)
+ sales to rest of world	(iv)
+ sales of intermediate goods to other trading enterprises	(v)
+ sales of capital equipment to other enterprises (both trading and financial)	(vi)
+ net additions to stocks of all kinds	(vii)
− purchases of intermediate goods from other enterprises	(viii)
− purchases from rest of world	(ix)
+ wages paid to public servants	(x)
+ wages paid to employees of financial enterprises	(xi)

Items (v) and (viii) cancel out. Item (i) is consumption expenditure, items (vi) and (vii) make up gross investment expenditure, items (ii) and (x) make up government expenditure, items (iii) and (xi) make up financial enterprises expenditure, item (iv) is exports and item (ix) is imports.

Hence GNP *equals* consumption expenditure (i) *plus* gross investment expenditure [(vi) and (vii)] *plus* government expenditure [(ii) and (x)] *plus* financial enterprises expenditure [(iii) and (xi)] *plus* exports (iv) *less* imports (ix). Therefore GNP *equals* GDE. Now GNP = GDE, but GNP = GNI; hence GDE = GNP = GNI.

The various components of these national accounting concepts for Australia in 1964–65 are shown in Table 2.1.

The equality of GDE and GNI may be demonstrated in another way. GDE is the total expenditure, net of imports, on final goods and services in a particular period. Consider the purchase of a bottle of beer from a hotel. Its market price may be broken down into the following components: indirect tax, import content, depreciation allowances and the incomes of the owners of the factors of production employed in the various trading enterprises associated with its production. Suppose that, of the original expenditure of 60 c., 15 c. is indirect tax paid to the government, 10 c. is the barmen's wages, 15 c. is the owner's gross surplus of which 5 c. is depreciation, and 20 c. is paid to the brewery for the bottle of beer. Similarly, this 20 c. can be broken down into its various components: wages of 2 c., gross surplus of 5 c. of which 2 c. is depreciation, and material inputs of 13 c. of which 3 c. is for an imported bottle and 10 c. is for malt purchased from the maltster. The 10 c., in turn, can be broken down into its components.

In Table 2.2 (i) the allocation of the sales receipts of the four enterprises is traced through the various stages of production. The total sales receipts are resolved into their four components: indirect tax, material inputs, depreciation and the net incomes of the owners of domestic factors of production. In Table 2.2 (ii) it is shown that the values added at each stage of production are equal to the wages and gross surplus associated with that stage, plus any indirect tax component; to include items other than the final expenditure of 60 c. *less* the import component of 3 c. in GDE or GNP would involve counting more than once the value of the domestic economic activity involved in the production of the bottle of beer.

Gross national product and net national product

GNP at market prices measures the total value of the production of goods and services gross of the allowance for the depreciation of capital equipment which occurs during the year. If the whole of GNP were used up for current purposes, the economy would not maintain its capital intact. This could continue for only a few years without damage to the productive capacity of the economy.[1] By deducting

---

[1] In war-time, the level of replacement expenditure is considerably less than the levels considered desirable in peace-time. This inevitably leaves a legacy for the post-war period of an obsolete and well-worn capital stock.

TABLE 2.1. *GNP, GNI and GDE, Australia, 1964–65 ($m.)*

(Source: *National Income and Expenditure, 1964–65*)

Sector	GNP		GNI		GDE	
Trading enterprises	Value added	17,348	Depreciation	1,432	Gross investment expenditure	4,830
			Company income	1,854		
			Surplus of public enterprises	452		
Personal			Wages and salaries	9,804	Consumption expenditure	11,540
			Income of unincorporated businesses	3,528*		
			Personal income	13,332		
Government	Value added	1,656†	Indirect taxes *less* subsidies:	2,054	Government expenditure	2,838
Financial enterprises	Value added	120†			Financial enterprises expenditure	340‡
					GNE	19,548
					Plus Exports	3,004
Rest of the world					GME	22,552
					Less Imports	3,428
Total	GNP	19,124	GNI	19,124	GDE	19,124

* Includes imputed income to owner-occupiers of houses.
† Estimate.
‡ Includes statistical discrepancy.

TABLE 2.2. *Components of the final expenditure of 60 c. on a bottle of beer (in cents)*

(i) Sales receipts

Trading enterprise	Sales receipts or value of output	equals	Indirect taxes	plus	Material inputs		plus	Wages	plus	Gross surplus	
					Imports	Domestic				Net surplus	Depreciation
Hotel	60 (bottle of beer)	=	15	+	.	20 (bottle of beer)	+	10	+	10	5
Brewery	20 (bottle of beer)		.		3 (bottle)	10 (malt)		2		3	2
Maltster	10 (malt)		.		.	4 (barley)		3		2	1
Farmer	4 (barley)		.		.	.		2		1	1
Total	94	=	15	+	3	+ 34	+	17	+	16	+ 9

(ii) Value added

Value added

Trading Enterprise	Value of output	less	Value of inputs	equals	Value added
Hotel	60	−	20	=	40
Brewery	20	−	13*	=	7
Maltster	10	−	4	=	6
Farmer	4	−	.	=	4
Total	94	−	37	=	57

Distribution of value added

	Value added	equals	Indirect taxation	plus	Depreciation	plus	Incomes produced	
							Wages	plus Net surplus
Hotel	40	=	15	+	5	+	10	+ 10
Brewery	7	=	.	+	2	+	2	+ 3
Maltster	6	=	.	+	1	+	3	+ 2
Farmer	4	=	.	+	1	+	2	+ 1
Total	57	=	15	+	9	+	17	+ 16

* Includes imported bottle, 3c. (The value added created in the rest of the world.)

from GNP depreciation allowances, which are estimates of the amount of capital equipment used up in the productive process, *net national product at current market prices* (NNP) is obtained. It measures the *net* volume of goods and services produced whilst maintaining capital intact; it indicates the volume of production which can be used for current purposes without diminishing the economy's capital equipment. By analogy, *net investment expenditure* is gross investment expenditure less depreciation, and it measures the net increase in the capital stock (including inventories) over the year.

Market supplies and expenditures

The sum of GNP and imports of goods and services is *market supplies* or, as it is described in *Australian National Accounts,* the *national turnover of goods and services;* it comprises the total supplies of goods and services coming on to the market of the domestic economy. These market supplies are matched by the five categories of final expenditure: namely, consumption expenditure, gross investment expenditure, government expenditure, financial enterprises expenditure and exports. This *gross market expenditure,* which emanates from both domestic and foreign sources, is matched by the available supplies of goods and services which are both produced domestically and imported from overseas.

Finally, it should be noted that the equalities between the various aggregates set out above are *accounting identities* and do not 'prove' anything. The identities emerge because of the definitions of the items under consideration. They are of the same character as the accounting identity: revenue $\equiv$ expenses + profit. As long as profit is defined as the excess of revenue over expenses, this identity always holds. To show that a given equality is an identity, the symbol, $\equiv$, will be used, and, in the following chapters of this book, the symbol $=$, is used for equalities other than identities.

3

THE PRODUCTION–INCOME–EXPENDITURE CIRCUIT AND NATIONAL ACCOUNTING IDENTITIES

In this chapter, the basic viewpoint of the economic process adopted in the analysis of the determination of the level of economic activity is described and the national accounting identities which correspond to the economic models of the later chapters are set out. The units in which the macroeconomic quantities of these chapters are measured are then discussed.

1. The production–income–expenditure circuit in a two-sector economy

(a) A simplified economy

The economic process can be pictured as a flow system. In a simplified economy, which has only personal and trading enterprises sectors and in which there is neither investment expenditure nor saving,[1] the services of the factors of production flow from the personal sector to the trading enterprises. The latter organizes the factors to produce consumer goods and services, which flow back to the personal sector. These are real flows, as distinct from money flows; they comprise services rendered and goods and services produced. They have, as counterparts, money flows, that is, income payments for the services of the factors of production, and payments for the purchase of the goods and services produced. This process is shown in figure 3.1. The real flows are shown by the solid lines, the money flows by the broken lines.

It is most important to appreciate that the real and money flows are counterparts of one another. Any given economic pattern can be described either in real or money terms, but for reasons of practical measurement it is much easier to describe economic activity in money terms.[2]

---

[1] This implies that all personal disposable income is devoted to consumption expenditure. For a discussion of personal saving, see below, pp. 26–28.

[2] The assumptions involved in, and limitations of descriptions of real activity by monetary dimensions are discussed in section 4 below.

In the simplified economy illustrated in figure 3.1 all production consists of consumption goods and services, and all incomes earned in the production process are spent on consumption goods. Such an economy has a self-sustaining flow of expenditure, production and income; that is, there are no leakages from, or injections into, the circular flow of income between the households and the trading

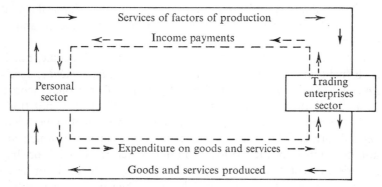

Figure 3.1.

enterprises. The following symbols are used to denote the national income concepts of this economy:

Y GNP (gross values added by trading enterprises);

Y_p personal disposable income;

C consumption expenditure.

All quantities are measured in market prices. The basic identities of this economy are:

$$C \equiv Y, \tag{3.1}$$

$$Y \equiv Y_p, \tag{3.2}$$

$$Y_p \equiv C. \tag{3.3}$$

Identity (3.1) indicates that final expenditure (which, in this case, consists only of consumption expenditure) matches production; (3.2) indicates that all of the incomes earned in the production process are distributed to the personal sector; and (3.3) that all of these incomes are spent on consumption goods.

(b) Leakages and offsets in the two-sector economy

Suppose now that part of personal income is not spent on consumption goods. Personal disposable income not spent on consumption goods is *saving*. Viewed in isolation, saving is a *leakage* from the circular flow of consumption expenditure, production and income. Because some part of the income received is allocated to uses other than expenditure on current output the saving leakage, if it were not offset, would cause the flow to shrink with each round of the income–expenditure circuit.

However, not all expenditure arises from personal income, nor is it all spent on consumption goods. In particular, *investment expenditure* or *capital formation* is not directly related to personal income. In a *closed, two-sector economy*, that is, one which does not trade with the rest of the world, and has no government, investment expenditure is defined as current expenditure on goods which are not consumed in the period. Trading enterprises build or buy factories, machines and plants, and add to their stocks, in order to maintain or increase production. They do so because they expect that by combining capital with labour they will make profits. Such expenditure is not financed directly out of the sales receipts from consumers' expenditure but from the retained income of the enterprises, together with external finance from new share issues and borrowings. Such expenditure is an *injection* into the expenditure–income flow, and acts as an offset to the leakage through saving.

The following are the basic identities of the closed, two-sector economy in which saving, S, and investment expenditure, I, are occurring:

$$C+I \equiv Y \text{ (expenditure matches production),} \qquad (3.4)$$
$$Y \equiv Y_p \text{ (production is distributed as income),} \qquad (3.5)$$
$$Y_p \equiv C+S \text{ (income is disposed of).} \qquad (3.6)$$

From which it follows that

$$S \equiv I. \qquad (3.7)$$

The first three identities describe current income relationships; the fourth is a capital account.

(c) The equality of saving and investment

This equality of saving and investment is an important national accounting identity which holds in the simplified two-sector economy,

26

and which follows from the definitions used. But it is most important to note that saving and investment expenditure are *not* the same thing. Saving refers to personal disposable income which is allocated to purposes other than the current purchase of consumption goods and services. Investment expenditure refers to expenditures on goods other than consumption goods. The saving by an entity could be in the form of the acquisition of a financial asset, for example, an increase in the entity's holding of money or bonds; or in the form of the acquisition of an existing asset, for example, a block of land or an existing house. On the other hand, a farmer may save part of his current income and use the proceeds to buy a new tractor. It can be said, therefore, that an act of saving may, but need not necessarily, coincide with an act of investment expenditure by the saving entity. The savers may be, and usually are, different entities from the investors, and governed by different motives.

(d) *Saving, money flows and the finance of investment*

Some personal saving may be regarded as being made available to trading enterprises to finance their investment expenditure. But, it must be stressed that the unspent income of a given period is not in general the direct source of finance of the investment expenditure of the same period. It is possible, for example, that the current investment expenditure of firms is directly financed by borrowing from households which are not currently saving; that is, the investing firms may currently not be saving at all, and the households which are currently saving may not be transmitting any of their money balances to the investing firms.

Money flows are not confined to flows of income and expenditure, though these involve money flows. It is possible to distinguish money outlays by entities associated with their expenditure on consumption and investment goods, and money outlays which are associated with reallocations of existing assets. Because income accrues to entities in the form of money, an act of saving, other things being equal, will mean initially an increase in the money balances of the saving entities. The *wealth* of an entity is its stock of assets, both real and financial, in excess of its obligations to other entities. This wealth represents the accumulated savings of the entity over the past. Individual entities are continuously rearranging the form of their wealth-holding, for example, by exchanging money for shares, or a block of land for money, and these asset transactions also involve money flows. The change in the money balances of an entity over a period can exceed or fall short of its current saving, because of this reshuffling of assets.[1]

(e) Company saving

So far it has been assumed that persons are the only entities which save; also the problem of accounting for depreciation has been assumed away. In fact, enterprises save by retaining part of their surplus or profits. These funds may be used in their own businesses or loaned to other entities. If profits gross of depreciation are considered, *gross company saving* (or *retained company income*) can be split into two categories: *depreciation allowances, D,* and *undistributed company income, U.*

Depreciation allowances lead automatically to funds being retained in trading enterprises instead of being distributed to the owners of the factors of production. Such funds need not be held as cash. They may be used in the enterprise to buy financial assets or to finance the holding of stocks or to buy new capital equipment. Furthermore, those trading enterprises which are incorporated as public or private companies usually retain a further portion of their net profits as *undistributed company income.* Unincorporated trading enterprises are deemed to distribute all their surplus (after allowing for depreciation and interest payments) to their owners, so that any saving from the incomes of these entities is included in *personal* saving. Total saving by the private sectors therefore consists of personal saving and gross company saving. This total is known as *gross private saving.*

(f) Gross and net investment

Capital equipment is used up in the production process; part of the current expenditure on capital equipment therefore serves to maintain the existing stock intact rather than to augment it. The symbol, *I*, refers to gross investment expenditure and that portion of it which serves to maintain capital intact is *conventionally assumed* to equal depreciation allowances.

This convention can be misleading for three reasons: first, the lengths of life of items of capital equipment implied in the calculation

---

[1] Total money flows are recorded by another national accounting technique, the flow-of-funds. A set of such accounts for Australia is presented in A. S. Holmes, *Flow-of-Funds, Australia, 1953–54 to 1961–62* (Staff Paper, Reserve Bank of Australia).

of annual depreciation allowances are often not true reflections of their actual economic lives. Secondly, depreciation allowances, as measured by accountants and the taxation authorities,[1] usually ignore changes in the replacement costs of fixed assets; this can lead to serious problems in periods of rapidly changing prices. Thirdly, actual replacement expenditure usually occurs when capital equipment is retired and scrapped, that is, it is related to the close of the economic lives of the assets concerned. Depreciation allowances, on the other hand, reflect the using up of all items of capital equipment that are currently engaged in production, whether they are near the end of their lives or not. Consequently, when the overall stock of capital equipment increases from year to year, the current depreciation *allowances* of a period, which relate to the current stock of equipment, may exceed current *expenditure* on the replacement of those items which were installed when the overall stock of equipment was smaller.

However, the practical problem of measuring the rate of growth of the 'actual' capital stock is not particularly relevant to the present discussion. This book is concerned primarily with an analysis of the determination of the level of economic activity in the short run. It is shown later that this depends primarily upon the level of spending; it is spending which constitutes a demand for production. It follows that it is gross investment expenditure (the spending upon capital goods) and not the 'actual' net increment to the capital stock for a period, which is relevant to the argument.

The basic identities have to be modified to take account of depreciation allowances and undistributed company income. GNP, GNI and GDE are always identical, but personal disposable income is now less than GNI by the amounts of depreciation allowances and undistributed company income. Personal saving no longer equals investment expenditure, I, but *total gross saving*, $S+D+U \equiv I$. The identities therefore are:

$$C+I \equiv Y, \tag{3.8}$$

$$Y \equiv Y_p+D+U, \tag{3.9}$$

$$Y_p \equiv C+S. \tag{3.10}$$

From which it follows that

$$S+D+U \equiv I. \tag{3.11}$$

[1] The latter are the main basis of the estimates of depreciation allowances published in the *Australian National Accounts*.

2. The full economy

Government expenditure on goods and services, G, financial enterprises expenditure on goods and services, F, and exports of goods and services, X, are injections of final expenditures made independently of the personal income–consumption–expenditure flow. As such they are offsets to saving, akin to investment expenditure. Taxation, both indirect and direct, and imports, are analogous to saving, in that they too are leakages from the circular flow of income–expenditure–production. These further offsets and leakages are now considered in the context of the national accounts and basic identities of an economy which has a government sector, a financial enterprises sector and which trades with the rest of the world. Such an economy may be referred to as an *open, five-sector economy* or a *full economy*. This contrasts with the *closed, two-sector economy* of the previous section. The ultimate purpose of this book is the analysis of the determination of the level of economic activity, and the possibility of controlling it, in a full economy such as Australia.

Government expenditure is final expenditure on goods and services which represent collective consumption or social capital formation for the whole community. Typical examples are defence expenditure; road construction; the maintenance of government schools and hospitals together with the employment of their staffs; garbage collection. The amount of such expenditure is determined by what the government considers to be the appropriate relative shares of the public and private sectors in the use of the resources of the economy.

The task of the financial enterprises sector is to assist in financing the economy's activities. As will become clear in later chapters, it is final expenditures on goods and services which determine the levels of employment of the labour force and capital equipment of an economy. From this viewpoint it is expenditure by the financial enterprises sector on goods and services which is the relevant item of GDE. In fact, this sector's expenditure on goods and services is relatively small—in Australia it is approximately equal to 1 per cent of GNP. For this reason it is ignored in subsequent chapters. However, the financial operations of the sector have important consequences through their influence upon the expenditure of the other sectors (see, in particular, chapters 6, 7 and 13 below).

Exports, the purchases by overseas countries of the products of the domestic economy, are a further injection of expenditure into the circular flow of domestic income, production and expenditure.

Indirect taxes are a leakage from the flow, in that they are those portions of the sales proceeds of commodities which do not accrue as income payments to the factors of production, but are collected by the government. Direct or income taxes are levies on the incomes earned by companies and persons. Direct taxes represent those portions of these incomes which are not available for spending or saving (in the case of persons) and for distribution or gross saving (in the case of companies). Direct and indirect taxes less subsidies (which conceptually are negative indirect taxes) are referred to by the symbol, T.

Imports, M, are a leakage from the point of view of the domestic economy because expenditure on them creates income in the oversea economy, not in the domestic economy. In summary, the leakages from the flow of income in the full economy are saving, taxation and imports; and the offsets are investment, government and financial enterprises expenditures and exports.

In the open economy GNP can be defined on a *geographical* or a *residential* basis. The former refers to the production of final goods and services by the factors of production resident in the domestic economy, irrespective of whether or not they are owned by residents in the economy. Some firms in the domestic economy may be foreign-owned, or controlled; the operations of such firms give rise to demand for domestic labour and capital and add to domestic market supplies. General Motors-Holden is an obvious example of an American-owned firm operating in Australia.

Residential GNP refers to the incomes which accrue to persons who normally live in the economy, regardless of where the production which is the source of this income occurs. If the incomes earned by, say, Australian-owned, overseas-located assets are more than the incomes earned from Australian-located, overseas-owned assets, residential GNP will be more than geographical GNP and vice versa. The *Australian National Accounts* is concerned with GNP defined on a geographical basis. In the analysis of later chapters this complication is usually ignored. It is assumed (unless the contrary is specifically indicated) that there is no international ownership of assets, which implies that current international income flows arise from expenditures on exports and imports of goods and services only.

The basic identities of the full economy[1] are:

$$C+I+G+X-M \equiv Y, \tag{3.12}$$

$$Y \equiv Y_p+D+U+T, \tag{3.13}$$

$$Y_p \equiv C+S. \tag{3.14}$$

From which it follows that

$$S+D+U+T+M \equiv I+G+X. \tag{3.15}$$

The difference between G and T is the *government deficiency*, $B\,(=G-T)$; this is the amount which the government sector has to borrow in order to finance its current and capital expenditures. It measures the increase in the indebtedness of the government sector. In the *Australian National Accounts*, the net current expenditure of governments, G_c (the expenditure on goods and services which are regarded as being fully consumed in the budget period), is distinguished from the *capital* expenditure of governments, G_k. The public authority surplus on current account, $T-G_c$, is also distinguished in the *Australian National Accounts*. For the purpose of the analysis of the overall level of economic activity in the short run, the division of G into G_c and G_k is not relevant and, in this book, only the aggregate $G\,(\equiv G_c+G_k)$ is used. Similarly, the concept of the surplus of current revenue over current expenditure is not used.

The difference between X and M is the *oversea balance on current account*, $R\,(\equiv X-M)$, or the *rest of the world deficiency*. It shows the extent to which the rest of the world's purchases of the exports of the domestic economy are not covered by the foreign exchange that was earned by the rest of the world from the sale of imports to the domestic economy. It represents the increase in the rest of the world's indebtedness to the domestic economy.

Both B and R can be negative. A negative value for $B\,(G < T)$ represents a government surplus; in the case where the value of R is negative $(X < M)$, the domestic economy is borrowing from the rest of the world or drawing upon its holdings of foreign exchange in order to finance the excess of its imports over its exports.

Identity (3.15) shows the balance of the leakages and offsets in the economy. It is the counterpart for the full economy of the identity,

---

[1] The expenditure of the financial enterprises sector is ignored for the reasons given on p. 30 above.

$S \equiv I$, in the closed, two-sector economy. It may also be written as follows:

$$S + D + U \equiv I + B + R. \tag{3.16}$$

Since GNI $\equiv$ GDE, the excess of expenditure over income by any one or more sectors must be offset by the excess of income over expenditure of other sectors. The excess of total private saving, $S + D + U$, over gross investment expenditure, I, is the surplus of income over expenditure of the domestic non-government sectors and this surplus is matched by the sum of the deficiencies of the government and the rest of the world sectors; that is, the total saving by the domestic private sectors is equal to the sum of gross private investment expenditure and the lending of these sectors to the other two sectors. It may be that one or both of these are in surplus; but it is impossible for all sectors to be in surplus, or all to be in deficit, at the same time. It is again stressed that these equalities follow entirely from the definitions of the items in the accounts. The *causal* relationships between the leakages and offsets is discussed in later chapters.

3. The national accounts of the Australian economy

A simplified form of the national accounts of the Australian economy is shown in Table 3.1. The income flows associated with the values added by the trading enterprises and government sectors are traced through their initial distribution to their final distribution. The latter is matched against final expenditures in order to obtain the surpluses and deficits and these are shown in the national capital account.

This national capital account shows the capital expenditure, and the surpluses of income over current expenditure, or *capital funds accruing*, for the economy. In terms of the symbols used in this book it is:

$$I + G_k \equiv S + D + U + (T - G_c) + (M - X). \tag{3.17}$$

This identity states that the value of the gross increment to the domestic capital stock is equal to the sum of gross private saving, the budget surplus (government saving), and oversea borrowing. It was explained above that, for the main purpose of this book, the division of G into G_c and G_k is not relevant. However, in order to convert the total leakages and offsets into the national capital account—and so to find the gross increment to the capital stock for the period—it is necessary to distinguish between G_c and G_k, and rearrange the terms, as in Table 3.1.

33

TABLE 3.1. *The national accounts of the Australian economy, 1962–63 ($m.)*

(Source: *Australian National Accounts, 1948–49 to 1963–64*)

Sector	(1) Production	(2) Initial distribution	(3) Final distribution	(4) Final expenditure
Trading enterprises	Value added 14,576*	Depreciation 1,262 Company income 1,600 Surplus of public enterprises 360	Depreciation 1,262 Undistributed company income 384 Dividends and interest 648	Gross investment expenditure 3,578
Personal		Wages and salaries 8,072 Income of unincorporated businesses 2,946† Personal income 11,018	Personal disposable income 11,210 Company taxation 568	Consumption expenditure 10,018
Government	Value added 1,382	Indirect taxes *less* subsidies 1,718	Net taxation 3,102 Net direct tax 456	Government expenditure 2,264§ Statistical discrepancy‡ 220
Rest of world				Exports 2,452 *less* Imports 2,574 −122
Economy	GNP 15,958	GNI 15,958	GNI 15,958	GDE 15,958

(arrow values in flow diagram: 6,690)

TABLE 3.1 (cont.). National capital account, 1962–63 ($m)

Expenditure		Capital funds accruing	
Gross investment expenditure	3,578	Personal saving	1,392
Government capital formation	628	Undistributed company income	384
		Depreciation allowances	1,262
		Government surplus on current account	1,266
		Imports less exports	122
		Less Statistical discrepancy ‡	220
	4,206		4,206

* Includes value added of financial enterprises.
† Includes imputed income to owner-occupiers of houses.
‡ Includes financial enterprises expenditure.
§ Government capital formation: 628; government expenditure on current goods and services: 1,636.

This book is concerned with the analysis of the short-run determination of the level of GNP. It is argued that the *planned aggregate expenditure* of the sectors upon domestic production determines the level of domestic income,[1] and there is a detailed analysis of the factors determining consumption expenditure, investment expenditure, government expenditure, exports and imports.

4. GNP in real and money terms

(*a*) *The interpretation of aggregates measured in current money prices*

The aggregate concepts developed in this chapter—GNP, GNI and GDE—are measured in terms of money; in the Australian case in Australian dollars. Thus, GNP is the sum of the values added of the enterprise and government sectors, measured as the difference between outputs valued at the current prices of the year concerned and inputs, similarly valued; GNI is the sum of the gross incomes of the factors, measured in terms of the rewards to factors currently ruling, plus net indirect taxes; and GDE is the sum of the expenditure on goods and services, each category of which is valued, either directly or indirectly, at current market prices and net of their import content valued at market prices.

For practical purposes it is necessary to express the multitude of things which make up production and expenditure in terms of a *common unit*. This is done by multiplying the quantities concerned by their respective prices per unit. Only in this way can essentially dissimilar things, for example, bottles of beer, motor-cars, teachers' services, be treated as an aggregate. Nevertheless, the valuation procedure should not obscure the main significance of the national accounting quantities, which comprises flow of actual goods and services matched by final expenditures, values added in the economic process, and services rendered in the factor markets and production process, for which money payments are made. Suppose, for example, that the standard of living of a nation is being considered. It is not the particular money value of GNP per head of its population which is relevant to the discussion, but, rather, the amount of goods and services per head of population which is available for consumption and capital accumulation. Or, to take another example, when considering the level of economic activity, it is the physical amounts of

---

[1] Subject always to the limitation of the physical capacity of the economy. This limitation is discussed in detail in chapter 5.

goods and services which entrepreneurs plan to produce, and the associated employment created for labour and capital equipment which are relevant, not the money values of current production plans.

Because the principal interest is in the *real* flows of goods and services, account must be taken of the fact that the prices of commodities change over time. Comparison of GNP's as between years may be a most misleading indication of the change in actual production of goods and services over the period. For example, the GNP of Australia in 1938–39 was $1,824 m., measured in terms of 1938–39 prices; the GNP for 1961–62 was $14,562 m., measured in 1961–62 prices. The eightfold rise in money GNP in no way indicates the rise in the production of goods and services between the two years, because, over the same period, prices generally had risen threefold. The observed change in GNP between any two years may reflect changes in the production of commodities, or in their prices, or—and this is obviously what happens in practice—changes in both production and prices.

In order to observe changes in production, the GNP's of different years must be valued in terms which eliminate the effect of the price changes. This is done by valuing the physical production of different periods by the same set of prices. The resulting aggregates are said to have been valued at *constant prices*; the period to which those prices are actually related is termed the *base period*. GNP so valued is called *GNP valued in constant (base period) prices* or *GNP in real terms*. Movements in GNP in real terms reflect movements in the production of goods and services, as contrasted with movements in GNP at current prices, which reflect changes in the general level of prices as well as changes in the production of goods and services.

(b) *The conversion of money aggregates to real aggregates*

In principle, GNP can be expressed in terms of constant prices by revaluing all the individual goods and services which compose it at the prices of a base year. In practice, paucity of data makes this an impossible task. It is customary to compute GNP at constant prices by dividing GNP at current prices (or its major components) by appropriate *price indexes*. This is known as deflating current-price values to obtain constant-price values; and the indexes used are called *deflators*.

A price index attempts to measure changes in the general level of prices of those commodities to which it refers. This is done by selecting a representative basket of commodities, and valuing it at the prices of the periods under consideration. The ratios of the costs of the basket under the various price régimes to the cost of the basket in the selected base period are the price index numbers.

This can be illustrated by a simple case of two commodities. Suppose the representative basket comprises 10 units of bread and 4 units of steel, and the prices of bread and steel are 20 c. and 200 c. a unit respectively in the base year. The basket will cost 1,000 c. If, in the next year, the prices change to 40 c. and 300 c. respectively, the basket will cost 1,600 c., and prices can be said to have risen in the ratio 1·6:1. Suppose that in this simple economy over the same period GNP has changed from 10,000 to 20,000 c. in current money prices. If the price index calculated above can be regarded as representative of the prices of the goods and services entering GNP, an estimate of GNP in the second period valued at base period prices can be made by dividing 20,000 c. by 1·6. The division gives 12,500 c. as the GNP valued at constant (base period) prices. Thus, while money GNP has doubled, GNP in real terms has increased only by 25 per cent.[1]

(c) The real GNP of Australia, 1948–49 to 1963–64

In figure 3.2, the real GNP of Australia for the years 1948–49 to 1963–64, using 1953–54 as the base period, is compared with the money GNP of the same period. The chart has several obvious features. The very rapid rate of increase of prices in the early 1950s is clearly revealed; thus GNP in money terms rose by 33 per cent between 1949–50 and 1950–51, compared with a rise in real GNP of only 5 per cent. There were considerable checks to the rise in real production in 1951–52, 1956–57 and 1961–62. Finally, it can be seen that the rate of increase of prices was considerably less in the second half of the 1950s and early 1960s.

---

[1] The 100 per cent increase in money GNP results from the multiplication, not the addition, of its price and quantity components. Thus

$$P_1 = p_1(1+x_1), \quad P_2 = p_2(1+x_2),$$
$$Q_1 = q_1(1+y_1), \quad Q_2 = q_2(1+y_2),$$

where x_i and y_i are the percentage increases in p_i and q_i respectively, $i = 1, 2$. Therefore,

$$\sum_{i=1}^{2} P_i Q_i = \sum_{i=1}^{2} p_i q_i (1+x_i)(1+y_i).$$

Chapters 2 and 3 have been concerned with the description and definition of the aggregate concepts and the units of measurement which are used in the analysis of the determination of the level of economic activity in the following chapters. The conceptual and practical problems involved in estimating GNP in both money and real terms are ignored in subsequent chapters.[1]

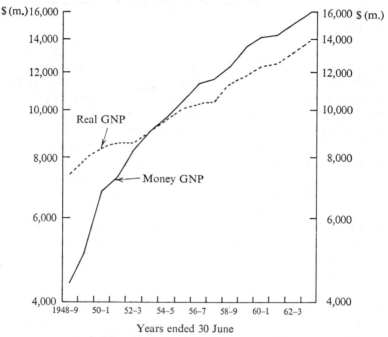

Figure 3.2. Ratio chart showing GNP in current prices and in average 1953–54 prices, Australia, 1948–49 to 1963–64.

[1] For a discussion of these conceptual and practical problems, see Appendix A of *Report of the Committee of Economic Enquiry*, vol. II (Commonwealth of Australia, May 1965), pp. A1–A25.

4

THE DETERMINATION OF THE
EQUILIBRIUM LEVEL OF REAL INCOME

1. Introduction

Study of the national accounts is useful in itself; it enables the complex relationships involved in a modern economy to be examined within an orderly framework. The information published in the *Australian National Accounts* shows in considerable detail how resources are allocated between alternative uses and how income is divided among broad groups in the community.

This information is a prerequisite for economic planning and policy-making. Is the rate of economic growth adequate? Is the income share of wage- and salary-earners changing? How important is the wool industry in the economy? What would be the effect on the availability of goods and services for other uses if defence expenditure were doubled? What will be the economic effects of the increased home construction associated with the anticipated marriage boom of the late 1960s? Is the Australian economy as dependent on export sales now as it was a decade ago?—these are but a small sample of the questions for which the national accounts provide a factual basis (although not a complete one) for rational discussion.

The particular use to which the national accounting framework is applied in this book is for the analysis of the determination of the short-run level of economic activity. In the discussion of national accounting it was shown that aggregate economic activity can be viewed from three aspects—production, income and expenditure. The equality of GNP, GNI and GDE does not imply that there is a causal link between them; the national accounting technique measures but does not explain the level of aggregate economic activity.

In the remainder of this book it is shown that the expenditure plans of economic entities play the key role in the determination of the short-run level of economic activity as measured by GNP in real terms. The procedure followed is to develop general principles within the framework of a simplified economy and then to consider successively more complex economies.

40

This chapter deals with the determination of the equilibrium level of economic activity of any *short period* in a closed, two-sector economy. By short period in this context is meant a situation in which the investment expenditure plans of businessmen (including their intended investment in stocks) are given, and all output within the period is produced by labour and raw materials working in association with the *existing stock of fixed capital*.[1]

The equilibrium level of economic activity is that level of aggregate output at which the production and expenditure plans of businessmen, and the expenditure plans of consumers, are all fulfilled. This does not necessarily coincide with the full employment of the labour force. The equilibrium level of economic activity may occur in a situation where some wage-earners who are prepared to work at the current money-wage rates are unable to find employment. This arises when the demand for labour corresponding to the equilibrium level of production is less than the available work-force. The relationship between the equilibrium level of production and the level of employment is discussed in the next chapter.

In any short period the economy tends towards an equilibrium rate of production and, once reached, this rate continues until the expenditure plans of consumers and/or businessmen change. The discussion of the process whereby equilibrium is achieved is deferred until section 3 of this chapter. It is necessary first to recapitulate the basic national accounting identities of the simplified two-sector economy; and to enlarge on the distinction between consumption and investment expenditures, between acts of saving and of investment, and between planned and actual quantities.

---

[1] This short period is 'shorter' than the period of time implied by a commonly used alternative definition, which requires only that the currently produced fixed capital goods cannot be used to produce current output. This latter definition does not preclude changes in investment plans; like the definition used in this chapter, it does imply that production is limited by the existing capacity of the fixed capital stocks in both the consumption and investment goods sectors. The determination of investment plans and the consequences of changes in investment expenditure are discussed in detail in chapters 9 and 10.

2. The two-sector economy

(a) The basic identities

The national accounting identities of the two-sector economy[1] are:

$$C+I \equiv Y. \tag{4.1}$$

The symbol, Y, is used throughout this book to represent *GNP at constant prices*.[2] This quantity is taken to be the basic indicator of the level of economic activity. It is also referred to as *real income* (or as income), *real output* (or as output or aggregate production) and as *aggregate supply*. Identity (4.1) expresses the truism that final expenditures, consisting of consumption and investment expenditures, equal production. If companies do not retain any income, then

$$Y \equiv Y_p. \tag{4.2}$$

That is, the initial and final distribution of incomes earned in the production process are the same:

$$Y_p \equiv C+S. \tag{4.3}$$

That is, personal disposable income is disposed of either as consumption expenditure or personal saving.

From these three identities it follows that

$$S \equiv I. \tag{4.4}$$

Identity (4.4) expresses the truism that saving (income which is not consumed) equals investment (production which is not consumed).

(b) Consumption and investment

In this analysis consumption expenditure by an entity is defined as its purchases of consumer goods and services; this does not necessarily coincide with the using-up of the goods. While it is the act of purchase which is relevant in the present context, it should be realized that the definition is more of a statistical convenience than a theoretically satisfying definition of consumption in the sense of the using of the

---

[1] There are two senses in which the economy discussed in this chapter is a two-sector economy: first, it has a trading enterprises sector and a personal sector. Secondly, the output is produced in the consumption goods and the investment goods sectors.

[2] With the exception of chapters 11 and 14, the analysis generally proceeds upon the assumptions that there are no indirect taxes and that the level of market prices is unchanged. In this case GNP at market prices is equal to GNP at factor cost measured in constant prices.

services of commodities. Consider the purchase of a dozen eggs: consumption expenditure occurs when they are purchased from the shop; consumption occurs when they are eaten at breakfast one week later.

The gap between purchase and using-up of a commodity is small in the case of most *single-use* goods, such as eggs. It is much longer in the case of *many-use* (*durable*) goods, such as furniture. The services of these goods are not entirely or even significantly 'consumed' in the year in which they are purchased. Expenditure on single-use goods tends to be more regular than purchases of durable goods. Purchases of single-use goods are also more closely related to the current incomes of the purchasers and reflect the pattern of recurring, every-day wants.

A feature of all consumption goods is that they are bought because of their anticipated ability to yield satisfaction. By contrast, investment expenditure is undertaken by businessmen in the belief that it will earn profits. Investment expenditure is not necessarily related to nor financed from the current incomes of the businesses concerned. In a nutshell, consumption expenditure is undertaken in anticipation of pleasure, investment expenditure in anticipation of profit.

Investment may be in the form of fixed investment, that is, in plant, machinery and buildings, or in the form of investment in stocks, that is, additions to their holdings of raw materials, partly processed and finished goods. Both forms of investment increase the sales capacity of an enterprise and both are made in the light of the balance between the cost of the investment goods, the cost of finance, and the expected additional net revenues. It is clear that the outputs of fixed investment goods and of raw and partly processed materials will be part of the investment output and expenditure of any period.

However, physical characteristics alone do not permit all finished goods which are produced ultimately for sale to the households sector to be unambiguously described as 'consumer goods'. From the viewpoint of the short period under consideration, some of these goods will be investment goods, that is, they will represent additions to the stocks held by businesses. Consider the case of a bottle of beer. In one sense this is a consumer good produced by an industry in the consumer goods sector. However, if at the end of the given period, the bottle of beer is still at the brewers or on the shelves of the bottle department of the hotel, it is an investment good and its value is included in the investment expenditure of trading enterprises. It follows that the value of the output of the consumer goods sector can exceed, or fall short of, consumption expenditure.

(c) Saving and investment

As was seen in chapter 3, personal saving is that part of the current disposable income of the household sector which is not spent on consumption goods. There are two aspects of saving: first, the decision not to spend, or, rather, to defer the consumption expenditure, and, secondly, the decision as to the form in which saving will be held—whether as financial assets (cash, bonds, shares, life-assurance payments, and so on), repayment of debts, or real assets. An act of saving results in a net increment to the wealth of the household.

Investment expenditure, on the other hand, involves the accumulation of newly created physical assets either to replace those worn out or obsolete—*replacement investment*—or to add to the already existing stock of assets and so to expand productive capacity—*net investment*. Investment expenditure also has two aspects: first, the decision to undertake the expenditure, which depends upon profit expectations, the cost of the asset and the cost and availability of finance; and, secondly, the decision as to how investment will be financed—whether to borrow additional funds, or to use retained profits, or a combination of the two.

Business saving is that portion of current gross business income which is retained by enterprises. In this chapter, it is assumed that all the gross incomes of trading enterprises are distributed to the personal sector, so that total saving consists wholly of personal saving. This would be realistic if all enterprises were unincorporated. Those entities in the personal sector who are owners of businesses may be thought of as reckoning their incomes net of depreciation allowances as available for consumption expenditure and saving. The more general case where some enterprises are incorporated, and business saving occurs, is discussed in chapters 9 and 10.

(d) Ex post *and* ex ante *concepts*

In this simplified economy $Y \equiv C + I$, and Y also $\equiv C + S$ so that it follows by definition that $S \equiv I$. S measures a particular allocation of part of income and I measures a particular allocation of part of output; the saving and investment decisions are made by different economic entities.

The equality of S and I is called an *ex post identity* (*ex post facto*, after the event); that is, it refers to what *has* happened in a period, and the quantities, S and I, are actual recorded amounts of saving and investment. Whenever the happenings of a period are reviewed it is found that $S \equiv I$. But it cannot be inferred from this that the amounts that people *plan* to save at the beginning of the period concerned, *ex ante saving* (*ex ante facto*, before the event), and the amounts that businessmen plan to invest at the beginning of the same period, *ex ante investment*, are equal either to each other or to the saving and investment which actually occur.

Assume that at the beginning of a period, persons expect that their disposable incomes will be such as to amount to $5,000 m. in the aggregate and, on the basis of this, they plan consumption expenditures amounting to $4,000 m. and saving amounting to $1,000 m. Assume further that businessmen in the aggregate plan investment expenditures amounting to $800 m., of which $700 m. is fixed investment goods to be made to order and $100 m. is planned additions to stocks of finished consumer goods. Suppose that, in the aggregate, businessmen do not accurately predict these planned expenditures and that the sum of their individual decisions results in an aggregate output of final goods to the value of $4,500 m., of which $700 m. is the fixed investment goods made to order and the balance of $3,800 m. is finished consumer goods. This production will create disposable income of $4,500 m.

If consumers spend the planned amount, $4,000 m., actual saving will be $500 m., not the $1,000 m. planned. Furthermore, actual investment expenditure will be less than the $800 m. planned. Businessmen will spend $700 m. on the fixed investment goods which were ordered; but consumers' expenditure exceeds the current output of consumer goods by $200 m. As a result, instead of there being an addition of $100 m. to stocks of consumer goods as planned, actual investment in stocks will fall by $200 m. Thus, aggregate investment expenditure will be only $500 m. ($700 m. − $200 m.) and will equal actual saving.

The *ex post* equality between actual investment expenditure and saving follows from the definitions used, and not because businessmen have accurately predicted the spending plans of enterprises and households. Actual investment expenditure is defined to include the element of unintended investment in stocks. This is equal to the difference between the actual and the planned increment (or decrement) to stocks; that is, it is equal to the difference between actual aggregate expenditure and the aggregate expenditure, including expenditure on stocks, which businessmen had anticipated when making their production decisions. In the case where businessmen correctly anticipate the *ex ante* aggregate expenditure, actual (*ex post*) investment expenditure will be equal to planned (*ex ante*) investment expenditure. This occurs in the equilibrium situation discussed in section 3 below.

The *ex post* national accounts[1] for the economy considered in the above example would be:

Value added	$m.	Incomes created	$m.	Expenditure	$m.
In consumption goods sector	3,800			Consumption expenditure	4,000
In fixed investment goods sector	700			Investment expenditure	
				(a) Fixed investment	700
				(b) Investment in stocks	−200
GNP	4,500	GNI	4,500	GDE	4,500

National capital account

	$m.		$m.
Saving	500	Fixed investment	700
		Investment in stocks	−200
	500		500

The distinction between *ex ante* and *ex post* situations, that is, between plans and actuality, plays a key part in the analysis of the determination of the equilibrium level of real income. In what follows the terms *ex ante* and *ex post* are used interchangeably with *planned* and *actual* respectively.

3. The equilibrium level of real income

Decisions concerning production and expenditure are made by individual businessmen and consumers. The level of real income and employment of, say, the next three months is determined by the interaction of the production plans of businessmen with the planned

[1] For purposes of economic control it is necessary to have estimates of planned expenditure. Although little information about expenditure plans is available, the *ex post* magnitudes published in *Australian National Accounts* are valuable information for the preparation of forecasts.

investment expenditure of businessmen[1] and the planned consumption expenditure of households. Businessmen estimate the expected demands for their products over the coming period; and in the light of these estimates, they set initial rates of production. Given their existing fixed capital stocks, their inventories, and the current prices of raw materials and labour, they will offer that level of employment which enables them to achieve this rate of production.

Planned consumption expenditure will be determined primarily by the incomes earned by persons as the production plans are implemented; planned investment demand will be influenced by the sales and profits experience of the past, and by businessmen's guesses about future profit prospects. In this simple economy it is assumed that fixed investment goods are produced only to order and that orders are placed at the beginning of each short period. Businessmen are also assumed to set at the beginning of each period a desired rate of investment in stocks; this rate will be determined in the light of their past experience, the initial level of stocks, and the expected rate of sales. Within the period the rate of production of consumption goods can be varied—the output decision can be revised daily in many industries. It is assumed, however, that changes in the rate of production within the period do not lead to a revision of the planned rate of investment in stocks or in fixed equipment.

There is therefore both a supply and a demand aspect involved in the determination of real income. The supply aspect is the planned production which gives rise to the *aggregate supply* of goods and services, that is, real income. The demand aspect is the planned expenditures on consumption and investment goods; this is also called the *aggregate demand* for goods and services.

Real income is said to be at its equilibrium rate of flow per period,[2] when the production plans of businessmen, and the expenditure plans of consumers and businessmen, are realized. As is shown below, such a position is reached when aggregate supply and aggregate demand are equal, and this implies that planned saving equals planned investment. Once this situation is reached, unless expenditure plans are expected to change businessmen have no incentive to change production. It should be noted that this situation does not necessarily

---

[1] For simplicity, in this chapter, investment by households in housing is ignored, so that only businessmen are regarded as investing.

[2] Income, output and expenditure are flow concepts, but for the sake of brevity, the term 'equilibrium level' is used in lieu of 'equilibrium rate of flow per period'.

correspond to the maximum possible rate of output, nor with the employment of the entire work-force.

Consider a situation in which total planned expenditures are greater than the aggregate supply and the accompanying real income. Such a situation may arise because, overall, the guesses of business-men concerning the total demands for their products were too pessimistic, so that too little production was undertaken. If, as will be assumed in this chapter, there are ample stocks on hand, planned expenditures can be met by running down these stocks whenever current production is less than current demand. But the unexpected run down of stocks would mean that some businessmen would not be accumulating stocks at the rate desired. That is to say, actual investment would tend to be less than planned investment. The failure of plans to match actuality—the disparity between *ex post* and *ex ante* investment expenditure—would lead businessmen to increase their rate of production because it would be apparent that the rates of production at the beginning of the period were based on estimates of current demand which were too pessimistic, and that their profits could be increased by raising the level of production.

If, however, businessmen's estimates of demands at the beginning of the period were too optimistic so that aggregate supply initially exceeded the aggregate demand associated with it, an unexpected accumulation of stocks would occur. In this situation *ex post* invest-ment initially would exceed *ex ante* investment; businessmen, in the interests of increasing their profits or of reducing their losses, would revise their production plans and reduce the employment offered until the rate of production matched aggregate demand and stocks accumulated only at the desired rates.

In the first situation there were forces operating to increase the rate of production and, in the second, to reduce it. However, should current production be such that it matched the current demands associated with it, that is, should aggregate supply equal aggregate demand, plans and actuality would coincide, and *ex post* investment would equal *ex ante* investment expenditure. Moreover, if the current production of consumption goods matched current planned and actual expenditure on them, planned saving would equal actual saving, and it would also equal both planned and actual investment. That is, the *composition*, as well as the total, of real income would correspond to planned spending. In this case there would be no unintended change in stocks; provided that there were no changes in the factors underlying planned expenditure, the current rate of production, and of real income and employment, would be maintained.

The real income of any short period, then, tends to settle at that unique level at which aggregate supply matches aggregate demand, which is also the level at which planned saving is exactly offset by planned investment expenditure. Moreover, this is a stable position within the bounds of the short period; any chance departure from it sets up forces which bring the rate of production back to this level.

It is quite possible for real income to be in equilibrium in the aggregate even though its composition is not in equilibrium. Thus the rate of output of consumption goods may exceed the demand, while the reverse situation applies for investment goods. In such a situation the consequent movements in stocks will encourage a greater rate of production in one sector, and a lesser rate in the other.[1]

There is no guarantee that this equilibrium rate of output will give rise to a demand for labour equal to the supply offered, that is, will correspond to full employment. Businessmen make their plans in order to achieve the most profitable level of production, and, given the aggregate demand situation, their profit interests lead them to produce the equilibrium level of output. Corresponding to this is a certain demand for labour (and the other productive factors). If this demand for labour falls short of the number of workers seeking work there is unemployment. This is discussed further in section 3 of chapter 5.

4. The process of the attainment of equilibrium

The basic argument of the book is that economic activity in the short run tends to that level where aggregate demand and aggregate supply are equal. In later chapters more complex economies are considered; however, the general process whereby equilibrium is

---

[1] It is assumed in this chapter that fixed investment goods are produced only in response to orders, and that there are ample stocks of consumer goods. It follows that, in this case, attainment of the equilibrium level of total output implies that the composition of output as between consumer goods in general, and investment goods, is also in equilibrium. In practice, the composition of the output of consumer goods is changing continuously as disequilibrium in individual markets (resulting from such factors as changes in consumer preferences and the introduction of new goods) are corrected. Furthermore, some fixed investment goods, for example, commercial buildings, are produced in anticipation of demand. Analysis of the composition of aggregate output involves *microeconomic* analysis; this is a separate field of study which is complementary to *macroeconomics*, the analysis of the determination of aggregate output, and of its major components.

achieved can be illustrated by means of the simple two-sector model. Three alternative presentations of the process are given in this section: first, there is an explanation which makes use of simple diagrams; secondly, a general analysis in algebraic form is set out; and finally, a particular arithmetic illustration is given.

(a) Diagrammatic illustrations

In order to explain the process of the determination of the equilibrium level of income by means of diagrams, it is necessary to discuss briefly the determination of the rate of planned consumption expenditure. This is discussed in detail in chapter 8. Initially, a simplifying assumption is made concerning the rate of planned investment expenditure for the period, but this is dropped later. The determination of investment expenditure is discussed in detail in chapter 9.

The equilibrium level of output and real income is determined by the response of producers to the levels of spending planned by households and trading enterprises. As explained above, a characteristic of the short-period situation is that the level of planned investment expenditure is given. Planned expenditures which are related to (influenced by) short-run changes in income are described as *induced* expenditures, whereas those expenditures which are independent of such changes are described as *autonomous* expenditures. For the present, planned investment expenditure, I, is assumed to be autonomously determined and is written: $I = \bar{I}$. It is not necessary to distinguish planned fixed investment from the planned investment in stocks. In figure 4.1, autonomous planned investment expenditure is denoted by the line, II.

For the present it is assumed that the planned spending in real terms by households, c, is wholly dependent upon personal real disposable income, Y_p; for simplicity, it is assumed to be a constant proportion of Y_p, that is, $C = cY_p$, where c is positive and less than one. As $Y = Y_p$ in the simplified economy being examined, the form, $C = cY$, is used in this chapter. These assumptions are modified later, but for the present it may be noted that they accord broadly with reality.

(i) *The equality of aggregate demand and supply.* Prior to the last two paragraphs, the symbols, C, I and S, have always referred to *ex post* values. They were so used, for example, in the national accounting identities. However, in the two previous paragraphs, and in what follows, unless the contrary is specifically stated, these symbols are always used to denote *ex ante* (planned) values (which may coincide with actual values).[1]

Planned consumption expenditure rises with the level of real income but not by as much as the latter does. This is illustrated by

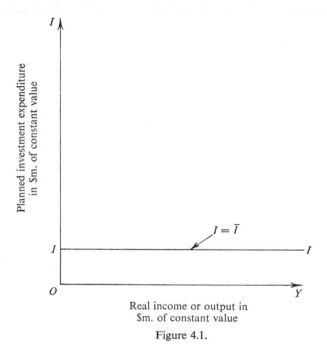

Figure 4.1.

figure 4.2, which shows the total planned expenditure on consumption goods, C, which would occur at different levels of real disposable income, Y_p (which in this case equals Y), given that the institutional and other factors which affect consumption expenditure remain constant. This relationship is called the *aggregate consumption function* or the *aggregate propensity to consume schedule*;[2] it is shown by OC in figure 4.2.

---

[1] This is in accordance with common usage. Some writers do not always make this distinction explicit and the reader must then establish from the context whether the value referred to is *ex ante* or *ex post*.

[2] There are alternative forms of the aggregate consumption function. For example, planned consumption expenditure may be related to the anticipated disposable income of the coming short period (as in the example of p. 45); or it may be related to the disposable income of some past period or periods.

It is a schedule in the sense that it shows a *series of possibilities* for a given period. Thus, when disposable income is OA, planned consumption expenditure is AB; and when disposable income is OC, planned consumption expenditure is CD. It is not a time series; that is, it is not an historical statement recording the actual consumption expenditure associated with actual levels of real income at different

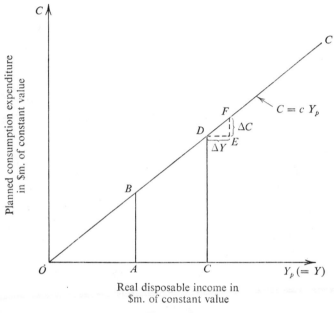

Figure 4.2.

times. The *slope* of the schedule, c, is called the *marginal propensity to consume, mpc*; the *mpc* is the ratio of the change in planned consumption expenditure to the small change in real disposable income which gave rise to it; for simplicity, it is assumed here to be constant. In figure 4.2 the *mpc* is measured, for example, by

$$EF/DE \; (=\Delta C/\Delta Y).$$

Total planned spending by households, $C = cY_p$ (which in this particular case may be written $C = cY$) and by firms, $I = \bar{I}$, are now added together to give the aggregate planned expenditure associated with each level of real income, that is, the aggregate demand schedule, $E = cY + \bar{I}$. In figure 4.3, this schedule is the line, EE.

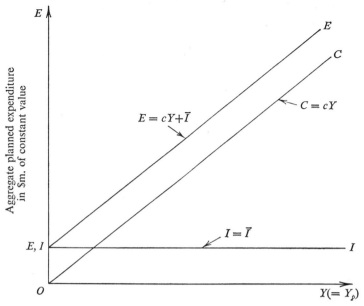

Figure 4.3.

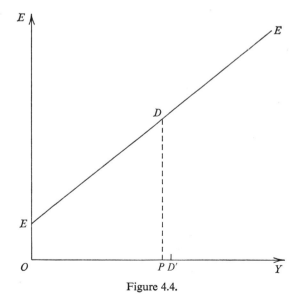

Figure 4.4.

At the beginning of each short period, in the light of their anticipations of aggregate demand, businessmen set a certain rate of output. Suppose that this initial rate is that indicated by *OP* in figure 4.4.

This rate of production gives rise to a matching flow of income, and corresponding to this will be a certain rate of planned spending by households; this, together with planned investment expenditure,

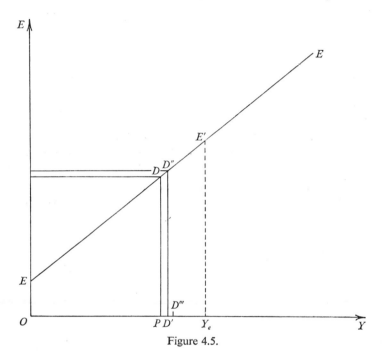

Figure 4.5.

gives rise to a unique level of aggregate demand, *PD*. Whether this is a stable position depends upon whether the *planned* rate of expenditure equals the *actual* rate of output. The two rates can be compared by marking off the amount of planned expenditure, *PD*, on the real income (horizontal) axis; the distance *OD′* equals *PD*. In the particular case illustrated in figure 4.4, at the output *OP* planned spending exceeds output by *PD′*, so that there will be a tendency for stocks to be depleted. As a result, businessmen will increase the rate of output.

It should not be thought that the equilibrium rate of output will be *OD′*. When output is increased to this level, there is an induced increase in desired spending resulting from the increase of PD' in households' real income. At the output OD', aggregate demand will be $D'D''$ ($=OD''$), as shown in figure 4.5, and there will still be a tendency for stocks to be depleted. However, the stock depletion will be at a lesser rate because the rise in output results in additional induced consumption expenditure of only c times it.

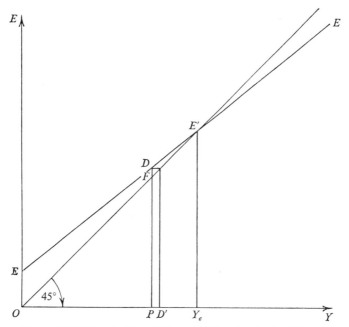

Figure 4.6. Determination of the equilibrium level of real income.

Output will increase until the equilibrium level, OY_e, is reached. This level has the characteristic that the aggregate planned spending associated with it equals the level of output, that is, $Y_eE' = OY_e$. There is then no *unplanned* movement in stocks and no incentive to change the rate of output.

An alternative method of comparing planned spending with output involves the construction of a straight line from the origin with a slope of 45°. Since at any point on this line the vertical co-ordinate equals the horizontal co-ordinate, output can now be shown as a vertical as well as a horizontal distance. Figure 4.6 shows the same information as figure 4.5, together with the 45° guide line.

At the original non-equilibrium level of output OP ($= PF$), stocks tend to be depleted at a rate FD ($= PD'$). The 45° line enables the immediate identification of the equilibrium level of output, OY_e, at which planned expenditure, Y_eE', equals actual output. Y_eE' and OY_e represent respectively the planned expenditure and actual output associated with the intersection of EE with the 45° line; this intersection shows the unique position where aggregate demand equals aggregate supply.

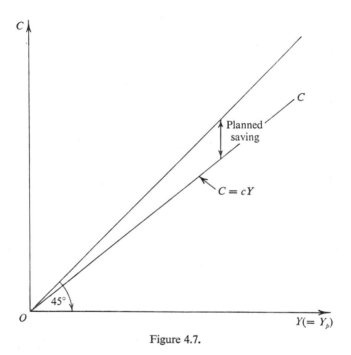

Figure 4.7.

The 45° line has a second function. It enables the planned saving corresponding to each level of real disposable income to be identified. Figure 4.7 shows the 45° line and the consumption function. The distances between the two lines represent planned saving, $S = sY_p$; s is the *marginal propensity to save*, *mps*, which is the ratio of the change in planned saving to the small change in real disposable income which gave rise to it. As disposable income is allocated between planned consumption expenditure and planned saving, $S = Y_p - cY_p = (1-c)Y_p$, so that $s = 1-c$. The *aggregate saving*

56

function, $S = sY_p$ is shown in figure 4.8 by the line OS. In this figure at any level of real disposable income, say OY_1, planned saving, Y_1S_1, plus planned consumption expenditure, S_1C_1, equals total real disposable income, Y_1C_1. The *mps* is measured, for example, by LM/KL.

(ii) *The equality of planned saving and investment.* In figure 4.9, the investment function of figure 4.1 is combined with the saving function of figure 4.8. This figure is used to show that an alternative way of describing the condition for the equilibrium level of output is that planned saving should equal planned investment. Consider the case

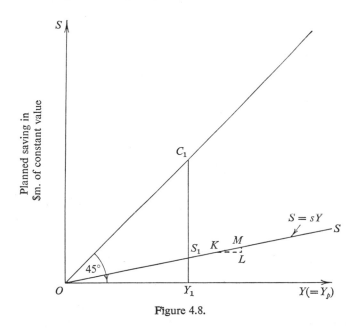

Figure 4.8.

where businessmen plan an output, OY_1. The total demands upon output are given by planned consumption expenditure, S_1C_1, and planned investment, Y_1I_1. Aggregate demand exceeds output by S_1I_1 ($= Y_1I_1 - Y_1S_1$), that is, by the *excess* of planned investment over planned saving. If it is assumed (as always) that there are adequate stocks, then total sales will be at the rate Y_1I_1 plus S_1C_1; but as current production is at a rate of only Y_1C_1, the balance, S_1I_1, will be supplied from an unplanned reduction in stocks. In response to this, the rate of output will increase. If, alternatively, the initial

57

output were OY_3, planned consumption expenditure would be at the rate, S_3C_3: given planned investment Y_3I_3 ($= Y_1I_1$), the total demand at output OY_3 would fall short of actual output by the excess of planned saving over planned investment, that is, I_3S_3 ($= Y_3S_3 - Y_3I_3$); and, as a result, the rate of output would be reduced.

It can be seen that at the income level, OY_e, planned saving equals planned investment. This is equivalent to the statement that households' planned spending on consumption goods plus planned invest-

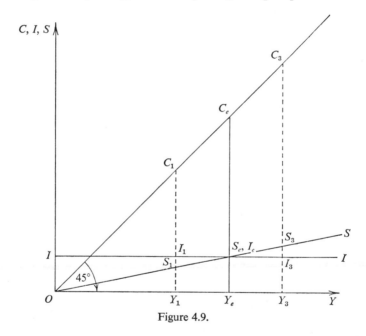

Figure 4.9.

ment matches actual output. Thus the determination of the equilibrium level of real income can be shown in terms of the relationship between planned saving and planned investment.

This alternative approach focuses attention upon the fact that differences between planned saving and investment give rise to unplanned investment or disinvestment in stocks, as shown by the hatched areas in figure 4.10. Actual investment equals planned investment *plus* unplanned investment in stocks (which can be negative). At non-equilibrium levels of output, the unplanned investment in stocks matches the disparity between planned saving and planned investment, so that *actual* investment expenditure equals actual (and planned) saving.[1] It can be seen from figure 4.10 that planned investment equals actual investment only at the equilibrium level of output.

Unplanned changes in stocks draw the attention of businessmen to the fact that actual rates of sales differ from the rates that they had anticipated. It is these disparities which cause businessmen to change their rates of output until, at the equilibrium level, aggregate output coincides with the actual rate of aggregate sales, together with the desired aggregate rate of investment in stocks.

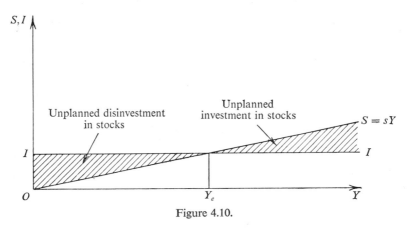

Figure 4.10.

(b) *Algebraic presentation of equilibrium*

The determination of the equilibrium level of output can be set out analytically as follows:

The equilibrium condition that aggregate demand equal aggregate supply is written as

$$Y = E.$$

Aggregate demand consists of consumption expenditure, which is a function of real income, and investment expenditure, which is given. Thus

$$E = C(Y) + \bar{I}.$$

[1] This assumes that consumers are not forced to save because of a lack of supplies of suitable consumer goods to match their planned spending. In peacetime there normally are ample stocks of consumer goods. It should be noted that in the case where fixed investment goods are produced in anticipation of a demand which does not eventuate, the unsold goods will accumulate as unplanned investment in stocks (see footnote on p. 49).

It follows that the equilibrium level of real income is given by the solution for Y of the equation

$$Y = C(Y) + \bar{I}.$$

The alternative equilibrium condition, that planned saving equal planned investment, can be derived from this latter equation by writing it

$$Y - C(Y) = \bar{I},$$

that is,

$$S(Y) = \bar{I}.$$

The above is the *general* case. In the particular case where consumption expenditure is a linear function of real income, that is,

$$C = A + cY,$$

the equation from which the equilibrium level of real income can be determined becomes:

$$Y = A + cY + \bar{I}.$$

It follows that

$$Y = (A + \bar{I}) \, \frac{1}{1-c}.$$

Throughout this book linear functional relationships are used frequently. This greatly simplifies the exposition, and (except where specifically noted) it does not avoid nor obscure any general principles.

(c) An arithmetic illustration

Suppose that for the economy described in the previous section, planned investment expenditure is autonomously determined at 500, and the consumption function is described by the expression: $C = \frac{3}{4}Y$; the quantities are $m. of constant value per period. With the above information, and assuming that planned demands can always be met either from stocks or from current production, Table 4.1 can be derived.

Suppose that the output decisions of businessmen in aggregate originally resulted in a rate of production of $1,700 m. Planned (and actual) consumption would then be $1,275 m.; planned (and actual) saving would be $425 m.; planned investment is $500 m.; but actual investment would be $425 m., that is, planned investment of $500 m. less the unintended run down of stocks of $75 m. Similarly, a real income of $2,300 m. would result in an unintended accumulation of stocks of $75 m. There are forces at work in both these positions which drive production to a level of $2,000 m. where the equilibrium condition that aggregate supply equals aggregate demand (or alternatively, that planned saving equals planned investment), is satisfied.[1]

TABLE 4.1

(1) Aggregate supply (real income) ($m.)	(2) Planned consumption expenditure ($m.)	(3) Planned saving (1)−(2) ($m.)	(4) Planned investment expenditure ($m.)	(5) Aggregate demand (2)+(4) ($m.)	(6) Unintended stock change (1)−(5) ($m.)	(7) Actual investment (4)+(6) ($m.)	(8) Actual saving (1)−(2) ($m.)
1,600	1,200	400	500	1,700	−100	400	400
1,700	1,275	425	500	1,775	−75	425	425
1,800	1,350	450	500	1,850	−50	450	450
1,900	1,425	475	500	1,925	−25	475	475
2,000	1,500	500	500	2,000	0	500	500
2,100	1,575	525	500	2,075	+25	525	525
2,200	1,650	550	500	2,150	+50	550	550
2,300	1,725	575	500	2,225	+75	575	575
2,400	1,800	600	500	2,300	+100	600	600

[1] Following the analysis of section 4(b) above, the equilibrium level of income can be derived algebraically as follows:

$$Y = C(Y) + I,$$

where $\qquad\qquad C(Y) = \frac{3}{4}Y, \quad I = 500,$

therefore $\qquad\qquad Y = \frac{3}{4}Y + 500,$

and so $\qquad Y = 2{,}000, \quad C = 1{,}500, \quad S = 500.$

THE CONCEPT OF FULL
EMPLOYMENT

The preceding chapter was concerned with the actual and equilibrium levels of output and employment. The equilibrium level was seen to be the outcome of the interplay of the forces underlying aggregate demand and those underlying the production decisions of business-men. It was said that there were no reasons why in the simple economy postulated, this equilibrium level should be the full employment level of activity. In this chapter, the elusive concept of full employment is further considered. The first step is to consider the different types of unemployment. The second section deals with two measures related to the extent of the departure of the economy from full employment; and in the final section, the influence of money wage changes upon the level of employment is considered.

It has been demonstrated that the equilibrium level of real output depends on the level of aggregate demand; clearly there is a relationship between the level of real output at any given time and the number of employed workers. However, this relationship is complex, and the level of employment is influenced by many other factors. Of these other factors, three are of particular importance—the composition of the level of output, the methods used to produce it and the intensity with which employees work. Given the methods of production used in each industry, a switch in the composition of output away from industries in which the share of wages in value added is large (labour-intensive industries, say, textiles) to industries in which the share of wages in value added is small (capital-intensive industries, say, oil-refining) will reduce the amount of employment associated with a given level of real output (as measured by GNP at constant prices). Similarly, given the composition of output, a switch to more capital-intensive techniques of production (because of innovations or changes in the cost of capital relative to labour) will operate to produce the same result upon the level of employment. Finally, a given level of output can be achieved with a smaller number employed, if the employed work longer hours or more intensively.[1]

To simplify the exposition it will be assumed that, in the short run, the production of each level of output is associated with the employment of a given number of workers. It follows from this assumption that an increase in output will result in a certain increase in employment, although not necessarily a proportionate one.

1. Full employment and types of unemployment

The physical upper limit to the potential short-run level of production of any economy depends upon four factors:

(1) The known natural resource endowment of the economy.

(2) The stock of capital, that is, the existing amounts of the various types of fixed capital equipment—machinery, plant and buildings, together with the accumulated stocks of raw materials, work-in-progress and finished goods.

(3) The state of knowledge. Two aspects of this may be distinguished: technical knowledge and administrative ability (in both the government and private sectors).

(4) The existing potential work-force and the willingness of its members to work at current money-wage rates.

These four factors set an upper limit to the amount of goods and services that can be produced in a given short period without coercing the work-force.

Full employment of the work-force is sometimes defined as that level of employment at which everyone willing to work at existing money-wage rates is able to find a job. Implicit in this definition is the assumption that there exist enough machines and other complementary factors to be manned by the potential work-force. That is, full employment of the work-force is assumed to occur at, or before, the point at which the existing capital stock is fully utilized. Such a situation may be described as one in which, in the short run, labour rather than capital is the main limitation to further increases in output. This is the case in the present-day Australian economy. It is possible to envisage situations where the capital stock is fully utilized, but where some workers remain unemployed. For example, in a

---

[1] The numbers of workers employed to produce a given output also depends upon whether businessmen expect the output to be sustained. If there is an increase in aggregate demand which it is believed is only temporary, firms will work more overtime and take on fewer new employees than they would if they expected the higher rate of output to be sustained.

country devastated by war the labour supply may be partially unemployed, not because of lack of demand for output, but because the supply of complementary productive factors necessary to make gainful use of the labour supply is inadequate.

The definition of full employment as that situation where all willing workers can find jobs is not, in practice, a workable one. It must be qualified in several important respects.

Any definition of 'full employment' must take account of the given institutions in the society; in particular, the proportion of the work-force which is unionized, and the degree of competition in the labour market. For example, if a minimum money-wage is set and middle-aged, married women who would be prepared to work as part-time domestic help at less than this wage rate cannot find employment at this wage, their unemployment cannot necessarily be attributed to a generally depressed level of economic activity. It may be that even if there were a shortage of most types of labour, as occurs at high levels of aggregate output, a large number of these women would remain unemployed; whereas if the minimum wage for domestic help were cut substantially many of those who desired to work at the lower wage could find work.

It would be an over-simplification to infer that a specific number of persons are precluded from employment because of the prevailing wage structure. In general those unemployed at any time are those whose services are valued lowest relative to the respective wage rates. But as aggregate demand for goods and services increases, employers will find it profitable (and largely unavoidable) to employ relatively less productive workers. Consequently, a pragmatic view must be taken of the magnitude of unemployment attributable to the prevailing pattern of wages. If, among a particular group of workers, the percentage of their number who remained unemployed at high levels of activity was persistently well above the percentage unemployed in the work force as a whole, a likely explanation would be that their wage rate was too high relative to the value placed on their services.

It is assumed that there is a given demand for labour associated with any given level of real aggregate demand. However, it takes time for potential employers and potential employees to make contact. Conceptually, the existing unemployed may be divided between two groups: first, those who would remain unemployed even if current demand conditions in the labour market were to remain constant for a sufficient time period for these frictions to be overcome. These workers may be described as the *involuntarily unemployed*. The second group are those who, although temporarily unemployed, would find jobs if sufficient time elapsed.

In Australia, there have been several years in the post-war period in which, according to almost all trade union leaders, academic economists, employers and government officials, there was 'full' or 'over-full' employment. The year 1965 was one such period but, throughout it, the number of applicants for jobs registered with the Commonwealth Employment Service was in excess of 30,000 (compared with the official estimate of the work-force of 4·5 million).[1] At no time in the post-war period has there been no person registered as unemployed, although in December 1950, at the peak of the strongest post-war boom, the number was reduced to 8,265, of whom 928 were in receipt of unemployment benefits.

The registered applicants for jobs may be divided into four categories. First, there are those *seasonally unemployed*; for example, shearers or fruit-pickers may be registered as unemployed in the off-season of their working year. Secondly, there are those *frictionally unemployed*; people may be registered as unemployed because, although there is some work available for them, they prefer to spend their time seeking for better-paid or more suitable work. Thirdly, registered applicants for work may be *structurally unemployed*; that is, their unemployment is a reflection of an excess supply of workers of their particular types, and not of a general decline in the demand for labour. This type of unemployment may arise from a shift in the pattern of demand for, or in the techniques of production of, goods and services. The acquisition of new skills takes time, and it is a

---

[1] People register as job applicants for two reasons: first, in order to be eligible for the unemployment benefit, and, secondly, to obtain information about jobs. The number of registered job applicants is not an exact measure of the number of persons seeking work; not all unemployed persons register. There are many reasons why they do not. Some expect to find work themselves (or through their trade union) before the elapse of the week necessary before the unemployment benefit is paid. Some do not consider that the Commonwealth Employment Service can help them find work and they are not eligible to receive the benefit; many unemployed women whose husbands are still employed are in this category. The proportion of unemployed persons who are registered as unemployed with the Commonwealth Employment Service varies with the overall demand for labour. When this is at high levels a greater proportion of unemployed workers are able to find work themselves. The incentive for employers to register vacant positions is influenced also by the level of demand for labour. When unemployment is at high levels, they are able to fill many vacancies with workers making direct contact with them.

particularly difficult process for older and less intelligent workers. Workers may not wish to shift to new areas, perhaps because they cannot sell their homes without losses. Consequently, workers from the declining industries may be unable to adapt themselves, at least in the short run, to the employment opportunities available in other industries or localities. Structural unemployment may also be the result of changes in the composition of the work-force. The new entrants to the work-force, in particular those who have just left school, may not have the particular skills required by employers. The residual group represents an approximate measure of the *involuntarily unemployed*.

It would not be correct to regard this residual as a precise measure of the involuntarily unemployed. To do so would be to assume that an increase in the general level of activity would have no impact on the other three categories. But, in fact, the higher is the overall level of aggregate demand, the more easily can the other three groups of workers find jobs. For example, if the general level of economic activity is high, a seasonally unemployed fruit-picker may find a temporary job as a labourer in the construction industry; the greater the variety and number of vacant positions the more rapidly will the frictionally unemployed find congenial jobs. In the case of the structurally unemployed, the higher is the level of aggregate demand, the easier it is for the worker to find another job in a new industry or location.

Furthermore, there is no unique pattern of aggregate demand. If, for example, there was general unemployment and the percentage of unemployment among coal-miners was particularly high because of, say, increased competition from petroleum, their unemployment could be described as structural if it arose from a change in technological conditions. In considering the measures to take in order to raise the general level of aggregate demand the government could take account of the industrial and geographical distribution of the unemployed. For example, it might initiate a railway construction project through the coal-mining region, and in this way create employment for the unemployed miners.

As the level of unemployment declines, the number of registered vacancies comes to exceed the number of registered applicants for work; employers find it is difficult to get workers with the particular skills they require. Consequently, there may be shortages of particular types of workers, while workers of other types, in general, the less skilled, are still unemployed. In fact, the unemployment may, in part, be attributable to the bottleneck in the supply of skilled workers necessary to work in association with the less skilled. Consequently, if aggregate demand is increased by given amounts, it tends to have a smaller impact on unemployment and a greater impact on unsatisfied employer demand, the lower is the level of unemployment.

It should be noted, however, that the response of production to these increases in spending is not confined to the increment of output resulting from the employment of persons formerly registered as applicants for jobs. The production per hour worked of those already in employment is likely to increase; for example, the retail and transport industries will be able to cope with increased business without proportionate increases in staff. Furthermore, the potential labour supply has two dimensions—the number of employed workers *and* the number of hours worked by each worker. If overtime is available, the existing labour force may be prepared, at least in the short run, to work longer hours, and if 'penalty rates' are offered, even more overtime may be worked. Finally, the increase in the labour supply will not be confined to the work performed by those formerly unemployed. When jobs are readily available, persons (such as married women) who were not registered as applicants for jobs will be drawn into the work-force. Consequently, a reduction in the percentage of the work-force who are registered as applicants for jobs from, say, 3 to 2 per cent, will be accompanied by an increase in output of substantially more than 1 per cent.

This discussion suggests that a pragmatic approach must be taken to the concept of full employment. It is not realistic to think that there is some finite number of workers prepared to work some given number of hours which comprises 'the labour force', and that this finite number, when 'fully employed', produces 'the full employment level of output', which represents the unique absolute maximum flow of production attainable.

In later chapters it is shown that when the number of registered unemployed reaches low levels, the rate of increase of prices quickens and the balance of trade deteriorates. The government must then choose a *set* of policy objectives, balancing its desires for low levels of unemployment and greater levels of output, against its desire for price stability and its desire to avoid balance of payment difficulties. There is really no useful point to be served in defining 'full employment' in isolation from this policy question.

In post-war Australia, all the major political parties have accepted *high* levels of employment as a desirable objective. It is doubtful whether any political party which permitted the percentage of the work-force registered as unemployed to rise above, say, 3 per cent could survive an election. At the other extreme, many people would regard a position where the number of job vacancies matched the number of registered unemployed as a reasonably satisfactory position of 'full employment'. But, even in this situation, further increases in aggregate expenditure would induce further increases in the labour supply and in output.

Individuals may find it convenient to adopt a particular definition of 'full employment'; for example, to say that it occurs when the ratio of registered applicants for jobs to the official estimate of the work-force is at some specified percentage. The members of the Commonwealth Committee of Economic Enquiry found it convenient to define full employment in terms of a *zone*, the lower limit of which is reached when registered unemployment as a percentage of the work-forces lies between 1·0 and 1·5 per cent. They considered that this lower limit should be set in the light of the seasonal factor in employment, so that they would consider 1·0 per cent as the lower limit of the zone during the months when the seasonal element of unemployment is lowest.[1]

In this book it is convenient to use the term 'the full employment level of income (or output)' in reference to a specific upper limit to economic activity. In practice, the government will design its policy measures with the aim of achieving some *target* level of activity. This target will be determined in the light of the prevailing economic and political circumstances, and it does not correspond to an absolute limit as determined by physical possibilities. Individuals may consider the chosen target level to be appropriate or inappropriate. However, the analysis developed in this book is not circumscribed by any particular practical interpretation which may be given to the term 'full employment'. The purpose of the book is to show how the level of economic activity is determined. Techniques are discussed which can be used to manipulate the economy towards any selected feasible target of activity. Consequently, it is neither necessary nor useful for the authors to give a precise definition of the term 'the full employment level of output'. There is a more detailed discussion of

[1] See paragraphs 2.25 to 2.30 of the *Report of the Committee of Economic Enquiry*, vol. II (Commonwealth of Australia, May 1965).

the relationships between the levels of aggregate demand, employment, wages, and prices in chapter 14, and the final chapter is concerned with questions of economic policy. In this book the term is used in reference to a *high* level of output without specifying whether this corresponds to, say, 1, 2 or 3 per cent of unemployed members of the work-force.

In chapter 4, the concept of the short-run equilibrium level of real income was discussed. It was pointed out that the physical factors which determine the upper limits to the potential level of output—the capital stock, natural resources, state of knowledge and the labour force—are not related to those factors which determine the equilibrium level of output—the expenditure and production plans made by individual households and businesses to promote their own interests. In the absence of positive measures by the government, it would be only a coincidence if the equilibrium level of output coincided with the full employment level of output. Aggregate demand may be such that the equilibrium level of output falls short of the full employment level; in this case the situation will be one of *deficient aggregate demand*—the case of a *deflationary gap*. Alternatively, if the equilibrium level of output implied by the level of planned expenditure exceeds the full employment level of output, there will be *excess aggregate demand*—the case of an *inflationary gap*.

2. Measures of deficient and excess aggregate demand

These two concepts can be explained with the aid of a diagram. Consider figure 5.1, which shows for a closed, two-sector economy, three aggregate demand schedules and the 45° line. Suppose that the full employment level of output is OY_f; and that the schedule of planned expenditures on consumption and investment goods, shown in the figure as E_1, implies an equilibrium level of output of OY_e. This falls short of the full employment level by $Y_e Y_f$. The amount of unemployment cannot be shown on the figure, but given the relationship between output and the demand for labour, there will be a specific number of unemployed workers corresponding to the gap between OY_e and OY_f.

Suppose that planned expenditures now rise and the new schedule is shown by the line, E_2, of figure 5.1. In this case, the equilibrium and full employment levels of output coincide. That is to say, with planned expenditures per period greater by an amount, BC, the full employment level of output has been achieved. BC measures the *deflationary gap*. It is the amount by which, in the initial situation, *planned expenditures* would have to be raised in order to raise *output* from $O Y_e$ to $O Y_f$. The deficiency of planned expenditures, BC, is less than the amount by which the actual level of output falls short of the full employment level, $Y_e Y_f$. The deficiency is measured in terms of

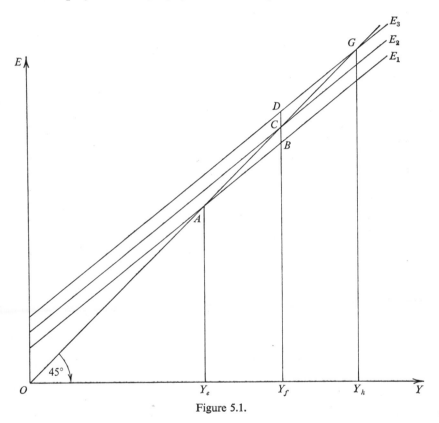

Figure 5.1.

planned expenditure, not in terms of potential output. It is shown in chapter 10 how an autonomous rise in planned expenditure of the amount, BC, results in a total rise in output of the greater amount, $Y_e Y_f$.

The other possibility is that the intersection of the aggregate demand schedule with the 45° construction line is to the right of the full employment level of output. Consider, for example, the aggregate demand schedule E_3, which intersects the 45° line at G in figure 5.1.

This implies an equilibrium level of output of OY_h; but this is in excess of the full employment level.

The level of real planned expenditure which would be made from the full employment level of income, OY_f, would be $Y_f D$. This exceeds the corresponding flow of production by the *inflationary gap*, that is, by the amount, CD.

Businessmen would find that their stocks were unexpectedly running down, and that their order books were continually lengthening. They would therefore have an incentive to raise their product prices and, also, to offer higher money-wage payments in an attempt to attract the additional labour needed to help them meet their expanding orders. An inflationary situation of rising prices and money costs would develop; situations of this kind are discussed in detail in chapter 14. However, if the excess aggregate demand is eliminated by reducing expenditures by the amount, CD, so that the aggregate demand schedule passes through C (as does the line E_2) the equilibrium and full employment levels of output will coincide.

The measures of deficient and excess aggregate demand are both defined in relation to the level of aggregate demand which calls forth the full employment level of output, but the two concepts are not symmetrical. Removal of a deficiency in demand involves not only a change in the level of planned demands but it also results in an increase in output; in figure 5.1 by an amount, $Y_e Y_f$. On the other hand, removal of excess demand reduces planned expenditures, but does not have a comparable impact on output, its effect mainly being on the rate of change of prices and on the length of order books.

3. Wage rates and employment in the two-sector economy

Where there is a disequilibrium situation in an *individual* competitive market the excess supply or demand gives rise to a price change which induces changes in the quantities supplied and demanded until the disequilibrium is corrected. This is true for an *individual* type of labour, say bricklayers, as well as for an *individual* product, say bricks. It is, however, not necessarily true that if there are disequilibria in most markets, price adjustments will remove the disequilibria.

In the case of the product markets considered in aggregate, it has been demonstrated that if the rate of aggregate expenditure exceeds the current rate of aggregate output, so long as the economy is operating *below* full employment, there will be an increase in the rate of production; because it gives rise to a lesser increase in aggregate real demand, the increased rate of output will be associated with a reduction in the excess aggregate demand (see pp. 54–55 of chapter 4).

If the economy is operating at full capacity, the excess demand will persist because it is not physically possible to expand the rate of output. It might at first be thought that in this case an equilibrium could be attained through an adjustment in aggregate demand consequent upon an increase in the price level. Such an adjustment is possible in an individual market where supply is fixed and there is excess demand; for example, if the current demand for first edition copies of *The Fortunes of Richard Mahoney* were to exceed the supply at the current price the price would increase until the number of willing purchasers and holders of the given number of copies was reduced to the given supply. In the case of an individual market where supply is fixed the rise in the price of the commodity causes potential buyers to revise their purchase plans; in the light of their unchanged money incomes and the unchanged prices of alternative products, some buyers will reduce their demands and thereby eliminate the disequilibrium.

When there is an excess of aggregate demand over full employment output, the prices of all commodities will tend to rise. In itself, this would tend to reduce demand, but a price increase cannot occur without *a matching increase in receipts of money income*. In the case of an individual commodity, the increase in income is an insignificant addition to aggregate personal income; furthermore, it is the sellers of the commodity, not the buyers, who receive the increment of income. When the prices of all commodities are rising the income aspect of the price rise cannot be ignored. The entities in the economy as *spending* units face higher prices, but in their capacity as *sellers* of services they receive corresponding increases in income. In the simplest case, if all prices rise by x per cent, money incomes will also rise by x per cent; no commodity will have become 'more expensive' in the sense that it is more costly relative to other goods or to incomes received. In these circumstances there is no *prima facie* reason to expect the process of price increases to reduce real expenditures on final products.[1]

It is obvious that an excess aggregate demand for products will be associated with disequilibrium in the labour markets—there will be

[1] This is a highly simplified exposition of the inflationary situation. A more detailed discussion is given in chapter 14.

an excess demand by employers for labour. It may not be so self-evident that equilibrium in the product market is compatible with continuing disequilibrium, in the form of an excess supply, in the labour market. The equilibrium rate of production is that rate which, given the level of expenditure, corresponds to the rate of sales and intended stock changes. Each firm endeavours to produce its particular rate of output at lowest cost and, in the light of the relative prices of productive factors, employs that quantity of labour (and other factors) which minimizes its costs. The consequent aggregate demand for labour may fall short of the number of persons willing to work at the current money-wage rates. The rate of production which, at the given level of real expenditure, yields maximum profits to enterprises, may involve the employment of only a part of the labour force which is prepared to work at the prevailing money-wage rates.

The labour market may not be (indeed, in practice, it rarely is) a competitive one. Wage rates may be largely determined by arbitration authorities (as is common in Australia) or by negotiations between unions and employers (as is common in the United States of America). Alternatively, the sense of unity among employees resulting from their trade-union membership may mean that unemployed workers refuse to under-cut the prevailing money-wage rate. For these (and other reasons) the current structure of money wages may be little affected by the existence of unemployed workers. But even if money-wage rates are determined competitively, a fall in the wage level will not necessarily cause an increased demand for labour. The fall in wage costs would induce employers to expand their employment only if expenditure on their products were to remain constant. But wages are simultaneously both a cost-determining factor and, as a source of income, a demand-determining factor.

Consider the simple case where prices are resolved into wages and gross profits, and where gross profits are a constant percentage of direct costs. Then a fall in money-wage rates of x per cent will reduce money incomes and prices by x per cent, and real incomes will remain unaltered. If real expenditure on consumer goods is determined by real disposable income, and if investment expenditure is given in real terms then the fall in money-wage rates will not cause any change in real expenditure; that is, the rate of activity in the product market will continue below that of full capacity, and the unemployment will persist.

This analysis is greatly simplified; it ignores many important factors, such as the possibility that a lower price and money-wage level (and hence a reduced transactions demand for money) may lead to a lower rate of interest which will encourage investment expenditure; or the possibility that a declining price level may cause potential purchasers to defer their expenditures; or that the fall in prices will reduce the real net disposable income of those who have debt commitments, and that it will improve the economic position of creditors, and persons whose money incomes are not reduced in proportion to the fall in prices. Also the argument applies to a two-sector economy. In an open economy, as is argued in later chapters, the fall in the price level of the domestic economy enables it to expand its output of export and import-substitute goods. However, the above discussion does serve to illustrate the important point that the elimination of unemployment requires an increase in the level of aggregate demand in real terms, and there is no reason to believe that a fall in money-wage rates will necessarily achieve this.

6

MONEY IN THE ECONOMIC PROCESS

In section 4 (*a*) of chapter 3 it was shown that by using prices (the ratios of exchange between goods and services and money) heterogeneous items can be expressed in terms of a common unit. Money, as the *unit of account*, greatly simplifies the task of *measuring* economic activity. But money also plays a positive role in *determining* economic activity.

In this and the following chapter the link between monetary factors and the process of income-determination is explained. The nature of money, the role of the banking system in the creation of money, and the role of the financial system in arranging the transfer of funds between entities are explained. It is shown that it is not possible to make a simple, direct causal link between changes in the quantity of money and changes in the level of economic activity. However, the demand for and supply of money do influence economic activity through their effect upon aggregate demand. Their influence is exercised in subtle and complex ways, but the main impact is through changes in the cost and availability of finance. Chapter 4 presented the basic argument of this book—that the level of economic activity is determined by the interaction of aggregate demand with aggregate supply. In that chapter the determinants of consumption and investment expenditures were discussed briefly. In the detailed discussion of chapters 8 and 9, it is shown that the cost and availability of finance play an important role in the determination of investment expenditures and that they may, on occasions, exert a significant influence upon consumption expenditures.

1. The nature and functions of money

In chapter 3, it was explained that the economic process can be viewed in its real dimension as exchanges of the services of productive factors for the goods and services produced within the trading enterprises sector. But these real exchanges are not made directly. They are carried out by means of money exchanges so that there is a second two-way flow—the money flows from firms to the suppliers of productive factors, and from the spending entities to firms for

75

goods and services. That is, money serves as the *medium for transactions*. Any entity wishing to acquire a good or service must either possess money to give in exchange, or else, in the case of credit sales, persuade the seller that money will be forthcoming at a later date. The use of money as the exchange medium is a prerequisite for the extreme specialization, and the consequent complex system of exchange relationships, involved in a modern economy.

In addition to being a unit of account, and medium for transactions, money serves a third function—as a *store of value*. An entity which contributes a service to the productive process receives money in exchange. In a sense a money payment is tantamount to a 'receipt' given by society as acknowledgement of the productive contribution of an entity; the 'receipt' gives the entity a claim to goods and services of equivalent value. However, exercise of this command over real resources can be deferred; this can be done by holding money or other financial assets, until the time when it is desired to exercise the claim.

Indeed it is mainly because money has this attribute of a store of value that fluctuations in economic activity occur. If the right to spend could not be deferred, the only motive for contributing to the flow of output would be in order simultaneously to withdraw an amount of equal value; consequently, the value of desired aggregate expenditure could not fluctuate independently of the value of desired aggregate production.

The domestic stock of money comprises those assets freely acceptable in the domestic market in exchange for any marketed item. The identification of the components of the stock of money follows from this concept. In Australia, the assets which serve as money are the public's holding of coins (manufactured by the Royal Mint), paper money (issued by the Note Issue Department of the Reserve Bank of Australia) and deposits in current accounts with the trading bank system. If, in time, other assets (such as savings bank deposits) came to be used as a means of payment, then this definition of the money stock would need to be revised.[1]

---

[1] Actually savings bank deposits and time deposits at trading banks are included in the Reserve Bank's definition of money. But, since they are not themselves used as means of payment, they are excluded from the present definition. For a further discussion of the concept of the quantity of money, see R. R. Hirst and R. H. Wallace (eds.), *Studies in the Australian Capital Market* (Melbourne: F. W. Cheshire Pty. Ltd., 1964), chapter 6.

2. The capital market[1]

The fact that the flow of production of final goods and services is matched by a flow of expenditure and income must be interpreted with care. Expenditure normally involves a cash transaction, but it may involve a credit transaction; in the latter case, the seller acquires a claim on a trade debtor. It was shown in chapter 4 that the *ex post* equality of production, income and expenditure does not imply that producers in aggregate will always find there are willing buyers at profitable prices for any level of output. Nor does it mean that each individual entity receives from the sale of currently produced goods and services exactly the amount of money and other claims which it incurs through its own expenditure on currently produced goods and services; indeed, for any given period, such a balance of money flows would hold for relatively few entities.

An entity whose current expenditure falls short of its current disposable income is saving. It is adding to its wealth, which is the sum of past net savings. Initially, the increment of saving is likely to be in the form of an increased money holding, but the entity is unlikely to want to hold permanently all of its increment of wealth as money; it may acquire more income-earning financial assets, such as government bonds, company debentures, savings deposits and so on; or it may reduce its indebtedness to other entities, for example, by repaying a bank overdraft or redeeming maturing debentures; or it may acquire real assets. Thus some part of the excess of its current saving over the capital formation financed from its own funds is channelled through the capital market, and becomes available to other entities.

Transactions in the capital market are not confined to the disposition of current saving but comprehend all trading in financial assets. The public holds a great stock of financial assets in the form of money, equities (shares or ownership claims), and fixed interest claims (savings and time deposits, debentures, mortgages and so on).

[1] Throughout this chapter the term 'capital market' is used in reference to financial dealings, and not to the production and sale of capital goods. The importance of determining the particular meaning of 'capital' in each particular context was emphasized in chapter 2; in particular, see p. 12. The capital market referred to in this chapter embraces not only transactions conducted through the organized financial sector (the banks, stock exchanges and financial intermediaries) but also informal arrangements such as loans negotiated on the golf course and trade credit extended directly by firms to buyers.

At each moment each entity must decide not only upon the rate at which it will currently save, but also whether or not to continue to hold its stock of wealth in the existing form. Should it convert some of its asset holdings to money and pay off some of its indebtedness to other entities? Should it reduce its money holding and acquire more income-earning assets? Should it borrow more to increase its holding of money or other assets? Should it reshuffle its non-money assets, for example, by selling equities and buying debentures? These are the sorts of choices continuously open to holders of financial assets.

Entities whose expenditure exceeds their current income (for example, firms which are expanding their capacity) can obtain the necessary finance by drawing on accumulated money balances, by converting to money other assets held (for example, by the sale of government bonds), by borrowing from financial intermediaries[1] and by borrowing from the general public. The financial transactions of the capital market embrace both the reshuffling of the assets of entities, as well as the raising of finance by entities whose expenditures on goods and services exceed their current incomes.

3. The cost of finance

The expenditure decisions of entities are influenced by the cost of finance. Those who want to spend in excess of their own financial resources must consider the cost of borrowing—the rate of interest that they will have to pay financial intermediaries, or the rate of return that they will have to offer in order to get the public to take up issues of securities.

There is a multitude of interest rates at any given time. Persons with little security to offer have to pay higher interest rates on loans from hire-purchase finance companies; others with large incomes and wealth can borrow more cheaply on bank overdraft. Small new companies will have to offer higher rates of return on their securities than will old-established, large enterprises; and so on. In general, at any moment of time, differences in interest rates tend to reflect differences in the length of loans or in the degree of risk, or differences in the service costs associated with the various forms of loans.

The different rates of interest tend to move together because borrowers and lenders are prepared to substitute between the

---

[1] Financial intermediaries are defined as institutions which borrow funds from one group of entities in order to lend to others. They are not concerned with physical production.

different forms of loans and securities. For example, an enterprise wanting additional funds to finance investment expenditure may be able to obtain funds by borrowing from lending institutions, such as banks or life assurance companies, or by the issue of its own securities. And entities with funds to lend can either take up securities issued directly by the spending entities, or they can lend their funds to financial intermediaries who in turn lend to the spending entities. When there is an increase in the rate of interest for a particular form of finance, borrowers tend to switch to alternative forms, and lenders tend to increase the amount made available in that form. As a result interest rates for the various forms of finance tend to move together.

However, the capital market is not perfectly competitive, so that, when 'money becomes tight' (to use the jargon of the market) not only do interest rates tend to rise, but credit also becomes 'scarce'. That is, individual borrowers are likely to find that, although they are prepared to pay the going market rates, they cannot obtain all (and in some cases, any) of the finance they desire. In a competitive market (for example, the wholesale fresh vegetable market) sellers ask the highest price consistent with selling their given supply. But in many financial markets the lenders do not set the highest possible rate of interest, given their rate of lending. For example, in most of the post-war period the Australian savings banks have had substantial waiting lists of persons wishing to obtain housing loans. That is, the banks could, in some periods, have charged higher interest rates and still made the same volume of housing loans. The existence of waiting lists (a form of credit rationing) for bank finance is largely due to the control by the Reserve Bank of bank interest rates. But interest rates in some other sectors of the capital market are not highly responsive to market forces. The reasons for the 'stickiness' of the interest rates offered and charged by financial intermediaries are complex; two factors of particular importance are the oligopolistic nature of the competition in some sections of the market, and the strong antipathy of the general public to increases in interest rates.[1]

There are three major factors which may cause a change in the

---

[1] For the sake of simplicity of exposition and brevity, reference is made in this chapter to 'the rate of interest' where the phrase 'the general level of the structure of interest rates' would be a more accurate term. Strictly, the term 'the rate of interest' is used in certain passages of this chapter to denote a complex index of both the cost and availability of finance. For a discussion of the significance of the availability of finance see chapter 9, section 6.

general level of the rates of interest. First, there may be a change in the demand for money associated with a change in the desired rate of spending. Secondly, the preferences of wealth-holders may change, so that on balance they wish to increase (or decrease) the proportion of their wealth held in the form of money. Thirdly, the stock of money may change. The first two of these factors will now be considered in some detail; the third is discussed in the next chapter.

4. The influence of monetary factors upon expenditure decisions

In chapter 4 it was argued that in the short run the equilibrium level of income is determined by the level of aggregate demand, subject to the upper limit of full employment. If, in the simplified two-sector economy postulated there, financial factors are to influence economic activity, it must be through their influence upon the expenditures of households and firms. At this stage in the development of the argument only the commonplace observations that spending is in part financed by borrowing, and that borrowing decisions are largely made in the light of the terms on which finance is available, need be made.

(a) The stock of money, the level of activity and the rate of interest

The method of analysis in this book is Keynesian; that is, changes in the level of economic activity in the short run are attributed mainly to changes in planned expenditures. Prior to the widespread acceptance of Keynes's arguments, a common approach to macroeconomic problems was to consider the quantity of money and the rate at which the quantity was spent. A useful starting-point for a consideration of the influence of monetary factors upon the level of planned expenditures is to examine this *quantity theory* approach.

In the first section of this chapter money was defined as the *stock* of financial assets possessing a particular attribute, namely, that they can be used to purchase any marketed item. Money is described as a stock because at each point of time, the amount of it existing can be identified. For example, at June 1965 the Australian public held approximately \$3,800 m. of money—\$800 m. as coins and notes, and \$3,000 m. in current accounts with the banking system. Since each act of expenditure requires that the spending entity has access to money or to credit, it might be thought that the size of the stock of money should be given central place as *the* determinant of the flow of expenditure. However, this would be warranted only if there were associated with each stock of money a uniquely determined rate of flow of expenditures. In fact, this is not so; for example, in Australia in the post-war period, there has been a general downward trend in the ratio between the stock of money and the flow of expenditure; in any short period it is quite possible that changes in the quantity of money and in the level of output will be in opposite directions.

The ratio between GNP at current market prices, Y_m, and the money stock, M, is designated the *income-velocity of circulation*, v, where $v \equiv Y_m/M$. For the year 1965, the value of v for Australia was 5·0 (compared with 2·5 for the year 1950). Income velocity reflects the rate at which the money stock is being transferred between entities in payment for *final* goods and services. It does not represent the rate at which money is changing hands, since many (indeed most) payments are for intermediate and financial transactions.

If v were a constant, control of economic activity would be a relatively simple matter. Both Y_m and M are measurable quantities and the calculation of v is a simple matter. It is shown below that the quantity of money can be regulated by the monetary authorities. However, expenditure can be increased without any increase, and in spite of a decrease, in the quantity of money. To note that in such a case 'the velocity of circulation has increased' adds nothing to the understanding of the economic process. The velocity of circulation is an *ex post* concept; it is knowledge of *ex ante* relationships which is necessary for effective economic control.

Because money is used as a medium for transactions there is a relationship between the level of planned expenditure and the amount of money which entities wish to hold. If entities wish to increase their rate of expenditure in money terms either because they wish to increase their real expenditures, or because there has been an increase in the level of prices and/or money wages, they will be able to give effect to this only if they can get access to money. For example, if a firm's rate of production doubles (and there is no change in the time lags between the receipt of sales income and the payment for inputs), the money needed to finance wage payments, stock holdings and trade debtors will double. Again, if the weekly income of a household is doubled and it wishes to double its rate of consumption expenditure (other factors, such as access to credit, given) it will need to hold increased money balances during the week. Conceptually a certain portion of the money stock in Australia can be regarded as being held by persons and enterprises in order to enable them to carry out their current rate of planned expenditure; this portion of the money stock is held to satisfy the *transactions motive*, and it constitutes *transactions balances*.

But entities hold money in excess of these amounts; and they do this despite the fact that they could earn a direct money income from their excess holdings if they exchanged them for other financial assets. Entities hold money above their current transaction needs for a variety of reasons; first, to be able to finance an anticipated increase in expenditure. For example, a firm contemplating an expanded investment programme may build up a money balance in anticipation of this. A household may hold money in order to be able to meet any unexpected forced expenditure, such as medical bills, or to be able to take advantage of bargain offers. Entities also hold money in order to be able to take advantage of favourable opportunities for investment in financial assets, or because they believe that in the near future the prices of financial assets will fall.

One way whereby entities requiring transactions balances in excess of their current money balances can obtain extra finance is to offer higher rates of return to holders of *idle balances*, that is, balances in excess of transactions needs. A higher rate of interest means that the opportunity cost of holding money—the potential reward which can be had by parting with money—is increased. An increase in aggregate expenditure is usually marked by increased borrowing and a consequent rise in the rate of interest. With a given money stock there will also be an increase in the velocity of circulation.[1]

Those who desire to increase their rate of expenditure may also obtain the extra finance by converting their non-money financial assets to money. If, for example, an enterprise has a holding of government bonds, it could sell these and use the proceeds to finance investment expenditure. However, to sell their bonds the would-be-

---

[1] An analogy may assist in understanding this concept. The university librarian measures the use made of the library's given stock of books, B, by R, the number of books borrowed per time period. The ratio $t \equiv R/B$ is the velocity of circulation of the stock of books. If the number of students increases but B does not increase proportionately, R will probably increase and the number of books on the library shelves at any point of time will decrease. If the pressure on the library stocks becomes sufficiently great, the ratio t will tend to reach a maximum because potential borrowers cannot get access to books. One method by which t could be further increased would be to introduce a charge for each day that a student held a book. This would promote a transfer of books from idle holders to active users.

investors will have to accept a lower price, which means an increased rate of return to the buyers;[1] because of the general interdependence of the various sectors of the capital market, the general level of interest rates will tend to rise.

In the argument above it was assumed that the stock of money was constant. Those who wanted to obtain greater holdings of money traded securities (either newly created or existing) with entities holding money. The associated increase in the rate of interest would depend upon the willingness of those holding money to substitute non-money assets in their portfolios of assets. In fact, there is a large volume of financial assets held by the Australian public, in particular the fixed and savings deposits held with the banks, which the owners can convert to money (trading bank current deposits and currency) without causing a matching fall in the money held by the other members of the public. Furthermore, because of the trading banks' practice of granting overdraft limits, potential spenders who have prearranged bank loans can draw upon these to increase their expenditure; in this case there is a matching increase in the quantity of bank deposits. If an increase in aggregate expenditure were financed mainly from these sources there would not be the same tendency for a rise in the rate of interest as in the situations where the spenders have to induce other members of the public to transfer a portion of a given money supply to them. For the purpose of the argument of this chapter and the next it is convenient to assume that all trading bank deposits are current deposits, and also to assume that the level of bank advances is determined by the banks' decisions, as influenced by the central bank. The more realistic case is considered in chapter 13.

[1] The rate of return to a bond buyer is not the nominal (or issue) rate of interest, but the interest receipts plus any capital gain (or loss) at redemption expressed as a rate of return on the purchase price. The calculation of rates of return is explained in chapter 9. In the case of a security which can be purchased for S, which carries interest payments of q each year, and which the buyer plans to sell at the end of n years at an expected price of T, the expected rate of return, ρ, is that rate of discount which satisfies the following equation:

$$S = \frac{q}{1+\rho} + \frac{q}{(1+\rho)^2} + \ldots + \frac{q+T}{(1+\rho)^n}$$

$$= \left(\sum_{i=1}^{n} \frac{q}{(1+\rho)^i} \right) + \frac{T}{(1+\rho)^n}.$$

It can be seen by inspection that, given q, ρ will be less the greater is S and the less is T.

(b) Portfolio preferences and the rate of interest

Equilibrium in the market for financial assets is possible because entities are prepared to substitute different financial assets one for another as their relative prices and rates of return alter. For example, consider the case where the only financial assets are money, and fixed-interest securities issued by trading enterprises. The rate of return which a person buying one of those securities would expect to earn over the period he contemplated holding it would be determined by the purchase price, the expected interest receipts, and the price at which it was expected it could be resold (or if it is to be held to maturity, the redemption proceeds).

Each person holding money has continually the opportunity to change his portfolio of financial assets by giving up money and acquiring these securities. A person who continues to hold money can, then, be presumed to consider it to have a value to him in excess of the expected rate of return on securities. As was explained in section 1 above, although money does not yield any interest payment, it does have the unique properties that it is the medium of exchange and a store of value free of the danger of a capital loss. In the case where a person anticipates that security prices will fall in the future, to the extent that the expected rate of return is negative, he will clearly wish to hold money. But even if the expected rate of return is positive, there are still advantages to be had from holding money; first, there is its convenience as the exchange medium; and secondly, people are rarely completely certain of the reliability of their expectations of the future of security prices. By holding some money they can hedge partially against the consequences of incorrect expectations.

Given the current prices of securities each entity will anticipate a rate of return to be had from the purchase of additional securities. This rate of return is foregone if the entity holds money. The entity's portfolio is in equilibrium when the advantage of holding a marginal dollar is regarded as being equal to the anticipated rate of return from the purchase of another dollar of securities. If, at any given time there are entities which consider that the advantages of holding a marginal dollar of money are not equal to the advantages of purchasing another dollar of securities, the financial market is not in equilibrium.

Consider the following disequilibrium situation: some entities consider there is a net advantage to be had from substituting securities for money in their portfolios; the other entities are satisfied with the composition of their portfolios. This could be described as a situation where there is an excess demand for securities, or an excess supply of money, at the current rate of return. In the short run both the quantity of money and quantity of securities are given. Those entities who wish to acquire additional securities can do so only if they can induce others to substitute money for securities in their portfolios. To do this they must offer higher prices for securities. This will reduce the rate of return to be had on securities,[1] and the net excess demand for securities will tend to be eliminated. There will be sales of securities from those initially in equilibrium to those initially in disequilibrium; the lower rate of return will both reduce the latter's excess demand for securities, and will also induce those initially in equilibrium to part with some securities. Exchanges of money for securities between the two groups will continue until the rate of return falls to such a level that all entities regard the rate of return from a marginal dollar invested in securities as being offset by the advantage obtained from the holding of a marginal dollar of money.[2]

So far the discussion has been based on the assumptions that there is no tendency for entities to reshuffle their assets if the volume of transactions is constant and an equilibrium portfolio holding has been achieved. In practice, wealth-holders are liable to change frequently their attitudes towards the benefits (and possible losses) to be had from holding securities and from making loans; the resulting reshuffling of asset holdings has implications for expenditure plans through its effect on the rate of interest.

Such reshuffling may be based on rational calculations; for example, the public may anticipate that the government plans to increase the rates of interest which it directly controls, namely, the rates of interest which it offers on its own new borrowings, and the rates of interest which it allows the banking system to charge. The rational wealth-holder who holds this view will anticipate that the whole structure of interest rates will go up (because of the inter-

---

[1] See footnote on p. 83.

[2] The argument implies that the marginal value of additional holdings of money declines. This is a reasonable view, since, with given rates of expenditure, the marginal convenience of money as a medium of exchange declines: and the importance attached to money as a hedge against a capital loss, other factors being constant, declines the greater is the proportion of money to securities in the portfolio.

dependence of the capital market), or, what amounts to the same thing, that the prices of existing assets yielding given nominal returns will fall.[1] Or they may be based on contagious waves of pessimism (or optimism)—a general revision of the folklore of the market place may lead to a consensus that 'business prospects are bad' and that it is 'a poor time to buy'. Such attitudes lead to attempts to hold less securities, a lesser willingness to subscribe to new issues of securities, and a lesser willingness to lend to institutions, individuals and customers, and so the general cost of finance rises.

If a wave of pessimism is allowed to develop unchecked it can lead to panic demands for money as people become fearful of a financial crisis. Such a panic may be self-justifying—people fear that stock exchange prices will fall; they fear that trade debtors may not be able to pay for goods; they fear that financial institutions may be unsound; and so on. And so they sell securities, refuse to extend credit, and withdraw loans made to financial institutions. In short, there is a reluctance to continue lending, and a desire to build up one's own money stock. The consequences of this are to cause the decline in stock-market prices and to bankrupt some traders and credit institutions. Australia experienced a mild form of this in 1960–61, when, for example, the index of the prices of ordinary shares traded on the Sydney Stock Exchange fell 20 per cent between September and December 1960, and over the following year several large credit institutions and trading enterprises encountered financial difficulties largely because of a change in the willingness of the public to lend as freely.[2]

In the absence of positive control by the government (or its agent, the central bank), monetary factors could cause substantial instability in aggregate expenditure in the short run; in particular the creation and destruction of the money supply by the banking system, and the waves of optimism and pessimism generated in the capital market would cause commensurable variations in the ease with which finance could be obtained. Likewise, instability could occur in the long run;

[1] If new issues of securities carry a higher nominal (contractual) interest rate, no rational buyer will purchase an existing security bearing a lower nominal rate of interest but similar in other respects until its price fell so that it yielded an equivalent rate of return. See footnote on p. 83.

[2] In terms of the analogy of the library, the counterpart of such a financial crisis would arise if students came to believe that the number of books available on the shelves was likely to decline sharply. Then (perhaps despite increased fines for holding them) students would hoard books in excess of those currently used, and the feared shortage would develop.

if the growth in the money supply did not match the growth in productive capacity, a greater proportion of the money supply would be absorbed in transactions balances, rates of interest will tend to be higher and, as a consequence planned expenditure (in particular that part financed by borrowing) might lag below that level which calls forth the full employment level of output. And even if, in the absence of outside control, the financial system was not a positive source of economic instability, there would still be a strong case for its control; in the event that the level of planned expenditure tended to fall short of that needed to give full employment, it could be stimulated by making finance cheaper and more readily available.

For these reasons, in the advanced mixed-economies, the monetary authorities (the government and its agent, the central bank) exercise a continuous influence upon the financial system. In particular they are able to vary the quantity of money and the volume of bank loans, and because of the interdependence of the market, this enables them to influence the behaviour of the whole financial system. The next chapter describes the banking system and the techniques of control available to the monetary authorities.

7

THE BANKING SYSTEM AND THE
QUANTITY OF MONEY

People sometimes speak as if the quantity of money is—or directly determines—the level of spending. For example, an increase in economic activity may be attributed to the 'fact' that 'there is more money around'. In chapter 3 it was shown that the aggregate flow of economic activity during a period is measured by the GNP at constant prices, and in other earlier chapters it has been shown that, subject to the upper limit of full employment, the level of activity depends upon the response of businessmen to the level of aggregate planned expenditures.

The argument of the previous chapter was based upon the assumption that the quantity of money was constant. It was explained that, although production and expenditure involve money exchanges, the level of activity can increase without an increase in the quantity of money. Through the capital market funds can be transferred from holders of idle balances to those entities desiring to increase their rates of expenditure. Expenditure plans, however, are formulated in the light of the cost and ease with which finance can be obtained. It was shown that changes in the public's willingness to part with finance will affect the conditions upon which finance is available; and also that, other things being equal, an increase in the rate of expenditure will tend to increase the rate of interest. In this chapter the factors which determine the quantity of money are discussed. It is shown that, other things being equal, an increase in the quantity of money will increase the availability and reduce the cost of finance, and consequently will operate to stimulate expenditure. The first task is to examine the nature of the banking system.

1. The Australian banking system

(a) *The Reserve Bank*

The Australian banking system comprises a central bank (the Reserve Bank of Australia), the trading banks, and the savings banks. The Reserve Bank is a public authority created by the Commonwealth Government; it is controlled by a Governor, appointed by Cabinet, and a Bank Board. The latter's members include the Secretary to the Department of the Treasury. The Reserve Bank co-operates closely with the Treasury to achieve the Commonwealth Government's economic objectives.

The basic functions of the Reserve Bank are the regulation of the monetary system and manipulation of the financial system in order to promote the Commonwealth Government's economic policy. Through its Note Issue Department the Reserve Bank has the capacity to create an unlimited amount of paper currency; and through its control over the trading banks, and its own open-market operations with the public it can vary the level of trading bank deposits. It acts as banker to the Commonwealth Government. In effect, the Commonwealth Government has an unlimited overdraft with the Reserve Bank. The Government can make any volume of payments by writing cheques drawn against the Reserve Bank. If the Government does not have a credit balance in its account with the Reserve Bank it issues government securities to the Reserve Bank as formal acknowledgement of its indebtedness. When these securities mature, the Government may, if it wishes, merely borrow again to redeem the maturing securities. Each of these aspects of central banking is discussed in detail below.

There is one limitation on the capacity of the Reserve Bank to create the means of payments. Australian currency is not an acceptable medium for the settlement of international transactions. But the Reserve Bank has, as one of its functions, control over Australia's international reserves. These consist of gold, and foreign exchange holdings in the form of sterling, United States dollars and other currencies acceptable in foreign trade. Any Australian who obtains foreign exchange (for example, from the sale of exports or of securities), must sell it to the trading banks. The latter act as agents for the Reserve Bank, and they purchase the foreign exchange for Australian currency. The prices paid for foreign exchange, the official *exchange rates*, are determined by the monetary authorities.[1]

---

[1] The Reserve Bank publishes the rates at which it will exchange each particular foreign currency for Australian currency. These prices are the rates of exchange. For example, the price of £100 sterling is Aust. $250 (approx.), and the price of U.S. $100 is Aust. $89 (approx.). The rates of exchange vary within very narrow limits in the short run. A major change in the exchange rate between the Australian dollar and the key international currencies would represent a most far-reaching change in economic policy. Such a change would be made by the

Consequently, all Australians who want foreign exchange (for example, to pay for imports) must purchase it from the Reserve Bank, through the trading banks.

Clearly the Reserve Bank has tremendous potential economic power, and if this were used in a reckless manner, the Australian economy could be reduced to chaos. In fact these powers are used in conjunction with other economic controls to promote orderly economic conditions.

The functions of the Reserve Bank of Australia are reflected in the composition of its balance sheet:

Balance sheet 7.1

Reserve Bank of Australia (including the Note Issue and
Rural Credits Departments)

Balance sheet as at the end of June 1965*

Liabilities	$m.	Assets	$m.
1. Deposits held by		5. International Reserves	1,300
(i) Trading banks	20		
(ii) Savings banks	430	6. Australian government	760
(iii) Governments	N.A.	securities	
2. Statutory reserve deposits	660	7. Loans extended by Rural	240
3. Notes on issue	870	Credits Department	
4. Other (including 1 (iii))	430	8. Other	110
	Total 2,410		Total 2,410

* The items are rounded to the nearest $10m.; N.A. = not available.

Items 1 (i) and (ii) are bankers' deposits and reflect the Reserve Bank's function as banker to the trading banks and savings banks; Items 1 (iii) and 6 reflect the Reserve Bank's role as financier to the Government; Item 2 reflects its function as controller of the activities of the trading bank; Item 3, its control of the note issue; Item 5, its custody of Australia's holding of international reserves; in addition to reflecting the role of financier to the government Item 6 also enables the Reserve Bank to engage in security dealings with the banking system and the public. The Rural Credits Department provides finance for the processing and marketing of primary produce (Item 7). The work of the Department falls outside the basic functions of a central bank.

Cabinet, after discussion with the Reserve Bank and the International Monetary Fund. The pound sterling–Australian dollar exchange rate has been unaltered since 1932, and the U.S. dollar–Australian dollar rate was last changed in 1949.

(b) The trading banks

The trading banks are a part of the profit-seeking sector. The main sources of their income are from loans (which are mainly made in the form of overdrafts), the interest on their holding of government securities, and the charges made for banking services. After the payment of interest to depositors and operating expenses, the surplus is available to the owners.[1]

From one viewpoint the trading banks can be regarded as one among many sources of loan finance. The control of the rate of *bank* lending does not provide a *complete* control over the channels of finance. It is possible that, when the banks are reducing their loans, other financial intermediaries are expanding theirs, either by drawing on cash reserves or by raising funds from the public for relending. Furthermore, those requiring funds for spending may be able to obtain some part of their needs by the sale of other assets, or by the issue of their own securities directly to the public, or through trade credit. An increase in the rate of spending does not necessarily require an increase in the rate of bank lending. Nevertheless, the trading banks are the largest single source of loans; and, as is shown below, there are other important reasons for paying particular attention to the behaviour of the banking system.

When contrasted with other sources of finance, bank loans are seen to have many advantages—they are quickly negotiated; they carry a relatively low rate of interest and other expenses for the borrower are nominal;[2] the bank does not acquire any legal right to share in control of the affairs of the borrower; and the loan can be repaid immediately if the borrower wishes to do so. An increase in planned expenditures is almost invariably associated with an increased demand for bank loans. If these are not forthcoming some potential spenders may be able to substitute other sources of finance, but others, in particular small enterprises such as farms and small-scale manufacturers, may be almost exclusively dependent upon bank finance. And, in any event, non-bank finance may be a poor second-best because it is more expensive finance in the narrow sense of the

---

[1] The trading banks are discussed in detail in section 3 below. One of the major trading banks, the Commonwealth Trading Bank, is a public enterprise. It competes with the privately owned banks and, in general, operates on a profit-seeking basis.

[2] This is by contrast with, say, an issue of shares which will involve heavy expenses in the preparation of a prospectus, underwriters' fees, and advertising expenses.

direct money-cost, and possibly also in the broader sense of loss of some independence of management and loss of financial flexibility.

Apart from their position as major lenders, the trading banks have a unique role in the financial system because their liabilities comprise the largest part of the means of payment (the stock of money). This unique aspect of the trading banks follows from their willingness to transfer the current deposit claim of any depositor to another, or alternatively to redeem immediately any current deposit for notes or coins.

(c) The savings banks

The Australian savings banks have assets approximately equal to those of the trading banks. They accept demand deposits from the public and invest their funds in government securities and housing loans. As in the case of the trading banks, they keep their main cash reserves with the central bank. The balance sheet of the Australian savings banks in aggregate is given in Balance sheet 7.2.

Balance sheet 7.2

Aggregate balance sheet of the Australian savings banks as at
the end of June 1965*

Liabilities	$m.	Assets	$m.
Deposits of public	4,910	Cash reserves at Reserve Bank	430
Other	130	Other cash reserves	120
		Government securities	3,160
		Loans for housing	1,190
		Other	250
Total liabilities	5,040	Total assets	5,150

* The individual items are rounded to the nearest $10m. The liabilities and assets are those held in Australia. Minor amounts held overseas account for the difference between the totals.

The deposits of the public with the savings banks are approximately equal to the public's deposits with the trading banks. There are, however, some important qualitative differences between the two types of deposit claims. First, the savings bank deposits are not a component of the stock of money as defined in the previous chapter. Money, by definition, can be used to settle any transaction; the assets used as money in Australia can be converted from one form to another (that is, from notes to deposits and vice versa) without capital loss. Savings bank deposits cannot be used directly to settle transactions. They can be quickly and easily converted to notes and coins or trading bank deposits without capital loss, and for this reason some economists describe them as 'near-money'. Any asset can be converted to money but the speed with which this can be done and the difference between the purchase and redemption price vary greatly between assets. Savings bank deposits are at the upper end of the spectrum of assets ranked according to their liquidity—that is, their nearness to money.

Secondly, savings bank deposits cannot be held by incorporated profit-making enterprises. They are held mainly by entities in the personal sector. They yield a rate of interest, and are held by many households as permanent forms of saving. By contrast, trading bank current deposits are held primarily to finance current transactions. The rate of conversion of savings deposits to cash in order to make payments is small relative to the rate at which trading bank current deposits are used to make payments.

From one viewpoint the savings banks (despite their title) are a member of the *genus*, non-bank financial intermediaries. Like the life-assurance, pastoral finance and hire purchase and finance companies, they collect funds from the public for relending to other sectors; and (unlike the trading banks) their deposits are not transferred between entities in the settlement of debt. Those who lend to these enterprises regard their claims against them as a store of value which can be converted to money—in the case of the savings banks with maximum ease.

However, the savings banks are distinguished from the other non-bank financial institutions by their close relationship with the Reserve Bank. This has two aspects: first, their investment policies are closely supervised by the Reserve Bank; in particular, the monetary authorities have great influence over the rate at which the savings banks lend for housing. Secondly, they have large holdings of government securities, and most of their cash reserves are held at the Reserve Bank. If the public's desired rate of accumulation of savings bank deposits should decline, the savings banks are likely to continue their rate of lending for housing, to draw upon their cash reserves at the Reserve Bank, and to sell some of their security holdings to the Reserve Bank. This close relationship with the central bank distinguishes them from other financial intermediaries.

2. The public's holding of notes and coins

From the public's viewpoint it is convenient to use notes and coins to make certain transactions; for example, everyday small household purchases, and wage payments are financed mainly by currency payments. But for the great bulk of business transactions, and for the larger outlays by households, payments by cheque are much more convenient. A cheque is an instruction to the banker to transfer a deposit claim from one entity to another, or to convert a deposit claim to currency. Use of the banking system to make money transfers provides an entity with a means whereby it may check on the uses and sources of its funds; it enables payments to be handled by third parties, including the postal system, without fear of loss due to theft or accident; and it permits payments of any magnitude to be made with ease.

The public's holding of notes and coins is one of the least important of economic quantities. Apart from a few eccentrics, people hold notes and coins to finance current spending. The proportion of spending made by exchange of notes and coins is stable in the short run,[1] and so the public's demand for currency is determined by (rather than determines) aggregate expenditure. The banking system provides facilities for the unlimited conversion of deposits to currency, as the public desires.

On occasions in earlier (pre-central bank) times the public would become suspicious of the ability of the banks to meet demands for cash, and a 'run' on the banks would develop. For example, in 1893, such a run forced the majority of Australian banks to close for some period, and some did not re-open. Today the banks can obtain unlimited cash by drawing upon their bankers' deposits with the Reserve Bank.[2] The Reserve Bank can obtain notes by transferring some part of its assets to the Note Issue Department; the physical limit of the note supply is set only by the capacity of that Department's printing presses. In practice, of course, the power to print notes is used, along with other economic weapons, to promote the attainment of the ends of economic policy.

Paper currency and bank deposits represent exchange media *par*

---

[1] There is in fact a seasonal pattern reflecting such factors as Christmas spending and cash accumulations to tide over holiday periods.

[2] If it should prove necessary these deposits could be augmented by sale of government securities to, or loans from, the Reserve Bank.

excellence, because they can be produced without the use of many resources. By contrast the production of gold and other metallic currencies involves the use of substantial amounts of capital and labour. The major functions of money are to serve as a unit of account, a medium for transactions and a store of value. As long as the monetary authorities follow policies which result in a relatively stable price level, the public has no reason to lose confidence in the existing monetary system. Monetary mismanagement arises ultimately from inept economic administration, not from the particular material selected to act as the medium of exchange.

3. The determination of the level of bank deposits

Most of the money supply consists of the public's current deposit claims against the trading banks. Whereas the public's holding of notes and coins is, in the short run, determined by the level of activity, the level of trading bank deposits and advances plays an important part in determining economic activity; changes in them influence the costs and availability of finance. Consequently the Reserve Bank attempts to influence the behaviour of the trading banks in order to control economic activity.

(a) *A closed-circuit banking system with a passive central bank*

In this section the determination of bank advances and deposits is considered. To simplify the exposition it is assumed that the public makes all of its payments through cheques drawn on the banking system which comprises a Reserve Bank and the trading banks. It is also convenient to assume that all money transfers are made within a closed circuit; that is, that any cheque written is lodged to the account of another entity in the domestic private sector. It is further assumed that the banks can always find credit-worthy borrowers to whom they are prepared to make loans. These assumptions enable the quantity of money to be considered in isolation from the level of economic activity. In section 3 (*c*) below the assumption of the closed-circuit is abandoned and in chapter 13 the interaction between changes in economic activity and the money stock is considered.

In the closed-circuit system changes in the money stock are determined solely by changes in the asset holdings of the banks. The non-bank financial intermediaries can influence the rate of lending to the spending sectors, that is, to the households and trading enterprises, but, as is shown below, they cannot influence the total level of bank deposits. For the present it will be assumed that the only function of the Reserve Bank is to act as banker to the trading banks. Each bank keeps a credit balance with the Reserve Bank and indebtedness between the banks is settled by transfers between these credit accounts. The central bank is assumed to play a passive role; that is, it does not act to alter the aggregate cash reserves of the trading banks, nor to influence their investment policies. The balance sheet of this hypothetical banking system is of the following form:

Balance sheet 7.3

Aggregate balance sheet of trading banks

Liabilities				Assets
Deposits of public	D	Bankers' deposits with central bank		B
		Government securities		G
		Advances		A
Total $= D$			Total $=$	$B+G+A$

If a member of the public decides to transfer his deposit to another bank, or if he writes a cheque in favour of a client of another bank, this will mean that the bank receiving the deposits will have a claim against the bank from which the deposits are transferred. This claim will be settled by a change in the composition of ownership of item B; total deposits of the public and the total assets of the trading banks will not change. As the trading banks in aggregate acquire earning assets (G and A) they incur deposit liabilities (D) to the public. This happens in the following manner. The banks may buy bonds from members of the public; they pay for these by cheques drawn against themselves, which, when deposited in the sellers' accounts, increase their deposits. Banks make loans by granting overdraft limits to borrowers; when the borrowers use the overdrafts, they write cheques which increase the deposits of other members of the public. In the first case, the banks acquire assets—the debt of the government—in exchange for their own indebtedness in the form of deposit liabilities; and, in the second case, they acquire assets—the indebtedness of private borrowers—in exchange for their own indebtedness (also in the form of deposit liabilities). Given the assets acquired by the banking system, the quantity of money (bank deposits) is determined, and the public's transactions change only the composition of the ownership of the quantity of money. This change in ownership is, of course, of economic significance. For example, the transfer of deposits

96

to willing spenders increases aggregate expenditure; thus a successful issue of securities by a firm will enable it to carry out additional investment expenditure.

Money is involved in all the public's transactions, whether involving the exchange of goods and services or financial transactions.[1] If total bank assets are constant, an increase in the money holding of any entity must be at the expense of another's. If, in the aggregate, there is a desire to move out of money into other financial assets, this will force up the prices of financial assets, and make it easier for borrowers to obtain finance. This may increase the quantity of financial assets, but it does not lead to an increase in the public's holding of money. For example, if some households become more willing to hold debt claims against (lend to) consumer finance companies, this will reduce the cost of borrowing to the companies, and (in a competitive market) the cost of consumer borrowing will fall. As a result there may be some increase in borrowing for, say, car purchases. The stock of financial assets will be increased by the debt claims created between the households who lend to the finance companies, and those created between the finance companies and the ultimate borrowers. Expenditure and production will increase.[2] The stock of money will not have changed; only the ownership of bank deposits will have altered. Should wealth-holding households revise their attitude towards the net advantages of holding the debt of consumer finance companies and decide to convert to deposits some of the maturing claims, the companies will be forced to reduce their lending. The stock of financial assets will be reduced, but again only the composition of ownership, not the total level of bank deposits, will change.

In this closed-circuit system, the use of bank deposits to settle all transactions gives rise to two unique characteristics of banks *vis-à-vis* other financial intermediaries. First, when a borrower seeks a loan from a bank he does not ask the bank to transfer to him an asset in the bank's possession. The borrower desires an asset, money, but the banking system accommodates this by incurring increased liabilities.

---

[1] In one sense the sale of goods on trade credit does not involve the use of money. However, such a transaction may formally be regarded as a loan to the buyer of goods conditional upon him using it to purchase the seller's goods.

[2] It should not be thought that the increased spending by the households who borrow would be offset by the reduced spending by those who lend. The lending households' decision was to rearrange the composition of their wealth, not to alter the rate at which they spend.

97

Thus the quantity of money increases when the banking system acquires assets from the public.[1]

The second characteristic of the banks in this closed-circuit system is that they are unaffected by changes in the desired wealth-distribution of the public. Other financial institutions can survive only as long as the public is prepared to hold claims against them. When the public's willingness to hold such claims declines, the particular institutions are faced with a demand by the public to convert maturing claims to bank deposits. In the case of the banking system the equivalent pressure would arise if the public decided to move out of bank deposits into another form of money, namely, currency. Such a shift is precluded by the assumption of a closed-circuit; but, in the previous section it was explained why such changes are no longer likely in the real world. In brief, the non-bank financial intermediaries can create assets only as long as the public are prepared to lend to them. By contrast, the quantity of bank deposits held by the public is determined by the banks' willingness to acquire assets from the public, not by the public's willingness to acquire claims against the banks.[2]

(b) Reserve bank control of aggregate deposits and advances in the closed-circuit system

The central bank in an advanced mixed economy plays an active role in the determination of the quantity of money. In order to simplify the explanation of the techniques of central banking it is convenient, as a first step, to continue with the assumption of a closed-circuit banking system.

[1] Advances are an asset of the banking system. The same argument holds if the banking system increases its holding of government bonds, or of typewriters. The assets are acquired by writing cheques against themselves; the public hold the deposits so created as an increment to the stock of money.

[2] In practice, the public's willingness to borrow from the trading banks does influence the level of deposits. Suppose that there is a shift of deposits to bank borrowers so that overdrafts are paid off. Instead of this increasing deposits held by some entities and reducing those of others, it reduces both the indebtedness of the public to the banking system (that is, overdrafts decline) and the indebtedness of the banking system to the public (that is, deposits also decline). The banks may not be able to extend new loans immediately. The Australian trading banks are sometimes in the position that they cannot find acceptable borrowers on overdraft, and they cannot purchase securities from the public in the quantities desired because of the limited market in government bonds. The present assumption is that the banks are always able to acquire suitable assets from the public.

A feature common to all banking systems is the requirement (either legal or conventional) that each trading bank holds particular assets, designated *liquid assets* at least equal in amount to a prescribed percentage of its deposit liabilities. This percentage is called the *liquidity ratio*, which, in the Australian case, is called the *L.G.S. ratio*. For example, if the liquidity ratio were 0·2, a bank with deposits of $100 m. would be required to hold liquid assets of at least $20 m. If the central bank can control the trading banks' aggregate holding of liquid assets (the *liquidity base*) it can determine the upper limit to the deposits which the banks can create. Alternatively, (or as a supplement), the central bank can exercise control by varying the prescribed liquidity ratio.[1]

Obviously, effective central bank control requires that the assets prescribed for the liquidity base should not be assets that the banks (in aggregate) could acquire for themselves in significant amounts by purchases from the public. For example, if loans to private borrowers, or grand pianos, were included in the liquidity base, the banks could increase their holding of these assets by acquiring them from the public giving in exchange deposit claims against themselves; this would increase the liquidity base and deposits by equal amounts and would increase the liquidity ratio.

In all banking systems the liquidity base includes the trading banks' holding of cash reserves in the form of demand deposits with the central bank, together with their till money. Other assets may be included; in the Australian case the liquidity base, which is known as *L.G.S. assets*, comprises cash reserves and government securities.[2] The two main techniques used by central banks to reduce the trading banks' holdings of liquid assets are *open-market operations*, and the exercise of *statutory powers*. In the case of open-market operations the central bank sells some of its own holding of government securities through the stock exchanges. The public pays for these with cheques drawn against the trading banks. The central bank in

---

[1] In the example of this paragraph the upper limit to deposits could be reduced by 25 per cent either by reducing the liquidity base to $15 m., or by raising the liquidity ratio from 0·2 to 0·26.

[2] It is unusual for long-term government securities to be included in the liquidity base of a banking system, but it is possible in Australia because the market for these securities is narrow. The main trading is between a few large institutions who report their dealings to, and frequently trade with, the Reserve Bank. In order to enforce a pattern of security yields and prices, the Reserve Bank continually operates on the stock exchanges where the smaller parcels are traded.

this way gains claims against the trading banks, and reduces the bankers' deposits by an equal amount. This technique of open-market operations is not used extensively in Australia, primarily because it is inconsistent with keeping government security prices (and hence interest rates) within the limits desired by the Department of the Treasury.[1]

The alternative technique is to use statutory authority to reduce the liquidity base. In Australia each bank must keep, in a *Statutory Reserve Deposit Account* (*S.R.D. Account*), an amount equal to a prescribed percentage of its deposit liabilities. This percentage is known as the *S.R.D. ratio*. The main method used by the Reserve Bank to control the liquidity position of the trading banks is to vary this ratio. When the S.R.D. ratio is increased the appropriate amount is transferred from cash reserves of the trading banks (that is, from bankers' deposits) to the S.R.D. accounts. If these reserves are inadequate to 'meet the call', the trading banks will obtain additional bankers' deposits (for transfer to the S.R.D. Account) by the sale of some of their government securities to the Reserve Bank if they have an excess of L.G.S. assets over the agreed minimum; if they do not, they must borrow from the Reserve Bank at a penalty rate of interest set by the Reserve Bank. By agreement between the trading banks and the Reserve Bank, a trading bank which has to borrow to maintain the minimum L.G.S. ratio must contract its advances. A reduction in advances reduces the aggregate level of deposits of the trading banks, and it causes the individual bank concerned to win cash reserves from the other banks (see p. 107 below).[2]

The system of central bank control in Australia can be illustrated by use of a simple model; the assumption of a closed-circuit system is still made. A simplified general form of the balance sheet of the Australian trading banks treated as an aggregate is:

[1] Most of the Reserve Bank's dealings in government securities on the stock exchanges are made to prevent the price of bonds from moving sufficiently to bring the market rate of interest outside limits determined by the monetary authorities.

[2] The discussion in the text somewhat simplifies the system. It omits, for example, the significance of the banks' loans to dealers in the short-term money market, which are not included in the official liquidity base. For a more detailed discussion of the Australian banking system, see H. W. Arndt and C. P. Harris, *The Australian Trading Banks* (Melbourne: F. W. Cheshire Pty. Ltd., 1965); R. W. Davis and R. H. Wallace, 'Lessons of the 1960 Bank Credit Squeeze', *Australian Economic Papers*, June 1963; and R. R. Hirst and R. H. Wallace (eds.), *Studies in the Australian Capital Market*, chapters 6–8.

Balance sheet 7.4

Aggregate balance sheet of the Australian trading banks

Liabilities		Assets	
Deposits of public	D	Cash reserves (= till money plus bankers' deposits)	C
		Government securities	G
		S.R.D. Accounts	S
		Advances	A
Total liabilities	D	Total assets	$C+G+S+A$

The actual balance sheet for June 1965 is given in Balance sheet 7.5. For the present, the distinction between fixed and current deposits is ignored.

Balance sheet 7.5

Aggregate balance sheet of the major Australian trading banks*
Actual as at the end of June 1965

Liabilities	$m.	Assets	$m.
Deposits		Cash Reserves	
(i) Fixed	1,790	(i) Deposits at Reserve Bank	20
(ii) Current	2,950	(ii) Other (till money)	140
		Government securities	890
Tota	4,740	S.R.D. Accounts	660
Other	150	Advances	2,630
		Other	490
Total liabilities	4,890	Total assets	4,830

* The individual items are rounded to the nearest \$10m. The liabilities and assets are those held in Australia. Minor amounts held overseas account for the difference between the total.

By an agreement between the Reserve Bank and the trading banks, the latter maintain their L.G.S. assets, $L = C+G$, at a level at least equal to the L.G.S. ratio, r, times D, that is, $L \geqslant rD$. This arrangement dates from 1956 when r was set at 0·14. Since then it has been increased twice, first to 0·16, and then to 0·18. In general, the Reserve Bank intends that r should be a stable ratio—a fulcrum around which changes in the S.R.D. ratio, s, can operate.[1] As the interest earned on the Statutory Reserve Deposit Accounts is nominal (the rate is less than 1 per cent per annum), the banks keep this asset to the minimum; that is, $S = sD$.

[1] From the viewpoint of the effect upon D and A, a given increase in r has the same impact as a given increase in s. The banks would prefer an increase in r because the income yield on G is several times that on S.

101

For the simplified case illustrated by Balance sheet 7.4 the following identity may be written:

$$D \equiv L + S + A.$$

If the banks aim to maximize A, their most profitable asset,[1] they will strive for the position where $L = rD$ and $S = sD$, that is, where $A = (1 - r - s)D$.

If $L > rD$, the banks have *excess reserves*, E, equal to $L - rD$,[2] and they will be able to increase their loans by ΔA. As explained above, an increase in loans to the public leads to a matching increase in deposits; thus $\Delta A = \Delta D$. This increase in deposits reduces E for two reasons. First, with given L, E would be reduced by $r\Delta D$. But ΔD gives rise to $\Delta S \ (= s\Delta D)$, which reduces L by a matching amount. Thus, the decline in excess reserves is: $r\Delta D + s\Delta D$, that is, $(r + s)\Delta D$. To reduce excess reserves to zero requires that this equals the initial excess reserves. This will be achieved when:

$$(r + s)\Delta D = E,$$

that is,

$$\Delta D = \frac{1}{r + s} E.$$

Since

$$\Delta A = \Delta D, \quad \Delta A = \frac{1}{r + s} E.$$

An example will illustrate the argument. Assume $r = 0{\cdot}15$, $s = 0{\cdot}1$, and that, initially, the aggregate trading bank balance sheet is:

Balance sheet 7.6

Situation of excess reserves

Liabilities		Assets	
D	100	L	25
		S	10
		A	65
	100		100

---

[1] This is a somewhat simplified account of their behaviour. While the rate of interest charged for overdrafts always exceeds the bond rate the former involve the risk of bad debts and the latter, of capital losses (and gains).

[2] The banks hold cash reserves, C, of about 3 per cent of D. This has proved sufficient to maintain satisfactory levels of till money (at the branches) and bankers' deposits (clearing balances) at the Reserve Bank. As C yields no money return it is kept to the minimum. Thus excess reserves, E, will typically be in the form of government security holdings.

Then $E(= L-rD) = 10$, and the appropriate $\Delta A = \dfrac{1}{r+s}E = 40$. This increase leads to:

Balance sheet 7.7

Situation of zero excess reserves

	Liabilities		Assets
D	$100+40$	L	$25- \ 4$
		S	$10+ \ 4$
		A	$65+40$
	$\overline{140}$		$\overline{140}$

The Reserve Bank has the capacity to create (and destroy) excess reserves in the Australian trading bank system; it can do so by using open-market operations, or by changing the S.R.D. ratio. Consider first the case where the Reserve Bank purchases government securities of amount, M, from the public.[1] When the public banks the cheques received from the Reserve Bank in exchange for their bonds, deposits increase by an amount, $\Delta D = M$. The increase in deposits gives rise to an increase of $\Delta L \ (= r\Delta D)$ in the agreed minimum holdings of L.G.S. assets, and an increase in the amount in S.R.D. Accounts of $\Delta S (= s\Delta D)$. The excess reserves created, E, are equal to $(1-r-s)M$, and the expansion in advances which will eliminate them is

$$\Delta A = \left(\frac{1}{r+s}\right)(1-r-s)M.$$

For example, if Balance sheet 7.7 is used as an initial equilibrium position, and if it is assumed that $M = 10$, the position immediately after the open-market purchase is as given in Balance sheet 7.8:

Balance sheet 7.8

Immediate position after open-market purchase

	Liabilities		Assets
D	$140+10$	L	$21+9$
		S	$14+1$
		A	105
	$\overline{150}$		$\overline{150}$

[1] In the text only two categories of bond transactions—those between the trading banks and the public, and between the Reserve Bank and the public, are described. The reader should have no difficulty in tracing out the effects of the other possibility, namely, transactions between the Reserve Bank and the trading banks.

and $E \ (= L - rD) = 7 \cdot 5$. After the increase in advances of ΔA $= \dfrac{1}{r+s} E$, the new equilibrium is as given in Balance sheet 7.9:

Balance sheet 7.9

Equilibrium position after open-market purchase

Liabilities			Assets	
D	$150+30$	L		$30-\ \ 3$
		S		$15+\ \ 3$
		A		$105+30$
	$\overline{180}$			$\overline{180}$

An alternative, and more frequently used method of inducing an expansion in bank lending is to create excess reserves by use of the S.R.D. technique; that is, by reducing s. If s is reduced to s', this initially releases an amount from the S.R.D. Accounts of $(s-s') D$, which would be excess reserves. The increase in advances which would eliminate these excess reserves is

$$\left(\frac{1}{r+s}\right)(s-s')\,D.$$

For example, if Balance sheet 7.9 is used as an initial equilibrium position and if the S.R.D. ratio is reduced from $s = 0 \cdot 1$ to $s' = 0 \cdot 05$, the immediate result is as shown in Balance sheet 7.10.

Balance sheet 7.10

Immediate position after reduction in S.R.D. ratio

Liabilities			Assets
D	180	L	$27+9$
		S	$18-9$
		A	135
	$\overline{180}$		$\overline{180}$

Here $E = 9$. The consequent increase in advances of $\dfrac{1}{r+s} E$ leads to the new equilibrium described in Balance sheet 7.11.

Balance sheet 7.11

Equilibrium position after reduction in S.R.D. ratio

Liabilities			Assets	
D	$180+45$	L		$36-\ 2 \cdot 25$
		S		$9+\ 2 \cdot 25$
		A		$135+45$
	$\overline{225}$			$\overline{225}$

(c) Leakages from the trading bank system

For expositional purposes it was convenient to adopt the assumption of a closed-circuit banking system; that is, it was assumed above that any cheque drawn by one member of the public banking with a trading bank would be paid to another client of a trading bank. In fact, there are leakages of funds out of the trading bank payment circuit.

First, some cheques will be written for the withdrawal of currency. Secondly, some transfers will be made to savings bank accounts. Thirdly, some cheques will be drawn for payment to the government sector which banks with the Reserve Bank. And fourthly, some cheques will be for payment to persons outside the domestic economy. Corresponding to each of these outflows from the domestic trading bank payment circuit are the inflows as notes and coins are deposited, as transfers are made from savings banks, as the public banks payments received from the government, and as overseas entities make payments to Australians. In each case, then, it is the net result, the balance of the inflow and outflow, which determines the loss of deposits from the domestic trading bank system.

The impact upon the level of deposits and the liquid assets of the trading banks is the same for all four net outflows.[1] In each case the outflow will be matched by a reduction in the cash reserves of the trading banks. If the public makes a net withdrawal of notes from the trading banks the latter will have to draw on bankers' deposits to obtain further notes from the Reserve Bank. If there is a net transfer to savings bank deposits, the Reserve Bank will transfer bankers' deposits from the credit of the trading banks to the savings banks (see Balance sheet 7.1). As the Reserve Bank is banker to the government, a surplus of government cash receipts over cash outlays will mean that the Reserve Bank will hold net claims against the trading banks, and this will be settled by cancelling bankers' deposits. When an Australian buys from overseas, the buyer exchanges his bank deposit for foreign exchange, which the trading bank obtains from the Reserve Bank by drawing on its banker's deposit.

Changes in economic activity give rise to changes in the quantity of money; these are discussed further in chapter 13. For the present

---

[1] The treatment of net transfers to the savings banks is somewhat simplified. First, because some (minor) part of the cash reserves of the savings banks are held at the trading banks, and secondly, because the savings banks may respond to the increase in deposits in such a way as to cause a reverse flow. For example, if the public transfers deposits from the trading banks to the savings banks and the latter increase their housing loans, the trading banks will regain some part of their lost deposits.

it is sufficient to note that an initial net outflow from the public's trading bank deposits of an amount F (due perhaps to the increased purchase of imports associated with a rise in economic activity) will be matched by a fall in L.G.S. assets (initially as a fall in cash reserves). This will reduce the trading banks' actual ratio of L.G.S. assets to deposits. If initially the banks had no excess reserves they would reduce their advances by an amount, ΔA, equal to

$$\left(\frac{1}{r+s}\right)(1-r-s)F,$$

and the total fall in bank deposits would be $(F+\Delta A)$.

The above analysis points to two further characteristics of the trading bank system which distinguish it from financial intermediaries. First, the excess reserves of the trading banks (and hence their ability to lend) is directly and immediately influenced by the budgetary position and the balance of payments' position; this will be considered further in chapter 13. Secondly, the existence of excess reserves in the trading bank system permits an expansion in aggregate bank loans by some multiple of the excess reserves.

No other category of financial institutions has this ability to lend a multiple of its excess reserves. Consider, for example, the consumer finance companies in aggregate. Their excess reserves take the form of trading bank deposits in excess of the working balances necessary to sustain their current level of operations. If they expand their loans this results in a transfer of their bank deposits to the borrowers. At most they can lend 100 per cent of their excess reserves.

Much the same applies in the case of the savings banks. Their excess reserves are in the form of bankers' deposits with the Reserve Bank.[1] When they make housing loans most of the loan proceeds will be paid to the credit of trading bank accounts. If the savings banks use their excess reserves to subscribe to new loans floated by the Commonwealth government or to purchase securities from the Reserve Bank, their excess reserves will fall by matching amounts. If they purchase securities on the open market, except in the case where the seller lodges the proceeds in a savings bank deposit, there will be a matching loss of savings bank reserves.

In the case of the trading bank system as a whole it has been shown

[1] See, however, the footnote on p. 105. The savings banks maintain minimum ratios of certain types of assets to their total assets. For a full discussion of the Australian savings banks, see R. R. Hirst and R. H. Wallace (eds.), *Studies in the Australian Capital Market*, chapter 6.

that increased lending is associated with increased deposit liabilities. This leads to only a fractional loss of excess reserves through the increments of required L.G.S. assets and Statutory Reserve Deposit Accounts, together with the losses of cash reserves due to the leakages of deposits out of the trading bank payments circuit.[1]

Individual banks regard the granting of loans as involving a 'loss of cash' in much the same sense as the manager of an individual finance company regards the granting of a loan as resulting in a matching reduction of its cash reserves (trading bank deposits). The cash reserves of the trading banks are their bankers' deposits with the central bank. If one bank becomes indebted to another the indebtedness is settled by a transfer of these deposits between the two banks. Consider the case of one bank which expands its loans while its competitors' loans are constant. When an Australian trading bank extends a loan to a client it grants the borrower an *overdraft limit*. The borrower can make payments by cheques drawn upon the lending bank until his debit account reaches this limit. Some of the cheques will be drawn in favour of individuals who bank with the other banks, and so their deposit liabilities will increase. They will thus acquire claims against the expanding bank and these will be settled by transfers of bankers' deposits held at the central bank. If, for example, the borrower uses $1,000 of his overdraft limit, and 20 per cent of the cheques written are deposited with the expanding bank, this bank will acquire an income-earning asset of $1,000, incur additional liabilities to its own depositors of $200, and lose reserves of $800 to the other banks equal to the increase in the latter's deposit liabilities.[2] By comparison, when an individual non-bank financial intermediary grants a loan, it loses bank deposits equal to the loan and this loss is not matched by a direct increase in the assets and liabilities of the other non-bank financial intermediaries.

[1] An increase in lending by any group of financial intermediaries is likely to lead to an increase in the level of real income. The increment of saving associated with this rise may in part be held by the saving entities in the form of loans to the financial intermediaries. In practice the magnitude of this 'feed-back' to any particular group of non-banking financial intermediaries is unlikely to be important. On the other hand, increases in real income are likely to cause a significant drain on the cash reserves of the trading banks, in particular through increased expenditure on imports and tax payments to the government (see section 2 of chapter 13).

[2] An analysis of the behaviour of individual banks in a multi-bank system based upon less restrictive assumptions is presented in R. H. Wallace and P. H. Karmel, 'Credit Creation in a Multi-Bank System', *Australian Economic Papers*, September 1962.

4. Central banking and the cost and availability of finance

The differences between the trading banks and the other financial intermediaries are significant, and they explain in part the greater degree of control exercised over the banks. But the trading banks are but one of the many sources of finance for expenditures. Because of the interdependence of the capital market the Reserve Bank can, by controlling one sector, influence other sectors. Consider the case where the Reserve Bank wishes to stimulate expenditure, and takes action to reduce the cost and increase the availability of finance.

It can create excess reserves in the trading banks by, for example, reducing the S.R.D. ratio; and it can reduce the interest rates offered by the trading and savings banks to depositors, and the rates charged for bank loans. If the banks had been rationing bank loans, the creation of excess reserves will enable them to lend more, and the lower interest charges for loans will induce more borrowing. In a situation where a significant stimulus to spending is required, the monetary authorities are also likely to reduce the rates of interest offered on government loans.[1]

These measures will affect the rest of the capital market in a variety of ways. Some financial intermediaries, for example, the pastoral finance companies, borrow from the trading banks and lend to their own clients; the effect upon them is obvious. When bank loans are more easily obtainable, firms may be prepared to extend more trade credit. Firms which do not actually borrow from the banks may be more willing to lend on trade credit, because bank loans are more freely available should they be needed. This knowledge of the availability of bank finance should it be needed will influence many entities; for example, some persons may make purchases and run down their bank deposits if they believe that they can always improve their liquidity position by obtaining a bank loan.

A reduction in the controlled interest rates will cause some entities to switch funds between the various financial assets; it will promote a flow of finance to the non-bank financial intermediaries. If the borrowing costs of these financial intermediaries fall, competition between them may lead to a fall in their own charges. Furthermore,

---

[1] Such a reduction will make the securities issued by the private sector relatively more attractive. Because of its access to Reserve Bank finance, the Commonwealth Government is able to continue (or increase) its own expenditures even if support for its own loan raisings declines.

if they are competing with the banks for business, they will have an incentive to reduce their charges. For example, consider the case of the finance companies which offer home finance in the form of second mortgages. If the savings banks make more finance available on first mortgage, the finance companies will face a reduced demand for second mortgage finance because the savings banks charge lower interest rates and lend for longer periods.

The lower rate of return on bank deposits and government securities will increase the relative attractiveness of the return to be had from investment in equities, and this will tend to cause an increase in the prices of securities traded on the stock exchange. Furthermore, if the public interpret the change in banking policy as indicative of further expansionary economic measures, this will lead to expectations of greater company profits and add a second stimulus to equity prices. A rising share market is conducive to new issues by companies.

This is not an exhaustive list of the ways in which a change in banking policy can influence the capital market in general; it would be tedious, and perhaps impossible, to trace out all the ramifications of such a change. It must, however, be emphasized that the quantitative magnitudes of these effects are a matter of conjecture. In practice, little is known about such things as the likely increase in trade credit and the possible increased demand for equities. In some cases, (for example, the increase in trade credit extended) it may be that further empirical research will provide useful information which will enable reasonably accurate predictions to be made; but in other cases (for example, the effect of changes in banking policy on the stock market) the factors involved are so complex that accurate prediction may never be possible. Furthermore, the practical problems for policy-makers are not only to predict the impacts of policy changes upon the capital market, but also to predict the changes in expenditure plans which follow from the changed cost and availability of finance.

It is not necessary to discuss in detail the effects of a change in banking policy designed to restrain economic activity. They are, in general, the reverse of those following upon expansionary measures. However, two important exceptions may be noted. In the case of an expansionary policy, the monetary authorities can make funds available at lower cost. But if the public are not prepared to spend, or if businessmen are pessimistic about the prospects of making profits from further investment expenditure, the easier financial conditions will make no impact upon production. The case of a contractionary policy is not the opposite of this. If entities are eager to spend at a greater rate, their plans will be aborted if they cannot obtain additional finance. For example, if the only source of finance for increased expenditure is from bank advances, Reserve Bank measures to reduce bank loans would clearly make an impact upon planned expenditure.

In practice, the sources of finance are multifarious, and it is difficult to curb all the flows of funds; a person who is refused a bank loan to purchase a car may, for example, borrow from another financial intermediary (perhaps borrow against a life assurance policy, or from a consumer finance company), or from friends, or sell some assets, or run down his bank deposit.[1]

A second difference between an expansionary and a contractionary banking policy is that, in the latter case, the monetary authorities are frequently not prepared to engage in large scale open-market sales of government securities which would force up the general level of interest rates.[2] One result of this is that, while bank lending may be checked, entities can sell government securities without incurring capital losses. Since this procedure is an alternative source of finance to bank loans, the reluctance of the monetary authorities to allow bond prices to fall provides some entities with a means of continuing with their plans despite the overall policy of credit restraint.

Even if the authorities were prepared to use more aggressive monetary measures to restrain activity, two practical questions would remain. First, what degree of credit restraint would be necessary to achieve any desired curb to expenditure? And secondly, how far should the authorities rely on monetary policy as contrasted with other techniques of economic policy to achieve any given restraint of aggregate expenditure?

The next four chapters are concerned with a discussion of the determination of the expenditure plans of the personal, enterprises

---

[1] On occasions the monetary authorities have acted to reduce directly the flow of finance made available by the non-bank lenders. For example, the central bank has directed the trading banks not to lend to finance companies. In 1960 the Commonwealth Government passed legislation which, in effect, forced the life assurance companies to invest a greater proportion of their loanable funds in government securities; it also introduced a temporary taxation measure which put great pressure on the finance companies to reduce the rate of their lending.

[2] Among other reasons, they are reluctant to increase the interest payments of borrowers (in particular, the state governments strongly resist such increases), and to inflict capital losses on the holders of government debt.

and government sectors, and of the effects of changes in these plans upon the level of economic activity. The cost and availability of finance are shown to play a role in the determination of expenditure plans. In chapter 13, monetary factors are considered again in the context of the full economy. To that point, unless the contrary is explicitly stated, the argument proceeds on the assumption that the cost and availability of finance are given.

8

THE CONSUMPTION FUNCTION

1. Introduction

The components of aggregate demand in the closed, two-sector economy are consumption and investment expenditures. In this chapter and the next, the factors determining these expenditures are discussed in detail.

The aggregate propensity to consume schedule has already been defined (see chapter 4) as the functional relationship between planned

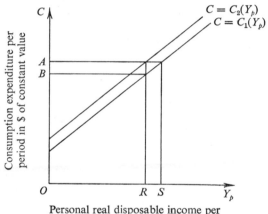

Personal real disposable income per
period in $ of constant value

Figure 8.1.

consumption expenditure, C, and personal disposable income, Y_p, for a specified period. This relationship has a key role in the determination of consumption expenditure, since the appropriate consumption function defines the planned consumption expenditure of households associated with any specified level of personal disposable income.

When a change in consumption expenditure is the result of a change in personal disposable income, the consumption function remaining stable, the change is said to be an *induced* change. Such an induced change is shown in figure 8.1 where, given that consumer behaviour is

112

described by $C = C_1 (Y_p)$, the increase in disposable income from OR to OS, results in an *induced increase* in consumption from OB to OA.

Alternatively, a change in consumption expenditure may be the result of a shift in the consumption function reflecting a change in consumer behaviour associated with changes in the factors *other than disposable income* which affect consumer expenditure. Such a shift is termed *autonomous*. The consumption expenditure-disposable income relationship shifts bodily and is described by a new function. In figure 8.1, $C = C_2 (Y_p)$ is the new consumption function consequent upon an autonomous increase of the original function.[1] The increase in consumption expenditure from OB to OA at the given level of personal disposable income OR is explained by the *autonomous change* in consumer behaviour. The distinction between induced and autonomous changes is of basic importance in the analysis of the determination of the level of economic activity. It is necessary therefore to examine the shape and stability of the aggregate consumption function.

2. The individual consumption function

To obtain the characteristics of the aggregate consumption function, the factors which determine the shape of consumption functions of individuals must first be established; the aggregate function is based upon these individual functions. By 'individual' is meant an individual 'income unit', which (as in the case of a family) may contain more than one person. An income unit is defined as a collection of people whose consumption and saving behaviour may be regarded as joint; that is, as far as consumption and saving decisions are concerned, they can be treated as one behaviour unit.

Because the most important single determinant of current consumption expenditure is current disposable income, the consumption function of an individual is written as a function of personal disposable income, $C_i = C_i (Y_i)$. Here C_i denotes consumption expenditure per period for an income unit measured in terms of constant prices, and Y_i denotes personal disposable income for an income unit per period, similarly measured. When the consumption function is

---

[1] An alternative approach is to regard consumption expenditure as a function of a number of variables including income (e.g. $C = C(Y_p, B, W)$, where B and W refer to the amount of consumer borrowing and the wealth of households respectively) and to suppose that the values of one or more of the variables *other than income* for $C = C_1(Y_p)$ differ from those for $C = C_2(Y_p)$.

written in this form, it is not assumed that income is the sole determinant of consumption expenditure. Other factors (for example, the rate of interest, personal wealth and expectations about prices) influence consumption expenditure and are discussed below. Writing $C_i = C_i(Y_i)$ assumes only that the influence of these other factors is held constant.[1]

The expenditure decisions of income units are determined by the command which their disposable money incomes give them over goods and services. For this reason, a consumption function relating the demand of households for consumer goods and services to their real command over goods and services is used.

The significance of this point is illustrated by the following example: suppose that the consumption expenditure of a particular income unit is described by the expression

$$C_i = 150 + \tfrac{4}{5} Y_i,$$

where both C_i and Y_i are measured in 1963 prices. Some values of C_i and Y_i for this function are shown in Table 8.1. Suppose that in 1963 the money disposable income of the income unit was $1,000. From the table it can be seen that its money expenditure on consumption would have been $950. If in 1964 the unit's money income were $1,200 and if no change in prices had occurred, its expenditure would

TABLE 8.1. *Consumption expenditure at given levels of real disposable income with $C_i = 150 + \tfrac{4}{5} Y_i$*

Y_i ($)	C_i ($)
1,000	950
1,200	1,110
1,400	1,270

be $1,110. However, if between 1963 and 1964 prices had risen by 20 per cent, the unit's command over real resources would be unaltered and there would be no reason for it to change its *real* con-

[1] A change in the value of any of these other determinants causes an autonomous movement of the consumption function (see figure 8.1 and footnote on p. 113). As long as such changes can be predicted, or are of relatively minor importance, it is possible to speak of predictable, stable, short-run equilibrium levels of economic activity.

sumption expenditure.[1] Its money expenditure would increase to $1,140, which is the equivalent in 1964 prices of an expenditure of $950 at 1963 prices. Had the income unit spent only $1,110, its consumption expenditure in real terms (that is, in 1963 prices) would have been only $916.7 ($= 1,110 \times \frac{100}{120}$).

In the discussion above a particular shape for the consumption function of the individual income unit is assumed, namely that, as disposable income increases consumption expenditure also increases, but by a lesser amount. This is the general relationship found by empirical investigations, and it is consistent with introspection and personal observation.

A most important concept in macroeconomics is the *marginal propensity to consume* (*mpc*), which is the ratio of the change in planned consumption expenditure to a small change in income which gave rise to it; that is, $mpc = \Delta C_i / \Delta Y_i$ (where the symbol, Δ, means 'a small change in'). Mathematically $\Delta C_i / \Delta Y_i$ is an approximation to the first derivative of C_i with respect to Y_i, (dC_i / dY_i). The *mpc* relates *changes* in C_i to *changes* in Y_i. It should not be confused with the *average propensity to consume* (*apc*) which is the *proportion* of each *given* level of disposable income devoted to consumption expenditure, that is, $apc = C_i / Y_i$. Both the *mpc* and *apc* describe properties of the individual consumption function, $C_i = C_i(Y_i)$. Their counterparts for the aggregate consumption function, $C = C(Y_p)$, are the *aggregate mpc*, $\Delta C / \Delta Y_p$, and the *aggregate apc*, C / Y_p (see section 3 below).

The nature of the *mpc* and *apc* concepts is illustrated by figure 8.2. In this figure, B denotes the *break-even point* at which $C_i = Y_i$, that is, all of the disposable income OV is spent on consumption goods and services; here $apc = 1$.

Empirical investigation has revealed that the most common individual consumption function has the properties that the *apc* falls continuously, and that the *mpc* is either constant or also declines. If the *mpc* declines as disposable income increases, then the *apc* will also decline. The case of constant *mpc* and declining *apc* arises when the consumption function is of the form: $C_i = A_i + c Y_i$. Here A_i may be interpreted as the consumption expenditure that the income unit

---

[1] When making its consumption-saving decision, the household is choosing between using the real resources at its command for enjoyment today, or for enjoyment in the future. In this example neither of the basic factors involved in making this decision (the real resources available and the preference for enjoyment today as against the future) has altered, so the distribution of real resources between today and the future will be unaltered.

would continue to make, at least in the short run (from non-income sources such as past savings), should its income receipts be zero. The great majority of income units have never experienced this disaster, and for these a consumption function of the form, $C_i = A_i + c Y_i$, is merely a mathematical description of their behaviour over the range of income actually experienced. The most common relationships between the *mpc* and *apc* are illustrated in figures 8.3, 8.4 and 8.5.

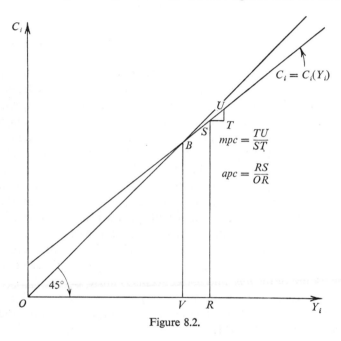

Figure 8.2.

Figures 8.3*a* and *b* illustrate the case of a constant *mpc* but declining *apc*, that is, $C_i = A_i + c Y_i$. The expression for the *mpc* is $\Delta C_i / \Delta Y_i = c$, and for the *apc*, $C_i / Y_i = A_i / Y_i + c$.

Figures 8.4*a* and *b* illustrate the case of a constant *apc* and *mpc*, that is, $C_i = c Y_i$.

The third possibility is that both the *mpc* and *apc* decrease as income increases, with the *mpc* < *apc*. This case is illustrated in figure 8.5, for the consumption function:

$$C_i = 50 + 0 \cdot 8 Y_i - 0 \cdot 0008 (Y_i)^2.$$

Corresponding to each propensity to consume schedule is a *propensity to save* schedule, which describes the same behaviour of

116

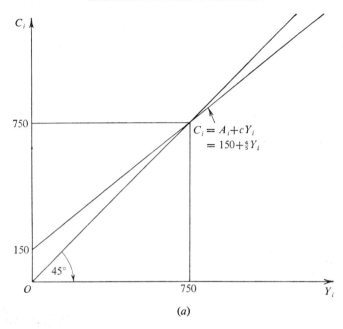

(a)

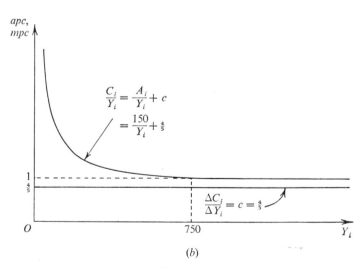

(b)

Figure 8.3.

the income unit, but focuses attention on another aspect of the same behaviour. Saving is defined as that part of current personal disposable income which is not spent on consumption goods, that is, $S_i = Y_i - C_i$. For the example above of $C_i = 150 + \frac{4}{5}Y_i$, the cor-

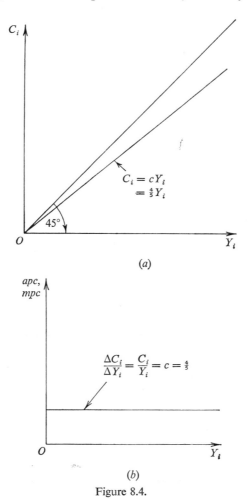

(a)

(b)

Figure 8.4.

responding saving function is: $S_i = -150 + \frac{1}{5}Y_i$. The *marginal propensity to save, mps,* is $(1 - mpc)$—in this case, $1 - \frac{4}{5} = \frac{1}{5}$. The *average propensity to save, aps,* is S_i/Y_i or $(Y_i - C_i)/Y_i$; in this case,

$$S_i/Y_i = -150/Y_i + \frac{1}{5}.$$

118

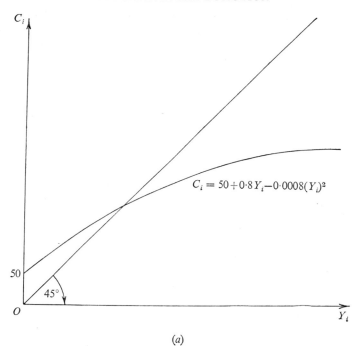

$$C_i = 50 + 0.8 Y_i - 0.0008(Y_i)^2$$

(a)

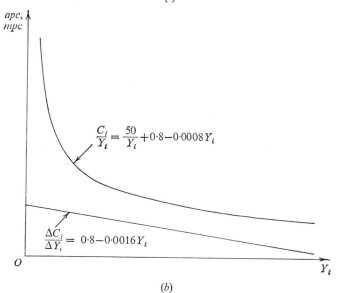

$$\frac{C_i}{Y_i} = \frac{50}{Y_i} + 0.8 - 0.0008 Y_i$$

$$\frac{\Delta C_i}{\Delta Y_i} = 0.8 - 0.0016 Y_i$$

(b)

Figure 8.5.

In the case of a consumption function which goes through the origin and has a constant *mpc*, the *aps* equals the *mps*. Where the saving function is of the form, $S_i = -A_i + sY_i$, the *aps* is negative for values of disposable income less than that corresponding to the break-even point and rises asymptotically towards the *mps*. This case is illustrated in figure 8.6.

As indicated on p. 113, each of the above concepts has a counterpart for the aggregate consumption function. In the case of an aggregate function of the form $C = A + cY_p$, the aggregate savings function is $S = -A + sY_p$; the aggregate *mps* is $\Delta S/\Delta Y_p$, and the aggregate *aps* is S/Y_p.

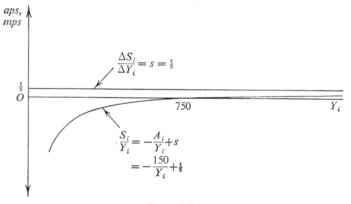

Figure 8.6.

3. The aggregate consumption function

The aggregate consumption function relates to consumption expenditure by consumers as a whole. It shows the total planned expenditure per unit of time associated with different levels of personal disposable income. While the aggregate function depends upon, and is built up from the consumption functions of the individual income units, the relationship between the individual and aggregate functions is complex and warrants a detailed discussion.

(a) The distribution of personal disposable income and the aggregate consumption function

The aggregate consumption function cannot be defined until the distribution of given levels of personal disposable income between the different income units in the community is specified. For each

120

distribution of a given level of total disposable income, there is, given the individual consumption functions, a corresponding level of planned aggregate consumption expenditure. This is illustrated by the following example.

Consider an economy which consists of two individuals, or groups of individuals, W and H. Suppose that W's consumption function is

$$C_W = 50 + 0.8 Y_W$$

and that H's consumption function is

$$C_H = 70 + 0.5 Y_H,$$

where Y_W and Y_H are the respective shares of W and H in the total personal disposable income, Y_p. Assume, first, that all levels of total personal disposable income are distributed in the proportions: 60 per cent for W and 40 per cent for H. The total planned consumption expenditure associated with different levels of aggregate personal disposable income is obtained by substituting the appropriate shares in the respective individual consumption functions and adding the resulting figures; the procedure is illustrated by Table 8.2. The *aggregate mpc* for any given distribution of disposable income is obtained by comparing the change in consumption expenditure with the change in aggregate personal disposable income. In this case it is constant and its value is between that of the individual's *mpc*'s.[1]

TABLE 8.2. *Aggregate consumption expenditure for a distribution of disposable income of 60 per cent to W and 40 per cent to H*

Y_p	Y_W	Y_H	C_W	C_H	C	mpc
800	480	320	434	230	664	0·68
900	540	360	482	250	732	
1,000	600	400	530	270	800	0·68

Next, suppose that the total disposable income is distributed in the proportions: 40 per cent for W and 60 per cent for H. Total consumption expenditure is now lower at each level of Y_p as also is the *aggregate mpc* (see Table 8.3). The effect of redistributing disposable income to the individual with the lower *mpc* is to reduce both the

---

[1] The aggregate *mpc* is a weighted average of the individual ones, namely, 0·8 for W and 0·5 for H. The distribution of Y_p determines the weights. Thus, the *aggregate mpc* $= (0.60 \times 0.8) + (0.40 \times 0.5) = 0.68$.

aggregate average and *marginal propensities to consume.* Thus, even if the consumption functions of all income units are known, the *aggregate propensity to consume* cannot be defined unless the distribution of disposable income between them is also known. There is one exception to this. If for all income units, the *mpc* is uniform and constant for all income levels, any redistribution of disposable income has no effect on aggregate consumption expenditure.

TABLE 8.3. *Aggregate consumption expenditure for a distribution of disposable income of 40 per cent to W and 60 per cent to H*

Y_p	Y_W	Y_H	C_W	C_H	C	mpc
800	320	480	306	310	616	0·62
900	360	540	338	340	678	
1,000	400	600	370	370	740	0·62

If the relative shares of Y_p are assumed to be the same at all levels of Y_p, the position and slope of the aggregate function reflect, in a relatively simple manner, the positions and slopes of the individual functions from which it is derived. For example, if the individual consumption functions are linear, the aggregate function has the form $C = A + cY_p$, where c is the weighted average of the individual *mpc*'s.

There are three main ways in which disposable income may be substantially redistributed in the short run between groups with different *mpc*'s. First, an increase in the progressiveness of rates of income tax, coupled with increases in social service payments such as child endowment and old age pensions, will redistribute disposable income from groups with low *mpc*'s (high-income receivers) to those with high *mpc*'s (large families and old age pensioners). Such government action could considerably raise the aggregate consumption function in the short run.

Secondly, in a situation where prices rise faster than money-wage rates, the share of wages in the values added of industries decreases and income is redistributed away from wage-earners who, in general, have high *mpc*'s. In this situation, the consumption function shifts downwards. The reverse movement occurs when prices fall faster than money wages so that the wage-earners' shares in values added rise.

The shifts in the aggregate consumption function in the above two cases occur when the *mpc* of higher income groups is less than that of lower income groups. The third case involves other considerations. In an open economy such as Australia, an important income-group in the community, namely, the primary producers, obtain large parts of their incomes by exporting products, the prices of which are determined, often independently of their actions, on world markets. If changes in these prices differ from changes in domestic prices and wages in Australia, a redistribution of income occurs between farmers, on the one hand, and profit-earners and wage-earners, on the other. For example, following the record peaks reached in the price of wool at the beginning of the 1950s, the trend in the price of wool and the prices of other major primary products has been downwards, while the levels of domestic prices and wages, which are the major determinants of farm costs, have risen.[1] The share of farm income in national income has declined over the period. As is discussed later in the chapter (see pp. 136–8) the *mpc* of farmers as a group may differ from those of other groups, especially in the short run when changes in farm income may not be regarded as 'permanent'.

(b) *Age composition and the aggregate consumption function*

Changes in the age composition of the population influence the level of consumption associated with given levels of Y_p but are unlikely to be an important cause of instability in the consumption function in the short run. Nevertheless, differences between the *apc*'s of the two communities with the same per capita disposable income may be explained, in part, by differences in the age compositions of their population.

The typical life-time pattern between consumption expenditure and income receipts for an income unit is shown in figure 8.7, where consumption expenditure and disposable income are shown on the vertical axis, and the age of the principal income-earner of the unit is shown on the horizontal axis. Typically, the rate of increase in earnings is greatest in the first decade of employment of the wage-earner; for salary-earners, earnings frequently rise at a steady rate up to retirement. Consumption expenditures tend to be greatest in the third decade of employment when the costs of maintaining a family reach their peak. Between the ages of 50 and 65 consumption expenditures may fall as the cost of maintaining dependants declines, and as

[1] Increases in farm productivity operate to reduce costs, but the actual increase has not been sufficient to prevent a decline in the share of farmers in the national income.

the income-earner prepares for retirement. On retirement consumption expenditure may stay at the level attained in the last working years, but is financed largely from past savings and/or pensions.

Suppose that the net saving of a typical income unit over its lifetime is nil (as is approximately true of all but the richest units). Provided that the population is growing steadily, there will still be positive saving occurring in any year, because the younger generation are more numerous than the older generation, and the saving of the

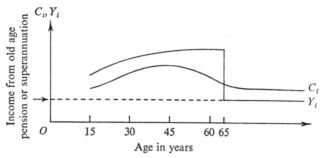

Figure 8.7. Typical lifetime disposable income–consumption pattern.

former offsets the dissaving of the latter. Furthermore, if a comparison were to be made between two communities with similar standards of living, each with a growing population, but in one the average age is 35 and in the other it is 50, the *apc* of the second community would be likely to be lower than that of the first. However, changes in the age composition of the population are unlikely to have significant effects in the short run.

4. Other factors which influence consumption expenditure

In the above discussion an aggregate consumption function based upon individual consumption functions of the general form, $C_i = A_i + c Y_i$, has been used. It was noted earlier that writing the consumption function in this form does not imply that disposable income is the sole determinant of consumption expenditure, but that other factors are assumed to have a constant influence. The more important of the other factors are now considered. Should any factor other than disposable income change, an autonomous shift in the consumption function (as illustrated in figure 8.1) will result. It is necessary to consider the likely magnitude and the predictability of such shifts.

(a) The rate of interest

Traditionally, the rate of interest was considered to have a marked influence on the saving from any given disposable income. Aggregate personal saving is the net outcome of the positive saving by some households and the dissaving by others. It was argued that as interest is the reward paid to savers, a rise in interest rates would encourage more saving. Furthermore, the cost of borrowing would increase and this would deter dissaving. This latter effect is not disputed. But, on both *a priori* grounds and from empirical studies, the impact of higher interest rates on positive saving remains uncertain.

This uncertainty arises from the double-edged impact of a higher interest rate. The reward for abstaining from an extra dollar of current consumption expenditure is greater the higher is the rate of interest. However, a person who increased his saving or continued to save the same amount from his current disposable income would be taking all the benefit of the higher interest rate in the form of a greater stream of goods *in the future*. But, if he wishes, he could reduce his current saving and so divide the benefit of his improved economic position *between the present and the future*.[1] *A priori*, there is no reason to expect one type of response to predominate: the issue is then an empirical one. To date, no conclusive evidence of a marked response of personal saving to changes in the rate of interest, at least over the normal range of interest rates, has been established.[2]

(b) Accumulated wealth

The amount of accumulated wealth owned by the income unit—its holdings of cash, bank deposits, bonds, shares and other property—is an important influence upon its current saving decision. Families frequently have a target of wealth accumulation; the target is often related to the family income, for example, it may be equal to two years' current disposable income. The saving of each period brings

---

[1] For example, a person who had been saving $100 per period on which an interest rate of 4 per cent was earned, could, if the rate of interest rose to 5 per cent, reduce his saving to $80 per period and the interest stream available to him in the future would remain unaltered.

[2] If saving were markedly responsive to the rate of interest, it would be possible to exercise control over aggregate consumption expenditure by varying the rate of interest. But even if it is not responsive there are other motives for varying interest rates, for example, to influence the flow of finance as between the various borrowers and lending institutions, or to influence directly the cost of investment.

the family closer to its target, raises the wealth-income ratio and reduces the incentive to save.

On occasions, such as in the immediate post-war years, many families may regard their wealth holdings as excessive; there was in fact an upward shift in the consumption function in the immediate post-war years as people reduced the wealth accumulated by 'forced saving' in war-time, when money incomes were high but consumer goods and services were in limited supply. In peace-time the effect of the accumulation of wealth tends to be significant only in the longer period. A more important short-term effect is that associated with changes in the liquidity and the market value of wealth. A situation of high and rising prices of financial assets, such as occurred in Australia in 1959–60, permits and encourages wealth-holders to increase their consumption spending.[1]

(c) Consumer borrowing and expenditure upon durables

Most of the items purchased by a household are relatively inexpensive, have a short life and are replaced at regular intervals. Food, drink, gas, electricity and newspapers are examples. Some durable goods, particularly the less expensive, are also purchased in a predictable pattern, for example, books, records and cheaper items of clothing. For the typical household, the monthly expenditure on non-durables and the cheaper durables is financed from current income, and it has a predictable pattern. There is a close relationship in the short run between these purchases in the aggregate and the current level of personal disposable income.

Purchases of expensive durable goods are not frequent transactions for individual households, but they comprise a large and growing component of total consumer expenditure. They are financed mainly by drawing upon accumulated liquid assets and by borrowing. As long as the individual households' purchases are made in a more or less random manner over time, aggregate expenditure on these items may be a stable function of disposable income. There are, however, strong forces which cause these large outlays to be bunched together.

The purchase of an expensive durable consumer good by a household is in many ways akin to the purchase of a fixed investment good

---

[1] A tax on capital gains such as the United States of America has had for many years, and as was introduced in the United Kingdom in April 1965, operates to reduce the effects of fluctuations in security prices on consumption expenditure.

by a businessman. Both durable household goods and fixed investment goods yield streams of services over lengthy periods. The
businessman in deciding his investment expenditure can value in money
terms the services from the investment good. The household considers the value to it of the flow of services from durable goods.[1] In
both cases the expenditure decision is made in the light of the value
of the services, the cost of the asset, the cost and availability of
borrowed funds, and the entity's own accumulated liquid assets.

For purposes of national accounting, the Commonwealth Statistician arbitrarily divides total expenditure by households between
the purchase of new houses, which is treated as 'investment expenditure',[2] and all other expenditures, which are regarded as 'consumption expenditure'. The components of aggregate consumption
expenditure in Australia in 1963–64, together with personal saving,
personal taxation and personal income, are shown in Table 8.4.

All expensive items purchased by households have two distinctive
characteristics which tend to cause expenditure upon them to be
unstable. First, the initial purchases and the timing of their replacement are flexible; and, secondly, the expenditures are financed largely
from sources other than current disposable income.

Consumer durable goods are a part of the *discretionary* expenditure
of households. That is (by contrast with expenditure on, say, basic
foodstuffs), the services that they provide fulfil less urgent needs or
needs that may be met by cheaper substitutes. If people are pessimistic about their future employment and/or income prospects, they
may postpone their purchases of durable goods, even though their
current disposable incomes are unchanged; and they may advance
their purchases if their expectations are optimistic. Moreover,
expectations about future movements of prices are more likely to
affect the timing of purchases of durable goods than of non-durables.
Thus, significant changes in short-period planned consumption
expenditure upon durable goods may occur independently of changes
in current disposable income.

[1] In some cases the household faces the alternative of continuing to purchase the
service from a trading enterprise or of itself investing in a durable asset, for
example, to use public transport or buy a car, to use a laundry or buy a washing
machine, to go to the cinema or buy a television set. In such cases the household's
calculations can be made largely in money terms.
[2] See chapter 2, p. 17, where it is explained that when a household buys a
new house, it is regarded as acting as a trading enterprise which makes this
investment in order to sell 'house-services' to itself. The notional flow of rent
of owner-occupied houses is included in GNP.

TABLE 8.4. *Components of personal income and consumption expenditure, Australia, 1963–64*

(Source: *Australian National Accounts, 1948–49 to 1963–64*)

Component	$m.	Per cent of Y_p
Food, drink and tobacco	3,514	29
Total clothing, etc.	1,176	10
Medical expenses and chemist's goods, etc.	644	5
Rent: Imputed	758	6
Other	270	2
Total household durables	836	7
Total travel and communication, etc.	2,052	17
Other	1,418	12
Total consumption expenditure	10,668	87
Remittances overseas and interest paid	280	2
Personal saving	1,330	11
Personal disposable income (Y_p)	12,278	100
Personal taxation	1,386	—
Personal Income	13,664	—

Furthermore, current expenditure on durable goods is also related to the stock of these goods already held. If, in the past, expenditures on these goods were bunched at particular dates, the replacement purchases are also likely to be bunched. For example, the introduction of television into a particular area leads to a rapid build-up of the initial stock of television sets by the existing population; thereafter, current sales must depend, in the main, upon the expansion of the population in the area, until the replacement of the initial stock falls due. It follows from these considerations that, if consumer durables become an increasing proportion of total expenditure, the relationship between aggregate consumption expenditure and current disposable income will become increasingly less stable in the short period.

The second characteristic of consumer durables is that their purchase is largely financed from non-income sources, particularly by consumer borrowing through hire-purchase finance. (This is illustrated for motor vehicles in Table 8.5.) Through consumer borrowing a consumer may make an immediate expenditure by

TABLE 8.5. *Purchases of motor vehicles by the personal sector and instalment credit finance of retail sales of motor vehicles, Australia, 1959–60 to 1963–64 ($m.)*

(Source: *Australian National Accounts 1948–49 to 1963–64*; *Monthly Review of Business Statistics*)

Year	Purchase of motor vehicles by the personal sector	Value of retail sales financed by instalment credit finance (including hiring charges, interest, insurance, etc.)*	$\frac{(2)}{(1)}$
	(1)	(2)	(3)
1959–60	467·4	468·8	100·3
1960–61	474·4	399·2	84·1
1961–62	454·2	366·4	80·7
1962–63	589·2	464·0	78·8
1963–64	673·2	529·6	78·7

* Statistics cover all schemes which relate primarily to the financing of retail sales of goods and in which repayment is made by regular instalment. Includes an (unknown) amount of purchases by the trading enterprises sector.

outlaying a small deposit. In future periods, the repayment of the loan by the household constitutes a form of contractual saving; that is, it is an allocation of disposable income for a purpose other than consumption expenditure. If consumers could not borrow, they would have to either draw on their savings, or delay their purchases until they accumulated savings. Wealth holdings and the capacity to save differ between households; consequently, the responses of consumers to the stimulus of a new durable good, or a new model, would be staggered over time. Where borrowing facilities are generally available the responses tend to be bunched together.

The effect of borrowing through hire purchase upon the consumption function can be analysed by means of a simple example. Consider an economy where, prior to the present time, there have not been any hire-purchase facilities.[1] Suppose that consumption expenditure in this economy depends solely upon disposable income and borrowing through hire-purchase loans. Prior to the introduction of hire-purchase finance, consumption expenditure is a function of

[1] This may be regarded as the simplest example of the more general case where hire-purchase facilities are extended to a wider range of goods.

disposable income only, that is, $C = C(Y_p)$. The immediate impact of the availability of consumer loans is to raise the level of consumption expenditure associated with disposable income, because households' spendable resources are increased—the consumption function shifts upwards.

The movement upwards will continue so long as consumer credit is expanding such that there is an *increasing* net supplement to spendable resources in each successive period. The actual net supplement to the spendable resources in any period is measured by the new loans granted *in excess of* the repayments on old loans.[1] If the net supplement is positive, there is an increase in the absolute level of outstanding debt, spendable resources exceed disposable income, and the consumption function will lie above its original position.

People will not wish to have continuously growing outstanding debts. There is a limit to the amount of repayments, as a proportion of current disposable income, which will be acceptable to a household.[2] Once the level of aggregate debt outstanding is stabilized and current borrowing matches current repayments, the net supplement to spendable resources will be zero, and the consumption function will revert to the original level. Current disposable income will be allocated between consumption expenditure and hire-purchase repayments (assuming other saving is zero). But, because new borrowings match repayments, total consumption expenditure will be at the same level as when financed only from current disposable income.

Should consumer incomes fall, the debt repayments arising from existing contracts will continue; however, new borrowings will fall, so that total consumption expenditure will be lower than when it was determined only by current disposable income; in this case, spendable resources are less than disposable income. The conclusion of the analysis is, therefore, that an increasing expenditure on durable goods, and increasing use of hire-purchase facilities, increase the likelihood of instability in the short-run aggregate consumption function. The

[1] This net supplement does not necessarily produce an equal increase in total consumption expenditure, because the purchases financed by credit may result in economies in other lines of consumption expenditures. For example, when a person buys a television receiver he will spend less on visits to the cinema.

[2] The repayments associated with any given amount of consumer borrowing can be reduced by lengthening the period of the loan (or by reducing the interest rate). Even if lenders were prepared continuously to extend loans on more liberal terms the rise in the ratio of debt to consumer income would check the willingness of consumers to borrow further.

consequences of such instability are discussed in chapter 10. The possibility for influencing consumer expenditure by variations in the cost and availability of consumer credit is obvious.[1]

In an economy where GNP is growing because of increasing population and/or technical progress, there will tend to be a trend increase in the level of outstanding debt associated with the trend increase in GNP. This will cause the consumption function to lie permanently above its position in the absence of consumer credit facilities. This point may be illustrated in reference to population growth. Consumer credit facilities enable households to purchase items earlier than they otherwise could. If, because of their ability to borrow, people are able, on the average, to buy their first cars at age 20 years rather than at age 25 years, in a growing population, the number of cars bought in any period will be greater than in the absence of credit facilities. This follows from the fact that in a growing population the number of births 20 years ago exceeds the number of births 25 years ago.

(d) Interdependence of households' expenditures

So far, the expenditure patterns of individual income units have been treated as independent of the income levels and expenditure patterns of the other units. But it is obvious that consumption behaviour is much influenced by the social values and the institutions of the society to which the unit belongs. The consumption pattern of the typical Sydney-sider, a member of an aggressive, extrovert metropolis, will differ, both in composition and total, from that of the typical resident of a more conservative city such as Adelaide, who has the same disposable income. The standards of consumption of friends

---

[1] Because the loans are relatively short term—usually less than four years—the loan repayments are dominated by the repayment of principal and changes made in the past in the rates of interest charged have had only a minor effect on the size of each repayment. On the other hand, a change in the length of the loan causes an almost proportionate change in the size of the regular instalments, and such changes are much more important influences upon consumer borrowing. In the United Kingdom, the monetary authorities have control over the length of loans which can be made, and they have been able to cause significant changes in these purchases by varying the maximum term of the loan. The Australian monetary authorities have no such power and changes in the length of loans result mainly from changes in the availability of finance to the finance companies. If they have difficulty in raising funds they give preference to borrowers who will repay in a shorter period. On the other hand, if they have difficulty placing all of their loanable funds they may extend the loan period to attract business.

and relatives, of income units on similar incomes, and in similar occupations, and of neighbours, all play a role in determining the consumption expenditure of the individual income units. Empirical evidence suggests that, if a particular unit receives an increase in income, but these other units do not, it will save more of the increase than if the other units were also to receive comparable increases. The difference between the two situations is illustrated in figure 8.8.

Assume that the current disposable income and consumption expenditure of the particular income unit are OR and RH respec-

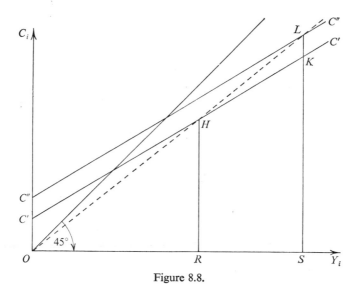

Figure 8.8.

tively. The unit's income is increased to OS. In the case where there is no increase in the incomes of the other units whose spending influences the behaviour of the particular unit its consumption expenditure increases only to SK. But where the other units also enjoy an increase in their disposable incomes, the particular unit's consumption expenditure from its income of OS is SL.

If the individual income unit's consumption function is defined as the function relating its disposable income and consumption expenditure, then, initially, the consumption function is $C'C'$. When the other units receive an increase in disposable income this causes an autonomous upward shift of the function to $C''C''$.

This interdependence is a plausible explanation of an apparent

132

paradox in consumer behaviour. Empirical studies of household spending behaviour reveal that when a cross-section of income units is taken at a given point of time, the relationship between consumption expenditure and the levels of disposable incomes is as described by $C'C'$ in figure 8.9. Units receiving relatively low incomes, such as OD, are dissaving; those at the disposable income level, OB, are spending amounts equal to their disposable incomes and those at

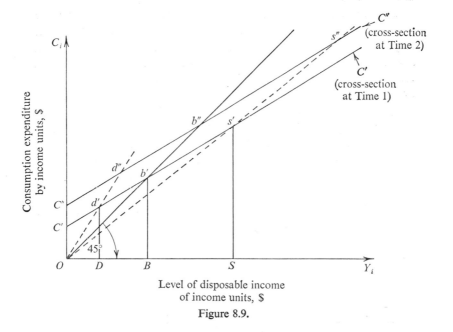

Figure 8.9.

higher levels, for example, at OS, are saving. The ratio of consumption expenditure to disposable income falls as the level of disposable income rises. As the general level of income of the community rises individual families receive higher incomes. Accordingly, over time, the spending of a typical income unit should follow the path $C'C'$. This would mean that over time the ratio of *aggregate* consumption to *aggregate* disposable income would fall. But this is not borne out by empirical studies; these show that, over time, this ratio remains approximately constant.

The interdependence of consumer spending suggests an explanation for this apparent paradox. Assume that $C'C'$ in figure 8.9 represents

133

a cross-section budget study at time 1. For the individual unit whose behaviour is illustrated in figure 8.8, a rise in its own disposable income from OR to OS leads to an increase in its consumption expenditure to SK; however, if this is accompanied by a proportionate increase in other incomes, the increase in its consumption expenditure is to SL. In this latter case (as can be seen from the guide line OHL) the individual income unit's *apc* remains constant; that is, $RH/OR = SL/OS$.

If the behaviour of each unit is similar to that of the unit described by figure 8.8, each unit would now spend the same proportion of its disposable income. The same units would be found to be dissavers, savers, or at the break-even point as in the initial study. A second cross-section study taken after the increase in income would, however, still show that the ratio of consumption expenditure to disposable income declined with the level of family income (as is shown by $C''C''$ in figure 8.9). This is not inconsistent with the ratio of consumption expenditure to disposable income remaining constant over time for individual income units. This is illustrated by figure 8.9 where the lines $Od'd''$, $Ob'b''$, $Os's''$ show the responses of three individuals to increases in their individual incomes when there is a general increase in incomes. If this behaviour is general, then, so long as the distribution of income does not change, the ratio of aggregate consumption expenditure to personal disposable income will be unchanged over time.

(e) The influence of the past

The consumption expenditure of a family is influenced not only by the behaviour of other units but also by its *own past consumption experience* which is influenced by the pattern of its own past income. Suppose that the wage-earner of a particular income unit has been regularly employed for some years, and is then put on half-time work. Initially, the level of family expenditure may be little reduced, because the unit has become accustomed to this living standard, and also because the short-time may be regarded as only temporary. This behaviour introduces a 'kink' into the individual consumption function as illustrated in figure 8.10. Initially disposable income falls from the accustomed level, OS to OR and consumption expenditure is reduced from SC_0 to RC_1. If, however, the short-time continues consumption expenditure is likely to fall to RC_2. In the short run the consumption function is described by C_0C_1, whereas in the long run, it is described by C_0C_2.

Alternatively, a family may be making *contractual saving*, for example, through life-assurance payments and hire-purchase repayments, and these may comprise a large proportion (or possibly all) of its current saving. When disposable income falls, the family either may not wish, nor be able, to vary its contractual saving;[1] in this case the fall in consumption expenditure is likely to be much greater than that predicted either by the 'kinked' or simple form of the consumption function of figure 8.10.

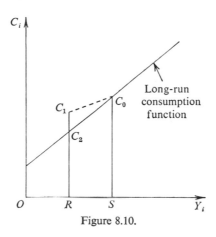

Figure 8.10.

Consider the case of a family whose consumption function would be OC as in figure 8.11 if in each period it were free to revise its total saving decision. Suppose that initially its disposable income is OS, and that of this C_0L is allocated to contractual saving, and SC_0 to consumption expenditure. If the family's income falls to OR and the family cannot revise its saving decision then C_1M of this income will be allocated to contractual saving, and RC_1 to consumption expendi-

[1] The example illustrated by figure 8.11 is the special (extreme) case of a household whose saving was initially entirely in the form of contractual payments, and which is not only unable to reduce these payments but also cannot reduce its overall saving by borrowing or selling assets. At the other extreme is the case of a household which, while continuing its contractual payments, can vary the amounts of its other forms of saving (and dissaving) to achieve total saving consistent with the consumption function. For example, a family might continue to pay its life assurance premiums, but exercise its ability to borrow against the security of the policy.

ture. The family's saving exceeds that which it would make, if it were free to revise its decision, by the amount $C_1 C_2$. The consumption function in this case is depicted by the kinked line $C_1 C_0 C$.

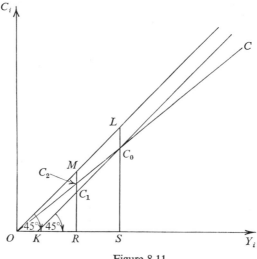

Figure 8.11.

(f) Expectations about future income

In planning current consumption expenditure, the income unit takes account of the pattern of the expected future income stream. To this point in the argument it has been assumed implicitly that the receipts of an income unit are received in an even flow; this enables consumption expenditure to be treated as a function of the present rate of flow of income, because this is the same as the future rates of flow. In fact, the income flow is not at a constant rate. If the income to be received over the whole lifetime of an income unit were known with certainty, it might be possible to plan a rational allocation of expenditures to give the most satisfying lifetime pattern of consumption. Since such complete knowledge is impossible, the expenditure plans of most income units are dominated by their expectations of income over the next few years. In the case of wage- and salary-earners, these expectations are likely to be based primarily upon immediate past experience, together with allowances for the pattern of wage and salaries in their particular types of work, and the general increase in the level of incomes because of increasing productivity.

136

Profit-earners in one-man businesses (including farmers) and persons whose incomes are mainly derived from dividends, are less able to forecast their immediate future incomes. Rather, they are likely to have in mind a *normal* level of income, about which they expect their *annual* incomes to fluctuate. They relate their annual consumption expenditure to this normal level (which may, for example, be some kind of average of the incomes of a number of the

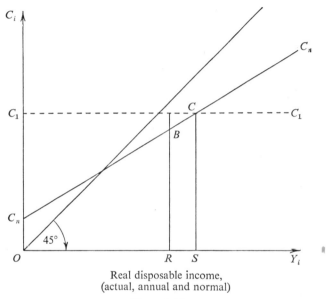

Real disposable income,
(actual, annual and normal)

Figure 8.12.

preceding years). In the case of Australian farmers, there is evidence that the main impact of short-term changes in their incomes falls upon their saving, whether directed towards the purchase of financial claims, or towards investment expenditures on their properties.

In these cases, current consumption expenditure is affected by a given change in annual income only when it is expected to be *permanent*. For example, there may be a long-term downward trend in the normal incomes of proprietors of small grocery stores because of increasing competition from discount houses and supermarkets. Temporary fluctuations in the incomes of the store-owners may have no impact on their current consumption expenditures, but as the trend becomes more and more apparent, they will gradually reduce their spending and adjust to a lower standard of living.

137

In figure 8.12 annual consumption expenditure is shown as related to normal income, which, together with annual income, is plotted on the horizontal axis. Suppose that normal income is currently thought to be OS. Then, if income fell to OR in the next year, consumption expenditure will not fall to RB unless the fall is regarded as a permanent fall, that is, a fall in normal income. The short-term consumption function is, therefore, $C_1 C_1$ as contrasted with the long-term function $C_n C_n$.

(g) Expectations about future prices

The final factor affecting consumption expenditure at given levels of disposable income to be considered is expectations about the future course of prices. Suppose that prices generally[1] have been increasing in the recent past and that the income unit expects this trend to continue in the future. Such an anticipation may lead to greater current expenditure in real terms out of any given level of real disposable income. In particular, the consumer is likely to buy durable goods, or goods which can be stored at little cost, before their prices rise further. If a purchase had been planned for the future it would pay the consumer to buy the item immediately, if the expected rise in its price exceeded the cost of borrowing, or the yield on accumulated savings held. Similarly, an expectation of a fall in prices may lead to the postponement of current expenditure.[2] Such an expectation about prices may be associated with speculation as to likely future rates of sales taxation. If the public anticipates that an increase in sales taxation will be made in the coming budget they will increase their rate of expenditure; if high rates of sales taxation are introduced to curb consumer expenditure (in real terms) they will be particularly effective if the public believes them to be temporary measures.[3]

[1] Changes in relative prices affect the composition of consumption expenditure but not necessarily its total.
[2] The estimate of normal income may be based not merely on past real incomes but also on expected future real incomes. In this case, expectations of falling future prices by an income unit which anticipates a constant money income flow would lead to an upward revision of the current normal income and would provide an incentive to increase current consumption expenditure. The opposite effect would occur where prices are expected to rise. The argument in the text assumes that this influence is out-weighed by the incentive to buy at the time when prices are lowest.
[3] For example, sales of motor-cars in Australia in the period November 1960–February 1961 fell sharply following the imposition of increased rates of sales taxation which the Commonwealth Government had stated were to be temporary. On the other hand, it was widely (and wrongly) believed that the 1965

In much of the argument of the later chapters, it will be assumed that the aggregate consumption function is stable, and of the form: $C = A + c Y_p$. The discussion in this chapter shows that this overlooks many refinements. It should serve to warn the reader that the consumption function is determined by a complex of factors, and that, in the short run, variations in influences other than changes in disposable real income may cause significant shifts in the consumption function. The effects upon the level of economic activity of such shifts is formally analysed in chapter 10 (see, in particular, section 3). For purposes of economic control, the problem is to predict such changes.

Commonwealth budget would provide for an increase in the rate of sales taxation on motor-cars, and in the months immediately prior to the budget sales increased; in the months after the budget the rate of sales fell markedly.

THE DETERMINANTS OF INVESTMENT EXPENDITURE

1. Introduction

Gross investment expenditure in countries such as Australia has been historically a highly volatile component of aggregate demand. The reasons for this behaviour are discussed in this chapter, which is concerned with the factors that lie behind planned investment expenditure per period.

It is convenient to divide gross capital formation by *all* sectors into four broad categories, namely, government investment expenditure, investment in housing, gross private fixed investment expenditure, and investment in stocks. Government investment expenditure (G_k) was discussed in chapter 2 where it was described as being determined by the policy decisions of the government.

The analysis of this chapter is concerned with the investment decisions of entities in the market sectors of the economy. For brevity, the analysis is cast in terms of investment in fixed equipment; the argument developed may be applied to the analysis of investment in stocks and investment in housing in so far as it is done by private landlords for rental.

In the Australian economy in the post-war period most of the investment in housing has been done by government agencies, for example, the Victorian Housing Commission and the South Australian Housing Trust, and by owner-occupiers. The decision by an owner-occupier to build can be fitted formally into the analytical framework of the chapter by treating the owner-occupier as matching his estimates of the money value to him of housing services against the relevant costs, in the same manner as do businessmen (see below). In Australia investment in housing is influenced at many points by the government. For example, the savings banks (the largest group of financial entities other than the trading banks) are closely controlled by the monetary authorities; they provide considerable total housing finance at low rates of interest. Finance through War Service Homes is also an important source of funds. By varying the interest rates, the size of loans granted, the period of the loans, and the total loans from these two sources, the government can influence the aggregate level of home construction. The rate of investment in housing is best regarded, along with the government's direct capital formation, as being largely policy-determined, and, therefore, an autonomous item from the point of view of short-period analysis.[1]

Planned gross private investment expenditure is the outcome of the decisions of individual businessmen made in the light of comparisons of the expected profitability of current investment opportunities with the availability and cost of finance. Investment expenditure occurs in established firms; it also occurs in the process of establishing new firms. In established firms it is possible to distinguish in principle between *replacement expenditure*, that is, expenditure designed to offset the wearing out and obsolescence of the existing capital stock, and *net investment*, that is, the expansion of the capital stock itself.

It was emphasized in chapters 3 and 4 that investment expenditure decisions and saving decisions are generally undertaken by different people, and for different reasons. This sharp distinction, however, is blurred in the case of business saving (retained company income) where, at least in the long run, there is a relationship between the amounts saved and invested; indeed, in some cases business saving may be made with investment plans in mind.[2]

Before discussing the factors which lie behind investment expenditure decisions, two concepts must be defined. These are *future values* and *present values*.

2. Future and present values

Suppose that a person has $100 and that the rate of interest which can be earned on a loan of three years is 5 per cent per annum. What will this $100 be worth in three years' time, that is, what will be the *future value* (in three years' time) of $100 *now*? At the end of the

---

[1] A detailed account of the institutions which supply finance for housing can be found in M. R. Hill, 'Housing Finance Institutions', chapter 3 of R. R. Hirst and R. H. Wallace (eds.), *Studies in the Australian Capital Market*, pp. 98–129.

[2] Investment expenditure by Australian farmers is believed to be closely related to their current incomes. Consequently, it is their marginal propensity to *spend* on consumption *and* investment goods which is relevant for the theory of income-determination. Indeed, if, as was argued in chapter 8, section 3 (f), the consumption expenditure of farmers depends upon their *normal* income, and if a given change in their current income is not expected to be permanent, it is only their expenditure on investment goods which is relevant. The only important group whose investment plans depend upon their income in the short period is farmers.

first year, \$100 earning 5 per cent per annum will have grown to: \$100 (1·05) = \$105; at the end of the second year, it will have grown to: \$105 (1·05) (= \$100 (1·05)^2) = \$110·25; at the end of the third year, it will have grown to: \$100 (1·05)^3 = \$115·7625. Thus, when the rate of interest is 5 per cent per annum, the future value in three years' time of \$100 now is \$115·7625. It is the value to which the original sum will grow by the end of the period, given the rate of interest. In general, if A is the original sum, r is the rate of interest per period, n the number of periods, and F the future value of A:

$$F = A(1+r)^n.$$

Now suppose that a person expects with certainty to receive \$115·7625 in three years' time and that the current rate of interest is 5 per cent per annum. What is the *present value*, that is, the value *now* of this amount to be received in three years' time? It is the maximum amount that a rational person would pay for a promised payment of \$115·7625 in three years' time in a market where there is only one rate of interest and no risk of default. This amount would equal the present sum which at the current rate of interest will be \$115·7625 in three years' time. In the particular example given, the present value is already known; it is \$100. In general, if B is the sum to be received at the end of n periods, r the rate of interest per period, and V the present value of B:

$$V = B/(1+r)^n.$$

It can be seen from the general expression for V, that V is greater, the smaller is the rate of interest. For example, if the rate of interest is 2·5 per cent, the present value of \$115·7625 in three years' time is \$107·4970; that is, \$107·4970 accumulated at 2·5 per cent for three years will amount to \$115·7625.

If a stream of positive receipts, $q_1, q_2, ..., q_n$, over n periods is expected, its present value is

$$V = \frac{q_1}{1+r} + \frac{q_2}{(1+r)^2} + ... + \frac{q_n}{(1+r)^n},$$

that is,

$$V = \sum_{i=1}^{n} \frac{q_i}{(1+r)^i},$$

where $\sum\limits_{i=1}^{n}$ is the symbol for 'the sum of the first to the nth terms'.

It can be seen that the present value of the stream of receipts is the sum of the present values of each receipt discounted at the specified rate of interest. If the value of V is known, a rate of interest (rate of discount) can be found such that the sum of the present values of the annual receipts equals V. It can again be seen from the general expression that there is an inverse relationship between V and r.

3. Two measures of the expected profitability of investment projects

(a) The expected rate of profit

The concept of present value is used in the definition of the expected rate of profit of an investment project. Suppose that a businessman is considering buying a machine which currently is priced at $\$S$. The expenditure on the machine of $\$S$ is called, variously, the *initial outlay*, or the *current cost* of the machine. (The 'initial outlay' could also be interpreted as the amount which a business man expects to spend in the coming period on the construction of a machine or plant within his business.) He estimates that the use of the machine in the business will add to his *net receipts*,[1] over the next n years (the expected lifetime of the machine) the stream: $q_1, q_2, ..., q_n$. The q_i's are the expected increases in his annual sales less the accompanying increases in wages, raw material and maintenance costs.[2] He also expects the machine to have a scrap value of K at the end of the nth year. The businessman wants to know the rate of profit which he can expect to earn on this project. This expected rate of profit, ρ, is defined as *that rate of discount which makes the present value of the expected net receipts (including any scrap value) equal to the initial outlay on the machine.* In terms of the symbols defined above, ρ is that rate of discount which satisfies the following equation:

$$S = \frac{q_1}{1+\rho} + \frac{q_2}{(1+\rho)^2} + ... + \frac{q_n+K}{(1+\rho)^n}$$

$$= \sum_{i=1}^{n} \frac{q_i}{(1+\rho)^i} + \frac{K}{(1+\rho)^n}.$$

In figure 9.1, V, the present value at different rates of discount of a stream of positive net receipts (including any scrap value) expected

---

[1] The terms 'initial outlay' and 'net receipts' are synonyms for the terms 'supply price' and 'quasi-rents' respectively used by J. M. Keynes, in *The General Theory of Employment, Interest and Money* (London: Macmillan, 1936).

[2] It should be noted that the net receipts are *gross* of depreciation allowances; the term, 'net', refers to the deduction of associated expected current operating costs, not the deduction of depreciation allowances.

from a specific investment project, is measured on the vertical axis; and r, the rate of discount, is measured on the horizontal axis. As explained in the previous section, there is an inverse relationship between V and r and this is shown by the downward sloping curve, VV, in figure 9.1. ρ is the particular rate of discount which gives a present value, V, equal to the initial outlay, S; this is to be found in figure 9.1 at the intersection of VV with the horizontal line drawn at the height of S.

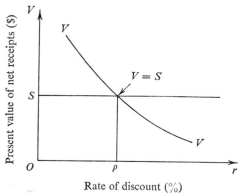

Figure 9.1.

There is a second way of interpreting ρ. If the expected rate of profit of an investment project with an initial outlay of S and a series of expected net receipts (including any scrap value) of $q_1, q_2, ..., q_n$ is ρ, it will be possible to provide a series of annual payments at a rate of ρ per year on the initial outlay, and to accumulate a sum of money which at the end of the life of the project will be equal to the initial outlay; always provided that the *cash surpluses* resulting from the differences between the annual net receipts and the annual payments (the amounts $(q_i - \rho S)$) can be reinvested at a rate of ρ.

This interpretation is illustrated in the following example. A machine costs \$713.5. The expected net receipts from it are \$200, \$250, \$200, and \$150 for its expected life of four years. Scrap value is ignored. The expected rate of profit, ρ, is 5 per cent. It can be seen from table 9.1 that an annual return of $\rho S = (0.05 \times 713.5) = \$35.7$ has been provided each year and that the remaining cash surpluses, $(q_i - \rho S)$, have been accumulated at 5 per cent and amount to \$713.5 by the end of the fourth year.

It is not easy to solve the equation for the expected rate of profit by

TABLE 9.1

Year	Accumulated cash surplus at beginning of year ($)	Interest earned on accumulated cash surplus ($)	Net receipt at end of year ($)	Return on initial outlay at end of year* ($)	Accumulated cash surplus at end of year ($)
1	—	—	200	35·7	164·3
2	164·3	8·2	250	35·7	386·9
3	386·9	19·3	200	35·7	570·5
4	570·5	28·5	150	35·7	713·5

* 5 per cent on $713·5.

analytical methods; in practice, trial and error methods leading to approximate solutions are used. One such method is described in the Appendix to this chapter.

The expected rate of profit provides a measure which aids decisions on whether or not projects are worth undertaking. It is also a means for comparing projects with differing initial outlays, expected net receipts and lives. The relevance of the concept for an analysis of the total and composition of planned investment expenditure is obvious.

(b) The present value of the project

The present value of an investment project is an alternative measure for assessing the profitability of different investment projects. Present value is calculated by discounting the expected net receipts (including any scrap value) of a project by the current rate of interest[1] and subtracting from this the initial outlay.

Let V' = present value of an investment project with an expected life of n periods;

q_i = expected net receipts of year i $(i = 1, ..., n)$;

K = expected scrap value at the end of year n;

S = initial outlay;

R = current rate of interest.

[1] Strictly, the appropriate rate of discount is the marginal cost of finance to firms; that is, the rate which must be paid for additional funds, or the interest foregone when firms use their own funds. The marginal cost of finance may include elements of imputed psychological cost, for example, those associated with rising fixed interest claims on uncertain, fluctuating future profits, or those which take account of the impact of new share issues on the returns to the old shareholders, as well as elements of money and/or opportunity costs.

145

Then,

$$V' = \sum_{i=1}^{n} \frac{q_i}{(1+R)^i} + \frac{K}{(1+R)^n} - S.$$

Essentially, then, the present value of a project is the difference between the present value of the expected net receipts and the initial outlay on the project. The present value depends inversely upon the rate of interest. In figure 9.2 the different present values corresponding to a range of interest rates are shown by the curve $V'V'$. OQ is the present value of the project if the current rate of interest is OP.

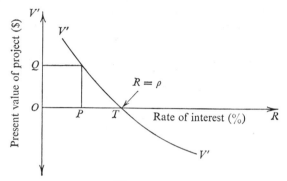

Figure 9.2.

It should be noted that the expected rate of profit of a project can be derived from figure 9.2. V' is zero where $V'V'$ cuts the horizontal axis. At this particular rate of interest the present value of the net receipts equals the initial outlay and OT indicates the expected rate of profit of the project.

It will be noticed in the descriptions of the profitability of investment projects, that, while S and (in the second description) R are known, the expected net receipts are estimates, derived from expectations about the future course of revenues and costs.[1] The more remote

[1] The initial outlay, S, may also be an estimated value, for example, when a businessman who is considering constructing a new plant within his business estimates its cost. Or, an investment project may contain several stages and take several years to complete, so that the outlays associated with the later stages must of necessity be estimates. An example of a multi-stage project would be the development of a housing estate over a number of years by a speculative builder. The expected rate of profit of a multi-stage project can be found by solving the following equation for ρ:

$$0 = \sum_{i=1}^{n} \frac{q_i - S_i}{(1+\rho)^i} + \frac{K}{(1+\rho)^n}.$$

[cont. on p. 147

in time are these estimates, the less the certainty with which they are held. The estimates involve predicting the future courses of quantities sold and of prices (both of the products sold and of the fixed investment goods), costs (labour, maintenance and raw materials), and tax rates. Moreover, the expectations can be held with varying degrees of confidence. It would be a mistake, therefore, to suppose that the estimates of net receipts are exact or firmly held; rather, they should be thought of as the averages of ranges of expected values. The confidence with which the expected values are held diminishes as the year concerned becomes more remote.

4. Long-run and short-run influences on expected revenues and costs

(a) *The influence of expected sales and costs upon investment*

This section is concerned with the factors which influence expectations concerning the levels of future revenues and costs and, therefore, the values of the expected rates of profits (or present values) of different investment projects. It is assumed that, at the beginning of any period, businessmen have in mind certain quantities of capital in relation to their output which will maximize their profits. This quantity of capital would be acquired if sufficient time elapsed without further changes in the expected levels of sales, prices, costs and technical conditions.

It is useful to distinguish two types of investment expenditure. Where more machines or other equipment of a similar type to the existing stock are acquired, this is described as *widening investment*. Widening investment is directed towards increasing output. *Deepening investment* occurs when machines or other equipment of a different nature from those in the existing capital stock are acquired in order that output can be produced at a lower cost.

Actual investment expenditure will include elements of both widening and deepening because not only do expected output levels change, but the costs of labour and of the existing types of capital also change, and through technical progress new types of capital

---

The present value of the same project is

$$V' = \sum_{i=1}^{n} \frac{q_i - S_i}{(1+R)^i} + \frac{K}{(1+R)^n},$$

where S_i = capital outlay in year i and q_i, K, R, ρ and V' are as defined in the text.

equipment become available. These latter changes mean that if the businessman continued to use the same production techniques his costs would exceed those possible by appropriate adjustment to the new situation.

It was assumed above that businessmen have in mind certain desired quantities of capital which they endeavour to achieve by their current investment expenditures. Given existing techniques and the level of the capital stock, the higher is the level of expected sales, the more likely it is that the current capital stock is below its desired level. It follows from this that the higher are the levels of expected sales, the *greater* will be the planned investment expenditures of any short period. Conversely, given the levels of expected sales, the greater is the capital stock, the more likely is it to equal or exceed the desired level. Consequently current investment expenditures will be *lower*, the greater is the current level of the capital stock in relation to expected sales.

In any period, t, there will be a maximum level to the potential flow of output from the existing capital stock. If this flow is less than the level of expected potential sales, there is, clearly, an incentive for investment expenditure to occur.[1] The investment expenditure of period t together with the consumption expenditure induced by the incomes generated by that expenditure will be elements of the actual sales of the period, and these sales will influence expectations of sales for the coming period, $t+1$. In turn the latter, together with the change in the capital stock for the period t, influences the planned investment expenditure for the period, $t+1$; and so on.[2] The approach

---

[1] From the point of view of investment decisions, the existing capital stock comprises those pieces of productive equipment which are expected to earn net receipts, given the current levels of expected product prices and wage rates. However, this definition may not encompass all equipment actually in existence. Businessmen keep in reserve machines which, though their expected net receipts are negative, can nevertheless be brought into production if there should be an unexpected rise in orders in the short run. These machines allow additional overtime to be worked or extra workers to be employed. It is the capital stock in this wider sense which sets the limit to output in the short run.

[2] The link between current investment expenditures, on the one hand, and expected sales and the existing capital stock, on the other, may be conveniently summarized by the following expression:

$$I_t = aS_t^* - bK_t,$$

where I_t = currently planned gross investment expenditure for the coming period t;
  S_t^* = the level of expected sales for period t;
  K_t = the existing capital stock at the beginning of period t;

in this book is to isolate the factors influencing the planned expenditures of each short period. An extension of this approach is to use *dynamic analysis* in which the events of any one period are functionally linked to the events both of the past and to those expected in the future.[1]

(b) Expectations, uncertainty and risk

The above approach may seem to suggest that all businessmen would make the same decision when faced with the same data about a specific investment project, that is, the net receipts, cost of finance and the initial outlay. In fact, the stream of net receipts is not known with certainty and businessmen's assessments of the advisability of implementing a given investment project will vary according to their individual assessments of the net receipts, and their willingness to bear risk.

Businessmen's expectations about the future course of product prices, costs and sales are determined, first of all, by what is currently happening to these variables—whether they are steady, rising or falling. Their individual experiences, both in the present and in the recent past, are the most tangible facts available to businessmen. In the absence of evidence to the contrary, businessmen are likely to assume that the future will be similar to the present. In a country such as Australia, which has experienced rapid rates of growth over most of the post-war period, the expectation with regard to, say, sales might be that the current *rates of growth* rather than the current levels would continue. Similarly, in a situation where prices and money-wage rates have risen steadily, it is more likely that businessmen would anticipate a continuation of these rates of growth rather than that the current levels would be sustained.

While immediate past experiences form the base on which businessmen's expectations are built, they will also be influenced by longer-run happenings in the economy. For example, the expected rate of growth of population, both by natural increase and by migration, will be important considerations for investment decisions; expected changes in the age structure of the population—for example, the

a and *b* are two constants showing the relative importance for current planned investment expenditures of unit changes in the values of expected sales and the size of the capital stock, respectively.

[1] For an excellent introduction to dynamic analysis, see R. C. O. Matthews, *The Trade Cycle* (Cambridge, 1959), chapters II and III.

numbers entering the teenage and young-married groups—will also influence total investment expenditure and its composition.

A further set of factors influencing expectations about the future courses of product prices, wages and sales are expectations about the impact of the periodic decisions on issues of economic policy; in particular, businessmen will speculate as to the measures to be introduced in the annual government budget, the likely increase in the basic wage, and the probability of changes in policies relating to international trade. Future sales and product prices are related to expected tax rates; income taxes affect the level of demand and indirect taxes affect the level of prices. In addition, the budget may offer incentives or disincentives to investment expenditure by introducing or changing taxation allowances for investment expenditure and for depreciation.[1] The expected results of decisions about the basic wage and margins are obviously relevant for expectations about future cost levels. Changes in tariff rates and the imposition, easing or abandonment of import controls affects the prices, costs and sales of many enterprises. An expectation of changes in the legislation relating to business behaviour is also a relevant consideration; for example, an attempt by the government to end resale price maintenance or to outlaw collusive tendering has obvious implications for the future level of prices and the competitive structure of different industries.

Current events are more than the base for current expectations.

---

[1] The taxation authorities have official rates of depreciation allowances which determine the amounts which firms may deduct from their gross profits to assess their taxable incomes. In 1962, the Commonwealth Government introduced investment allowances for certain types of fixed investment expenditure; firms are allowed to deduct in the year of purchase, 20 per cent of the purchase prices of specified assets as well as the annual depreciation allowance. Australian primary producers may deduct, in five equal annual instalments of 20 per cent each, the purchase prices of certain assets. These are referred to as special depreciation allowances for primary producers; they are an example of accelerated depreciation, which may be defined as any scheme whereby the depreciation allowances granted on fixed assets for taxation purposes, are initially at a greater rate, or are received in a shorter time, than normal statutory depreciation allowances. The introduction of an accelerated depreciation or investment allowance scheme, or changes in the rates and coverage of existing schemes, changes the *post-tax* expected rates of profit (or present values) of existing investment projects, thereby affecting the inducement to invest. For example, suppose that the *post-tax* present value of a given project with an initial outlay of $1,000, is itself $1,000. If the rate of interest is 5 per cent per annum and the marginal tax rate is 50 per cent, the introduction of a 20 per cent investment allowance will raise the post-tax present value of the project by $95.2381 $[= \frac{1}{2} \cdot \frac{1}{5} \cdot 1{,}000/1{\cdot}05]$, that is, by nearly 10 per cent.

If, for example, businessmen have recently experienced setbacks, say, disappointing levels of sales, they may view other factors such as a fall in share prices or an increase in the Statutory Reserve Deposit ratio in a pessimistic light. If this pessimism leads to a fall in current investment expenditure, the repercussions on the level of activity will tend to justify the original pessimism, and reinforce such a mood. Similarly, an optimistic assessment can be self-justifying and self-perpetuating. The observed fluctuations of investment expenditure can be explained, at least in part, in terms of such waves of optimism and pessimism.

Suppose, however, that all expectations are given, so that the profitability of the investment projects currently available to all businessmen in the economy can be described either by their expected rates of profit (or, alternatively, by their present values). It should be noted that, even with given expectations, businessmen will be *more confident* about actually earning the expected rates of profit on some projects than on others. That is, some projects will be assessed as *riskier* than others. Because of the existence of risk, normally businessmen will undertake a risky project only if the expected rate of profit exceeds that on a riskless project by a *margin of risk*.

The assessment of the riskiness of a given project will also differ as between businessmen. A businessman who is a 'gambler' by nature would require a lower margin for risk for a given project than would another who is unwilling to risk a loss, even though there may be a reasonable chance of a large gain.

5. Planned investment expenditure in the short period

Planned investment expenditure is the result of the aggregation of the investment plans of individual businessmen. In making his plans a businessman takes account on the one hand of the expected rates of profit and the riskiness of the various potential investment opportunities to him; and, on the other hand, of the cost of finance. If the expected rate of profit exceeds the cost of finance by the margin required to cover the risk element, the businessman would wish to undertake the project.

In practice some projects may not be implemented because, as a result of imperfections in the capital market, particular businesses cannot obtain the necessary funds. At this stage of the argument the simplifying assumption is made that there is only one rate of interest in the market and that borrowers are prepared to make available an unlimited amount of funds to any borrower prepared to pay this rate.

The decision by a businessman to implement an investment project is a highly subjective one. In the first place, the expected rate of return is based on *estimates* of the streams of net receipts and costs expected to be associated with the project. These estimates are formed on the basis of information of varying degrees of reliability. For example, expected receipts will be influenced by the productive capacity of the existing stock of fixed equipment relative to sales; and expected costs will be influenced by current trends in costs and knowledge of improved techniques. In the second place, the decision to invest is influenced by the businessman's required margin for risk, and this is entirely a subjective factor.

In a relatively few cases the businessman may have a high degree of confidence in his estimates of the net receipts and costs associated with a project. For example, a firm constructing a large office block where rentals are made on a long term basis, and where tenants are required to meet the maintenance costs, would regard the project as being almost riskless. In this case the expected rate of profit would be an objective calculation which could be matched against the objective rate of interest. The relative riskiness of such a venture would mean that the businessman would proceed with the project so long as the expected rate of profit was slightly above the market rate of interest. It follows that a change in the rate of interest would result in reconsideration of the desirability of going ahead with projects of this kind where the expected rate of profit is close to the market rate of interest.

Cases where the calculation of the expected net receipts and costs are highly objective are rare. For the bulk of investment opportunities, the estimates have a large subjective element, and normally the expected rates of profit must stand well above the market rate of interest if the project is to be undertaken. If the subjective margin required to cover the risk could be expressed in precise terms it would be possible to deduct this precise risk margin and compare the expected rate of profit *net* of risk with the objective rate of interest. However, the margin allowed for risk is usually large relative to the rate of interest, and cannot be formulated with precision.

For example, a businessman considering the installation of a new plant and faced with a market rate of interest of 5 per cent may, because of the element of risk, regard an expected rate of profit of

20 to 25 per cent as the minimum necessary to justify implementing the project. In this case the required margin for risk of 15 to 20 per cent is large relative to the rate of interest, and since, in practice, the market rate of interest varies within relatively narrow limits,[1] the businessman would not regard it as a major factor influencing his decision. Of course, if the rate of interest were to increase from, say, 5 to 10 per cent, this might be a significant factor influencing his decision, but changes of the magnitude experienced in practice would be unlikely to cause him to abandon the project.[2]

The view that changes in the rate of interest have little impact on investment decisions is reinforced by the following considerations. Businessmen commonly require investment projects to meet the 'pay-off' (or 'pay-back') period criterion, if they are to become actual investment expenditure. The 'pay-off' period criterion requires a project to 'pay for itself' over a period of time (said to be between two and five years for most items of plant and machinery) considerably shorter than its effective working life; that is to say, the sum of the expected net receipts of the first two to five years of the project's life should exceed or at least equal the initial outlay. In this way businessmen attempt to take account of the riskiness of investment expenditure and the greater uncertainty about the distant as compared with the near future. Changes in the rate of interest clearly have no direct impact on the ability of a project to meet this criterion.

The above discussion suggests that planned investment expenditure will not generally be highly sensitive to movements in the rate of interest of the magnitude experienced in post-war Australia. However, as indicated on p. 152 above, there is a class of projects for which an increase (decrease) in the rate of interest will inhibit (encourage) investment expenditure. These are long-lived projects, the returns to which can be predicted with a high degree of certainty.[3] A numerical

---

[1] Over the years 1945 to 1965 the long-term government bond rate has varied between $3\frac{1}{8}$ and $5\frac{3}{8}$ per cent, and the maximum bank overdraft rate between $4\frac{1}{4}$ and $7\frac{1}{4}$ per cent respectively. The maximum increase in the rates in any one year was $\frac{3}{4}$ and $1\frac{1}{4}$ per cent respectively.

[2] It is possible that the businessman would interpret an increase in the interest rate as indicative of a broad government policy designed to restrain aggregate expenditure. He may revise downwards his estimates of the likely net receipts associated with the project, and the gap between the expected rate of profit and the rate of interest may narrow so much that he abandons the project.

[3] However, much of the investment expenditure of this type is influenced by special factors. In the case of housing, for example, in Australia public authori-

example may be useful. Consider a landlord who can purchase a house for $10,000 which he can lease on a long term basis at $13.00 per week (the tenant to pay all rates, taxes and maintenance costs) and which the landlord expects will have a life of thirty years. If he can borrow the purchase price at 5 per cent per annum his weekly payment for interest and amortization of the loan will be $12.33, and he may regard the venture as worthwhile. But this could cease to be so if the interest rate were 6 per cent when his payment would be $13.75, or 7 per cent when it would be $15.30.[1]

It should also be noticed that the impact of a *given* change in the rate of interest on the present values of projects is greater, the longer are the lives of the projects concerned. The influence of a change in the rate of interest is magnified in the later years of a project's expected life. For example, a change in the rate of interest from 4 to 5 per cent per annum reduces the present value of $100 a year for five years by 2·8 per cent and that of $100 a year for twenty years by 9 per cent.

With the exception of those projects where the margin for risk is low and the expected rate of profit is close to the rate of interest, the level of planned investment expenditure is determined by the prevailing state of expectations and the degree of confidence on the one

---

ties are responsible for much of the construction, and private borrowers usually receive preferred treatment from the lending agencies. The savings banks, for example, co-operate with the Reserve Bank to promote a flow of home finance at a more stable rate, and with lower interest charges than would be available in an unregulated capital market. The loan raisings by the public authorities to finance their investment expenditures are also given special consideration by the banking system. The Commonwealth government is able to finance some part of its own capital formation from taxation receipts. The long-life investment expenditures of the rural sector—pasture improvement, fencing, construction of dams and so on—are given favourable treatment by the banking system, and also are encouraged by special taxation provisions.

[1] These values can be obtained as follows: the fixed periodical combined payment of interest and principal (q) is that value which, over the n periods of repayment, has a present value equal to the original amount borrowed (S), at the rate of interest, r. That is

$$S = \sum_{i=1}^{n} \frac{q}{(1+r)^i} = q\frac{(1+r)^n - 1}{r(1+r)^n} ,$$

that is

$$q = \frac{rS(1+r)^n}{(1+r)^n - 1} .$$

With $S = \$10,000$, $r = 6$ per cent per annum, and $n = 30$ years, $q = \$13.75$ per *week*. (It should be remembered that r and n, which are stated in years in this example, must be converted to their equivalent values in weeks.)

hand and the availability of finance on the other. The limiting factor in many cases is the availability of finance rather than the cost of finance. This is discussed in more detail in the next section.

6. The availability of finance

The argument of the previous sections is based on the assumptions that all investment expenditure is financed from sources external to the firm, and that borrowers can obtain an unlimited amount of finance at the current rate of interest. This latter implies that potential lenders[1] share the expectations of the potential borrowers that the rate of return on projects will exceed the rate of interest.

In practice the financial market is imperfectly competitive. On the one hand most established firms are able to finance their investment expenditures, at least in part, from funds internal to the firm; that is, from *retained company income*. On the other hand, lenders frequently do not have sufficient information with which to estimate the expected rates of profit; and in so far as a lender can make such an estimate it is likely to be more conservative than that made by the borrower. Thus, some firms may be unable to borrow all (and in some cases, any) of the funds they desire, despite their willingness and ability to meet the current market terms. This may arise because of the ignorance of lenders, or because of a situation of *capital rationing* imposed by the monetary authorities.

(a) Retained company income

In the previous chapters it was assumed that all saving was made by the personal sector. This implied that companies retained no income, and had to obtain the finance for an expansion of the scale of their operations from external sources. The argument will now be modified to take account of the fact that company saving does occur, and that it plays a dual role in the determination of economic activity. One aspect of current company saving is that it represents a leakage from the income–expenditure circuit; it is income which is not distributed to households, and consequently, other things equal, the greater is company saving, the less will be personal consumption expenditure. The other aspect is that *past* retained company income may be accumulated in the form of liquid assets, and may be a source of finance for an increase in the scale of operations of the enterprises.

---

[1] In this section the term 'lenders' is used in a broad sense, and refers both to persons lending funds on fixed interest terms and also to those subscribing equity capital.

The gross income of a company for a period *less* the company taxation payable is its *gross disposable income*. This is allocated between *depreciation allowances*, the distribution of dividends to the shareholders, and the residual item, *undistributed company income*; the sum of depreciation allowances and undistributed company income will be referred to as *retained company income* (gross company saving).

Over the period 1953–54 to 1960–61 the ratio of the gross saving of Australian companies to their gross disposable income varied between 59 and 67 per cent. By contrast, over the same period, the gross saving of persons and unincorporated businesses ranged between 11 and 15 per cent of their disposable income. The role of company saving as a source of company finance is illustrated by Table 9.2, which shows that the gross saving of companies for the seven-year period amounted to more than one-half of the sources of the capital funds of companies.

TABLE 9.2. *Sources and uses of funds by companies,*
1953–54 to 1960–61

(Source: *Report of the Committee of Economic Enquiry.* Some of the figures are provisional estimates.)

Net sources	$m.	Net uses	$m.
Gross company saving	4,720	Fixed capital	5,710
Issues of securities	1,910	Stocks	1,740
Borrowings from banks and other financial intermediaries	760	Other	920
Other	980		
Total	8,370	Total	8,370

Depreciation allowances are estimates of the extent to which the capital equipment of enterprises has lost value over the accounting period. They are book-keeping entries which result in retention of funds within the enterprise.[1] It should not be thought that each enterprise spends on purchases of equipment for replacement amounts

---

[1] The wear and tear on machines increases with their use but in practice companies cannot accurately estimate this. Furthermore, changes in the types of capital goods available and not their physical breakdown, together with the state of demand for the firms' outputs, determine the time at which machines are discarded. In Australia, the taxation authorities specify the rate at which capital expenditures may be written off as a cost incurred in the process of earning taxable income.

equal to the accounting provision for depreciation of the period. For example, if the effective life of a machine is five years, accounting provisions for depreciation will be made in each year, but only at the end of the fifth year is the decision made whether or not to purchase a replacement machine. And replacement is not automatic; there is in principle no difference between a decision to replace a piece of equipment and a decision to undertake new investment. The enterprise will consider the expected rate of profit upon investment in a replacement machine, and compare this with the advantages of using funds in alternative ways, such as the purchase of a different type of machine, or in overhauling the old machine, or of using the funds to acquire income earning financial assets, or of making a cash distribution to shareholders. Furthermore, the provisions for depreciation over the life of a machine do not necessarily accumulate as a cash balance; most commonly they are used in the enterprise.[1]

Companies retain income over and above the allowances made for depreciation for two main reasons. First, to accumulate additional funds to finance the activities of the company; and secondly, to avoid changing the dividend rate with each change in distributable income. Directors generally prefer to maintain a constant dividend rate, and they are reluctant to raise the dividend rate unless they believe the higher dividend rate can be sustained in the future. As a result, in the short run, undistributed company profits usually change more than proportionately to changes in company disposable income.[2]

From the viewpoint of their influence upon the determination of the level of economic activity in the short run, there is no point in distinguishing between depreciation allowances and undistributed company profits—both represent non-income generating allocations

[1] If a firm is not raising new funds from external sources, but its holding of, say, stocks is increasing while the trade credit that it receives is unchanged, then it would be possible to speak of the increase in stocks as being 'financed by the retained income'. However, where the funds of an enterprise are from more than one source and there are increases in more than one asset, it is not possible to identify the particular use made of any particular source of funds. In the special case where a firm's rate of output is constant, and the nature and prices of its machines remain unchanged, and the firm has a stock of machines the ages of which are divided evenly over the life span of the machine, the annual depreciation allowance would match the annual replacement expenditure. Such a stock of machines is referred to as a balanced stock.

[2] Consequently the dividend component of personal disposable income is relatively stable in the short run. Share prices fluctuations are also reduced because of the stabilization of dividend payments. Both these factors operate to stabilize the consumption expenditure of shareholders.

157

of gross company income. A detailed account of the influence of retained company income upon the level of real income is deferred to section 4 of the following chapter. At this point it is sufficient to note that, other things being equal, the greater the amount of retained company income the less will be personal disposable income and hence the less will be the level of economic activity.[1]

It is the role of company saving as a source of finance which is of particular relevance for the determination of investment expenditure. Typically, trading enterprises with accumulated retained income in the form of liquid assets—bank deposits, short-term loans, and negotiable securities—do not consider the possibility of long-term investment outside the firm.[2] If a firm considers there are profitable opportunities for investment within the firm, then retained income is likely to be used internally even though investigation might reveal that a higher rate could be earned outside the firm. Firms are concerned with their rates of growth and shares of the market, as well as with the earning rates of their funds.

There are advantages to management groups in financing their investment expenditure from internal sources. By contrast with new share issues this form of finance does not involve problems of control associated with changes in voting strength. Moreover, while in the case of borrowed funds, interest and principal repayments must be faced whether or not the investment project is as successful as was expected, in the case of retained funds the firm will earn at least the same absolute profit so long as the actual rate of profit is not negative. If the actual rate of profit should be lower than was anticipated the firm which finances its expenditure from retained income will not be embarrassed by the repayment of principal and payment of interest to outside lenders, nor will it necessarily have to

---

[1] In some cases, firms may plan to increase their depreciation allowances and their undistributed income in the coming year because they wish to increase their investment expenditure without using other sources of funds or reducing their liquidity. In this instance, an increment of saving by companies is matched by an increment of investment expenditure (though the latter frequently could have been financed from other sources). The consequences of this behaviour for the level of activity are analysed in chapter 10, section 4, footnote on p. 192.

[2] They may consider the possibility of absorbing another firm by making a take-over offer. This may be by a cash offer, or by the creation of new shares issued to the shareholders in the absorbed firm in exchange for their shareholdings. A successful take-over does not, in itself, involve investment expenditure in the sense in which the term is used in this book; viz. an increment to the physical capital stock of the economy. However, generally a take-over is made in the belief that additional investment expenditure will be profitable.

reduce the dividend rate, as may occur if new share capital is used to finance an unsuccessful activity.

An important factor to be added to the determinants of current investment expenditure is the level (and distribution) of the liquid assets holdings of firms. Other things being equal, the volume of accumulated liquid assets will be greater, the greater the income retained by firms in the past.

(b) Market imperfections and capital rationing

If financial markets were perfectly competitive, and if all potential lenders (including trading enterprises with retained income) had reliable information which enabled them to assess independently the rates of profit of all the potential investment expenditures, a uniform rate of interest for each category of finance (depending, for example, on the degree of risk) would emerge, and any firm could obtain un-limited finance if it were prepared to pay the appropriate rate. In fact, potential lenders usually have little accurate information about the likely rates of profit associated with new investment projects. As pointed out in the previous section, trading enterprises usually do not look beyond their own firms for investment opportunities. Large institutional lenders do, on occasions, investigate the likely profitability of projects, but it is more usual for lenders to investigate the overall financial security—the value of property, securities and guarantees—offered by the borrower. Individual persons rarely have reliable information about investment projects, and usually their decisions to lend or to buy shares are made in the light of the size and past performance of enterprises. Consequently new and small firms are at a disadvantage in raising external finance; indeed, some may be unable to raise any finance despite the fact that a careful appraisal of their projects might reveal that they have high expected rates of profit.

The attitudes of lenders influence the total level, as well as the com-position of actual investment expenditure. Lenders, like borrowers, are subject to changing moods of confidence; indeed, factors causing borrowers to become more optimistic such as improved export prices, increased government expenditure, or a boom in home building, will normally have a favourable impact on the willingness to lend. Lenders also pay particular attention to the published reports of companies, and to the behaviour of the prices of securities traded on the stock exchange. An improvement in these indicators may mean that funds are made available, whereas if lenders are less optimistic firms may be unable to raise finance for specific projects. Given borrowers' expectations of the rates of profit, a reduced willingness on the part of lenders to make funds available makes its impact upon actual investment expenditure partly through the increase in the general cost of finance. But, more important, because of the imperfections in the capital market, particular groups of potential borrowers will be unable to implement planned expenditures through lack of availability of funds rather than because the cost has increased.

The monetary authorities attempt to influence investment expenditure both by changing the rate of interest and by influencing the availability of finance. It was explained in chapter 6 that the monetary authorities determine specifically certain key interest rates; in particular, the rates offered on new loan raisings by public authorities, and the rates offered and charged by the banks. By changing these rates the authorities can divert funds between the various avenues; for example, an increase in the government bond rate may induce some lenders to substitute government bonds for, say, the securities of finance companies. Because of the inter-relationships of the financial markets, changes in controlled interest rates will result in sympathetic movements throughout the financial system.

The monetary authorities are operating continuously to influence the availability of finance.[1] The Reserve Bank of Australia can, through the techniques explained in chapter 7, alter the liquidity position of the trading banks, and thereby affect their lending. The Reserve Bank consults regularly with the trading and savings banks, and it may give them specific *quantitative* directions as to their appropriate rates of new lending; for example, they may be told that the new bank loans granted over the next six months should not exceed by more than 10 per cent those of the past six months. The directives issued may also be *qualitative*; that is, the banks are directed to adopt particular lending policies towards certain groups of borrowers; for example, those in export industries may be given preferred treatment whilst borrowing to finance the purchase of shares may be subject to particularly rigorous conditions.

[1] It was pointed out above (see footnote 2 on p. 153) that borrowers may revise their estimates of the expected rate of profit because of changes in the controlled interest rates. Changes in monetary policy may also cause lenders to become less optimistic.

Reasons were given above (see pp. 152–5) for believing that planned investment expenditures are unlikely to be highly sensitive to increases in the cost of finance; however, quantitative and qualitative controls of credit operate directly on the availability of finance. For example, in a credit squeeze, bank managers consciously ration out the limited quantity of new loans among the applicants; actual investment expenditure will be restrained by the squeeze because some unsuccessful applicants for bank accommodation cannot get finance from alternative sources, or if they could raise the finance it would be too expensive. The reduction in the availability of bank finance will lead to increased demands upon other sections of the financial system, and so force up the uncontrolled rates of interest. Consequently changes in the rates of interest and in investment expenditure may occur together, but the changed availability of finance is likely to be the more important causal factor—the higher rates of interest being concomitants of the smaller supply of credit.

Finally, planned investment expenditure may be frustrated not only by lack of finance, but also because the total of planned investment expenditures for the period exceeds the present physical capacity of the investment goods industries. This may lead to a lengthening of order books; or, it may lead to a rise in the prices of investment goods; or to a combination of both. Prices may rise both because higher money wages may be paid to attract extra labour to this sector, and because businessmen in the sector may take advantage of the shortage to increase their profit margins. There are two ways whereby the rise in prices will serve to bring about equilibrium between demand and capacity in the investment goods industries. First, the higher prices of investment goods will make given projects in sectors other than the investment goods sectors less profitable; and secondly, rates of profit will rise in the investment goods sector, and that will encourage greater capital formation there, so increasing that sector's productive capacity.

Appendix. A method for calculating the expected rate of profit

There is another interpretation of the expected rate of profit which was not discussed in the chapter. If a sum of money, $\$S$, is deposited in a bank at a rate of interest, ρ, it would permit, and only just permit, annual withdrawals of sums equal to $q_1, q_2, ..., q_n$. This may be illustrated by using the amounts in the example of pp. 144–5 of

161

the chapter. Here $\$S = \$713.5$; the q_i's are: \$200, \$250, \$200 and \$150; and $\rho = 5$ per cent per annum.

Year	Balance at beginning of year ($)	Interest earned during year ($)	Withdrawals at end of year ($)	Balance at end of year ($)
1	713·5	35·7	200	549·2
2	549·2	27·4	250	326·6
3	326·6	16·3	200	142·9
4	142·9	7·1	150	Nil

A rate of interest of 5 per cent per annum on the cash balances at the beginning of each year is just sufficient to allow the four annual withdrawals and leave nothing in the bank at the end of the fourth year.

The above interpretation leads to a simple trial and error method for calculating the expected rate of profit. The essence of the method is that a tentative value for ρ is arbitrarily selected, and a table such as the one above is worked through. If the final balance is found to be negative, then the tentative value of ρ selected must be smaller than the actual value of the expected rate of profit, since a higher rate of interest will be required to provide enough funds for the given withdrawals. Similarly, if the final balance at the end is positive, the tentative value of ρ must be greater than the expected rate of profit.

The following is a procedure which can be used to make an approximate estimate of the expected rate of profit, ρ.

(1) Make, by inspection, a rough estimate of the expected rate of profit. There are various guides to doing this. Perhaps the simplest is to calculate the average yield above cost per annum as a percentage of the initial cost, that is,

$$\frac{q_1 + q_2 + \ldots + q_n - S}{nS}$$

and round this off to the nearest whole per cent.

(2) Try this rate in a declining balance table such as the table above.

(3) If the final balance is negative, try a higher rate. If the final balance is positive, try out a lower rate.

(4) Continue this process (it will usually take only two or three trials), until a rate, say r_0 per cent, such that r_0 per cent yields a negative final balance and $(r_0 + 1)$ per cent yields a positive final

balance, is obtained. This locates the expected rate of profit between r_0 per cent and (r_0+1) per cent.

(5) Interpolate between r_0 and (r_0+1) in order to get an approximation to the expected rate of profit. To do this, write A for the negative final balance when r_0 is used and B for the positive final balance when (r_0+1) is used. Then ρ is approximately equal to

$$\left(r_0+\frac{A}{A+B}\right) \text{ per cent.}$$

Example. A machine with a life of six years costs \$3,000 and has expected net receipts accruing at the end of the years, of \$600, \$700, \$700, \$700, \$600 and \$400 respectively. Compute approximately the expected rate of profit.

(1) The average yield above cost per annum as a percentage of initial cost is

$$\frac{3700-3000}{6\times 3000},$$

that is, about 4 per cent per annum.

(2) With a rate of 4 per cent per annum the following table is obtained:

Year	Balance at beginning of year (\$)	Interest earned during year (\$)	Withdrawals at end of year (\$)	Balance at end of year (\$)
1	3,000	120	600	2,520
2	2,520	101	700	1,921
3	1,921	77	700	1,298
4	1,298	52	700	650
5	650	26	600	76
6	76	3	400	−321

(3) Clearly the rate of 4 per cent is much too low. Try 6 per cent:

Year	Balance at beginning of year (\$)	Interest earned during year (\$)	Withdrawals at end of year (\$)	Balance at end of year (\$)
1	3,000	180	600	2,580
2	2,580	155	700	2,035
3	2,035	122	700	1,457
4	1,457	87	700	844
5	844	51	600	295
6	295	18	400	−87

(4) The expected rate of profit must be even higher than 6 per cent. Try 7 per cent:

Year	Balance at beginning of year ($)	Interest earned during year ($)	Withdrawals at end of year ($)	Balance at end of year ($)
1	3,000	210	600	2,610
2	2,610	183	700	2,093
3	2,093	147	700	1,540
4	1,540	108	700	948
5	948	66	600	414
6	414	29	400	+43

Hence the expected rate of profit must be between 6 and 7 per cent.

(5) Interpolating, the following approximation to the expected rate of profit, ρ, is obtained

$$\rho \simeq \left(6 + \frac{87}{87+43}\right) \quad \text{per cent per annum,}$$

that is, $\rho \simeq 6 \cdot 7$ per cent per annum.

10

THE EFFECT OF CHANGES IN
EXPENDITURE PLANS:
THE MULTIPLIER CONCEPT

In this chapter the consequences of autonomous changes in expenditure plans for the level of economic activity in the two-sector economy are examined. Formally, this consists of an analysis of the impact on the level of real income of a change in either planned investment expenditure or a shift in the functional relationship between consumption expenditure and real income. The important concept of the *multiplier*, which indicates by how much real income will change as a result of these changes, is introduced.

Throughout the chapter it is assumed that the economy is operating below the full employment level of activity so that increases in demand can be met by increased production resulting from the employment of additional workers. In some cases production is assumed to respond only after a lapse of time. Businessmen are assumed to hold ample stocks of consumption goods; this implies that any unexpected changes in consumption demand can be met either by running down or accumulating stocks of goods, rather than by changing their prices. The production of fixed investment goods is undertaken to meet orders and not in anticipation and ahead of demand.[1] The prices of investment goods are assumed to remain constant.

1. The multiplier

The *multiplier*, k, is the ratio between the total change in real income, ΔY, and ΔE, the initial bodily shift of the aggregate demand function which occasioned it. That is,

$$k = \Delta Y / \Delta E,$$

[1] This is a simplifying assumption, which, however, makes no essential difference to the analysis—it merely removes the need to distinguish between stocks of fixed investment goods and stocks of consumption goods. As a first approximation, production to order is a characteristic of the demand for fixed investment goods.

ΔE is referred to as the *multiplicand*. It is explained below that ΔY exceeds ΔE because the initial (or autonomous) increment in aggregate demand gives rise to an induced increment of consumption expenditure. The total increment in income, ΔY, is matched by expenditure of $\Delta E + \Delta C$, where ΔC is the induced increment in consumption expenditure. It should be noted that ΔE may be a

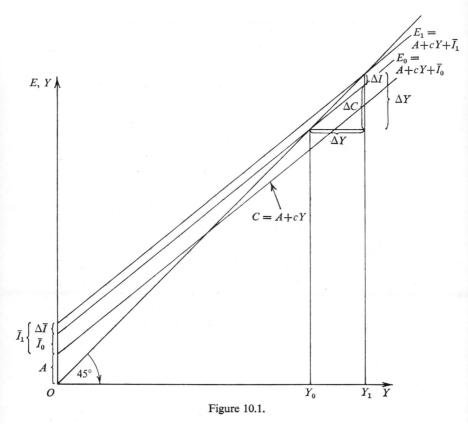

Figure 10.1.

bodily shift of the consumption function. This case is discussed in section 3 below. In the exposition of section 2 the example of an autonomous change in investment expenditure is considered.

Various methods by which the expression for the multiplier may be derived are set out in this section. The argument is developed in the context of a closed, two-sector economy in which initially $I = \bar{I}_0$; $Y_p = Y$; $C = A + cY$; and the aggregate demand schedule is

166

$E_0 = A + cY + \bar{I}_0$ (see figure 10.1). It is assumed that the equilibrium level of income (OY_0) has been established.

Suppose that planned investment expenditure rises from $\bar{I}_0$ to $\bar{I}_1$, and that the economy reaches the new equilibrium level, OY_1. As a result of the rise in planned investment expenditure of $\Delta I = \bar{I}_1 - \bar{I}_0$ ($= \Delta E$), real income has risen by $\Delta Y (= OY_1 - OY_0)$. It is clear from

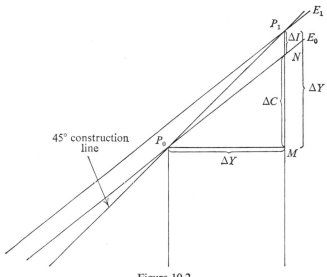

Figure 10.2.

figure 10.1 that $\Delta Y > \Delta I$ by an amount, ΔC, the induced increase in consumption expenditure. Persons originally brought into employment to produce the additional investment goods spend part of their newly created incomes on consumption goods. This in turn brings about increased production and employment in the consumer goods industries.

The ratio between the total rise in real income and the autonomous increase in investment expenditure, $\Delta Y / \Delta I$, is the multiplier, k. An expression for k can be obtained in several ways; first, consider figure 10.2, which is an enlargement of the two equilibrium positions of figure 10.1.

$$\Delta Y = P_0 M = MN + NP_1$$
$$= \frac{MN . P_0 M}{P_0 M} + NP_1$$
$$= \frac{MN}{P_0 M} \Delta Y + \Delta I.$$

167

$MN/P_0 M$ is the slope of E_0 (and E_1), and this equals c, the slope of the consumption function, that is, the *mpc*.[1] Therefore,

$$\Delta Y = c\Delta Y + \Delta I,$$
$$\Delta Y(1-c) = \Delta I;$$

that is,
$$\Delta Y = \frac{\Delta I}{1-c},$$

therefore
$$k = \frac{1}{1-c} \quad \text{or} \quad \frac{1}{s}.$$

That is to say, the multiplier is the reciprocal of one minus the *mpc*, or the reciprocal of the *mps*. It can be seen that the value of k is greater, the greater is the value of c. A given rise in investment expenditure will have a greater ultimate impact on the level of employment and income, the greater is the proportion of additional disposable income which is spent on consumption goods.

It should also be noticed that

$$\Delta C = c\Delta Y = \frac{c}{1-c} \Delta I,$$

and that
$$\Delta S = (1-c) \Delta Y = \Delta I.$$

The induced increase in saving matches the initial increment of investment expenditure. At the new equilibrium level of output the increased planned saving is just offset by the new higher level of planned investment production.[2]

Another method for deriving the multiplier is based on an analysis of the sequence of increments of income resulting from the initial increase in investment expenditure. This method is based on the expression for the sum to infinity of a geometric progression with a common ratio less than one.[3]

---

[1] As $\bar{I}_0$ and $\bar{I}_1$ are independent of income they affect the positions, but not the slopes, of the aggregate demand schedules, E_0 and E_1.

[2] At the new equilibrium level of output, the additional consumption expenditure made by income-recipients in the investment goods sector is just sufficient to take off the market the consumption goods not purchased by the additional income-recipients in the consumption goods sector. That is,

$$c\Delta I = s\Delta C \quad \left(= (1-c)\frac{c}{1-c} \Delta I\right).$$

[3] The method for summing such a series is as follows: let $a, ar, ar^2, \ldots$ be a geometric progression with a, the first term, positive and r, the common ratio, less than one. The sum to n terms (S_n) of this series is

$$S_n = a + ar + \ldots + ar^{n-1}.$$

[*cont. on p.* 169

The view of the income-creation process in this book is that expenditure calls forth production which creates income, which generates expenditure. Suppose that this were an instantaneous process; that is, suppose that any increase in expenditure immediately called forth the necessary production, that the income so created was immediately distributed to its owners and that part of it was immediately spent, and so on. With these assumptions, an autonomous increase in income-creating expenditure would instantaneously have its full impact on the level of income and employment.

Consider an economy in which the aggregate *mpc* is $\frac{4}{5}$ and where, initially, income is at its equilibrium level. Planned investment expenditure then rises by \$1,000m. per period. This will immediately lead to a rise in production and disposable income of the same amount. Four-fifths of the newly created income will be immediately spent on consumption goods, the increased production of which will be associated with an equal value of distributed income which will be associated with increased consumption expenditure, and so on.

This process is set out in table 10.1. It can be seen that the initial rise in expenditure of \$1,000,000, which is referred to as the *primary* 'round', calls forth *secondary* 'rounds' of expenditure, production and income. In the production column, ΔY, the primary and secondary 'rounds' are seen to be the terms of a geometric progression with an initial term of \$1,000,000 and a common ratio of $\frac{4}{5}$. The sum to infinity of the rounds is \$1,000,000 $[1/(1-\frac{4}{5})] = \$5,000,000$, the figure shown in the total row of the table. Similarly, \$4,000,000, the total figure of the consumption expenditure column, is the sum to infinity of a geometric progression with an initial term of \$800,000 and the same common ratio, $\frac{4}{5}$. As a result of the induced rise in income, saving immediately rises to a level where it is exactly offset by the initial rise in planned investment expenditure. The value of the multiplier in this economy is $5[= 1/(1-\frac{4}{5})]$.

Multiply both sides by r and subtract the resulting product from the original summation.

That is,
$$S_n - rS_n = a - ar^n,$$

that is,
$$S_n = \frac{a(1-r^n)}{1-r}$$

as
$$n \to \infty, \quad S_n \to \frac{a}{1-r} \quad \text{because} \quad r^n \to 0.$$

That is
$$S_\infty = \frac{a}{1-r}.$$

TABLE 10.1. *Instantaneous impact on real income of a rise in planned investment expenditure of $1,000 (all values in $'000)*

Round	Increment of investment expenditure ΔI	Increment of real income ΔY	Increment of consumption expenditure ΔC	Increment of saving ΔS
1	1,000 $\longrightarrow$	1,000 $\longrightarrow$	800	200
2	—	800 $\longrightarrow$	640	160
3	—	640 $\longrightarrow$	512	128
4	—	512 $\longrightarrow$	410	102
⋮	⋮	⋮	⋮	⋮
Total	1,000	5,000	4,000	1,000

That $k = 1/(1-c)$, where $c = mpc$, is the general form of the multiplier can be seen by taking a unit increase in planned investment expenditure. The consequent changes in investment, real income, consumption expenditure and saving are shown in Table 10.2. The nature of the various series of geometric progressions can also be seen in the table.

TABLE 10.2. *Derivation of the total effects of a unit change in investment expenditure*

Round	ΔI	ΔY	ΔC	ΔS
1	1 $\longrightarrow$	1 $\longrightarrow$	c	$(1-c)$:
2	—	c	c^2	$c-c^2 = c(1-c)$
3	—	c^2	c^3	$c^2-c^3 = c^2(1-c)$
4	—	c^3	c^4	$c^3-c^4 = c^3(1-c)$
⋮	⋮	⋮	⋮	⋮
Total	1	$\dfrac{1}{1-c}$	$\dfrac{c}{1-c}$	$\dfrac{1-c}{1-c} = 1$

If c were zero, the multiplier would be unity; the increase in production would be confined to the initial increment of investment goods. If c were unity, the multiplier would be infinite; there would be no leakages from the system through saving to check the expansion or

170

contraction of income resulting from any chance disturbance of aggregate planned expenditure. The fact that the economic system is not violently unstable suggests that c is less than unity—a proposition that has been argued already, for different reasons, in chapter 8. The stability of the system is therefore related to the size of the leakages from each round of expenditure—the higher is s, the smaller is the induced impact of any given autonomous change in income-creating expenditure.

Where $C = C(Y)$ is not a linear function, the *mpc* for any given value of Y is given by the slope of the function, dC/dY, at that point.

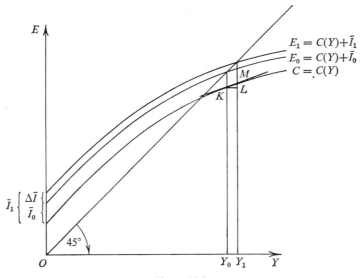

Figure 10.3.

This slope itself continuously changes so that the multiplier, $1/(1-mpc)$, is accurate only for small changes in aggregate expenditure. Such a case is illustrated by figure 10.3 where the value of the *mpc* falls continuously as income increases. At the income level OY_0, the *mpc* is equal to LM/KL. Initially planned investment expenditure is $\bar{I}_0$, and the equilibrium level of income is OY_0. If there is an increment of planned expenditure, $\Delta \bar{I}$, the new equilibrium level of income is OY_1. The increment of income, $Y_0 Y_1$, is approximately equal to $[1/(1-mpc)]\Delta \bar{I}$.

In order to simplify the exposition, linear functions are used to

171

illustrate the argument of this book. However, the argument developed is equally valid for the general case, and can be developed in general terms analytically. For example, in a closed, two-sector economy, let $C = C(Y)$ be the consumption function and $\bar{I}$ the autonomous level of investment expenditure. The equilibrium level of income will be given by the solution for Y of

$$Y = C(Y) + \bar{I}.$$

It follows that

$$\frac{dY}{d\bar{I}} = C'(Y)\frac{dY}{d\bar{I}} + 1,$$

$$\frac{dY}{d\bar{I}}(1 - C'(Y)) = 1,$$

that is,

$$k = \frac{dY}{d\bar{I}} = \frac{1}{1 - C'(Y)},$$

where $C'(Y)$ is the *mpc* at income Y.

2. Lags in the income–creation process

(a) The income–expenditure lag

So far, it has been assumed that the reactions of producers and consumers are instantaneous, so that the multiplier process is a series of timeless 'rounds' of expenditure, production and income which immediately carry real income and employment to their new equilibrium levels. However, in the real world, the process takes time; it is a lagged, not an instantaneous, process.

Businessmen need to be assured that a given change in demand will be sustained before they change their production levels; and there are technical reasons why production cannot be raised immediately. Income created by additional production may reach the factors of production concerned only after a lag. This is particularly relevant for dividend and interest payments, which are usually made only once or twice a year. Changes in consumption patterns may not occur immediately as a result of changes in income. Consumption expenditure tends to be a continuous process while income payments are periodic; apart from inertia, consumption expenditure may not immediately respond fully to a given change in income because income recipients may not regard the change as permanent (see chapter 8).

Three possible lags may be distinguished:

(1) The *expenditure–production lag*: the lagged response of production to expenditure changes.

(2) The *production–income lag*: the lagged response of the final distribution of income to production changes.[1]

(3) The *income–expenditure lag*: the lagged response of consumption expenditure to income changes.

The instantaneous multiplier analysis will now be modified to take account of lags; the simplest case, the income–expenditure lag, is considered first. It is assumed that producers correctly anticipate any change in expenditure on consumption goods and that the additional income so created is immediately distributed. Similarly, the income associated with any change in the production of investment goods is immediately distributed. However, the income–expenditure lag is introduced by assuming that the consumption expenditure of the current period is based on income received in the *previous* period. In this analysis, the period is assumed to be one month, so that planned consumption expenditure in January is a function of income received in December. Analytically, $C_t = C(Y_{t-1})$, where t is the current month.

The assumption that *planned* consumption expenditure of the next period is based on the *current* period's receipt of income, may be taken as implying that it is expected that this current flow will be maintained. It is further implied that even if this expectation is not realized in the next period, nevertheless, consumption plans are actually carried out; in this case, anticipated saving will not be realized. This amounts to the assumption that consumption expenditure always takes priority over saving, which is treated as a *residual*.

A lag between consumption expenditure and income may occur because people's spending tends to be habitual, and it takes time for them to alter their spending patterns; or because people believe that this month's income will be equal to last month's, and budget accordingly; or because people plan their consumption expenditures using an income period of more than one month.

The first case considered is that of an equilibrium position disturbed by a temporary rise in investment expenditure of $1,000,000 in January. Investment expenditure is assumed to *return* then to its

---

[1] The production–income lag is not discussed in detail in this book. As far as wage- and salary-earners are concerned, it seems reasonable to ignore it. Wages are usually paid weekly and are related to current production.

previous level. The aggregate *mpc* is again $\frac{4}{5}$. If there were no lags, the initial rise of $1,000,000 would immediately induce a further rise of real income of $4,000,000, due to the secondary rounds of consumption expenditure, and the rise of total production in January would be $5,000,000. In February, because planned investment returns to the level of December, production would return to the original equilibrium level; in effect, the instantaneous multiplier has operated in reverse.

However, when consumption expenditure lags behind income by one month, the changes in production are spread over time (see Table 10.3). In January, investment expenditure and production rise by $1,000,000 and the resulting increase in real income is distributed. Consumption spending in January is, however, related to income received in December, and so is not affected. The *total* change in expenditure, production and income in January is therefore an increase in planned and actual investment of $1,000,000; this is matched by a rise in *actual* saving of $1,000,000. Not all of this increment of saving is planned, for if disposable income were to be $1,000,000 greater in the next month, households would plan to save only $200,000 more. Actual saving therefore can be thought of as composed of two elements—ultimately intended (planned) saving—in this case, $200,000—and temporary (unplanned) saving—here $800,000—which exists for only one month.

The temporary saving is equal to the change in income over the month. This follows because this increment of income, $Y_t - Y_{t-1}$, must be allocated either to consumption or saving; but, *ex hypothesi*, this month's consumption expenditure is independent of this month's income.

In February, investment returns to its original level but an additional $800,000 is spent on consumption goods. This is immediately matched by increased production and distributed income. The increase in income of $800,000 has all been used for consumption purposes this month, so *actual* saving is zero. However, the saving appropriate to a *sustained* increment of income of $800,000 is $160,000 and in March households will anticipate saving $160,000, having planned to spend an additional $640,000 on consumption goods. Whether or not their *actual* saving in March is $160,000 will depend upon their actual income. In fact in March the increment of income is only $640,000—the fall occurs because of the households' attempt to save the extra $160,000. Since the actual increment of income in March is $640,000 and consumption expenditure (based on the previous month's income experience) is also $640,000, actual saving is zero (see Table 10.3).

TABLE 10.3. *Impact on real income of a temporary increase in planned investment expenditure, with an income–expenditure lag of one month ($ '000).*

Month	ΔI	ΔY	ΔC	ΔS		
				Saving planned for month t ($\frac{1}{5} Y_{t-1}$)	Change in income ($Y_t - Y_{t-1}$)	Actual saving ((1)+(2))
				(1)	(2)	(3)
Jan.	1,000 →— 1,000		—	0	1,000	1,000
Feb.	—	800 —← 800		200	−200	0
Mar.	—	640 —← 640		160	−160	0
Apr.	—	512 —← 512		128	−128	0
Ultimately	0	0	0	0	0	0
Total of the monthly changes	1,000	5,000	4,000	1,000	0	1,000

Ultimately, the economy will return to the equilibrium level of income of the month prior to the rise in investment expenditure. This must occur because any *sustained* departure from this level must be based upon a *permanent* change in desired spending. The change in spending on investment goods lasted for only one month, and the changes in consumption spending have been seen to be transitory. In the case of the lagged response of consumption expenditure to changes in income, the same *total* expansion in the output of consumption goods ($4,000,000) occurs as in the case of the instantaneous multiplier. But in the lagged case the increments of consumption output comprise a *diminishing stream* through time. The difference between the operation of the instantaneous multiplier and the lagged response for an income–expenditure lag of one period is illustrated in figure 10.4. The left-hand section of the figure illustrates the instantaneous multiplier; the right-hand section illustrates the multiplier process where there is an income-expenditure lag.

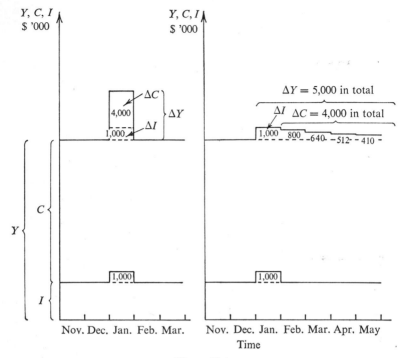

Figure 10.4.

Now consider the case where the increase in investment is permanent, that is, planned expenditure rises by $1,000,000 *per month*. In the case of the instantaneous multiplier, income expands immediately by $5,000,000. For the lagged case there is a smooth, convergent approach to the new equilibrium position. Each period the rate of flow increases (but at a decreasing rate) until the new level is reached. The particular example postulated is illustrated in figure 10.5. The general case is shown in Table 10.5 where a sustained unit increment of investment is assumed. Again, actual saving in the transition period between one equilibrium position and another can be viewed as the net outcome of the planned rise in saving and the change in disposable income. It will be seen that when income has risen by $1/(1-c)$ per period, planned saving again equals planned investment, and a steady rate of flow of real income has been attained.

176

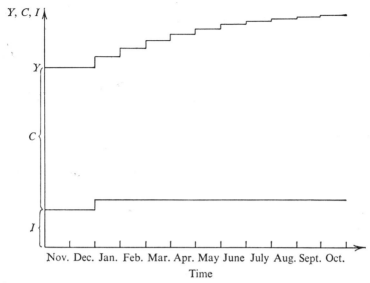

Figure 10.5. Impact on real income of a sustained increase in investment expenditure per period, with an income–expenditure lag of one period.

TABLE 10.4. *The impact on real income of a permanent unit change in investment expenditure per month, with an income–expenditure lag of one month*

| | | | | | ΔS | |
| | | | | Saving planned for month t $(1-c)\,Y_{t-1}$ | Change in income $(Y_t - Y_{t-1})$ | Actual saving $(1)+(2)$ |
Month	ΔI	ΔY	ΔC	(1)	(2)	(3)
1	$1 \longrightarrow 1$			0	1	1
2	$1 \longrightarrow 1+c$		c	$1-c$	c	1
3	$1 \longrightarrow 1+c+c^2$		$c+c^2$	$1-c^2$	c^2	1
4	$1 \longrightarrow 1+c+c^2+c^3$		$c+c^2+c^3$	$1-c^3$	c^3	1
$\vdots$	$\vdots$	$\vdots$	$\vdots$	$\vdots$	$\vdots$	$\vdots$
Ultimately	1	$\dfrac{1}{1-c}$	$\dfrac{c}{1-c}$	1	0	1

177

(*b*) *The expenditure–production lag*

For the case of a permanent change in investment expenditure with an income–expenditure lag it was shown that real income approaches the new equilibrium level by a smooth path, and that after a few periods it is close to that level. The higher rate of production of fixed investment goods is achieved immediately; the consequent induced consumption expenditure causes a smooth expansion of the rate of production in the consumption goods sector. Total production adapts smoothly to the change in aggregate demand.

However, when there is an *expenditure–production lag*, the approach to the new equilibrium level is not smooth; instead, the paths of expenditure and real income oscillate. In the example considered in this section, the oscillations eventually die out and a new equilibrium position of real income (as indicated by the instantaneous multiplier) is actually reached, although the real incomes of particular periods have values both higher and lower than the ultimate equilibrium value. But it should be noted that, by using slightly different assumptions, the oscillations may not be damped, and real income may fluctuate steadily or in ever-increasing oscillations around the equilibrium level associated with the instantaneous multiplier. This suggests that in certain circumstances, the forces operating in an economy may not result in income settling at a stable, short-run equilibrium position but may, instead, cause real income to fluctuate from period to period. An analysis of such fluctuations is outside the scope of this book. But it will be seen from the example which follows that the static theory of the short-run determination of real income (the theory which isolates the events of each short period) can be adapted to the dynamic case (the case where the events of any period are linked to those of the preceding and following periods).

To illustrate the impact on income, production and expenditure of the expenditure–production lag, a permanent change in the level of investment expenditure is examined for an economy where the rate of production is initially in equilibrium. In this economy, fixed investment goods are produced to order, so that there is no expenditure–production lag in the investment goods sector. Consumption goods, however, are produced in *anticipation* of demand; businessmen in the consumer goods sector expect the rate of sales in the current period to be the same as the rate of sales in the previous period and their production plans are guided by this expectation. It is assumed that businessmen wish to hold a *certain level* of stocks and that stocks always are sufficient to meet any difference between current production and demand. If sales fall short of anticipated demand, that is, if they are less than the sales of the previous period, the surplus output is absorbed as an unplanned increment to stocks, and this leads businessmen to attempt to restore the desired level of stocks by changing the rate of production. The rate of production in any period is therefore made up of two parts: the production to match the expected current rate of sales plus or minus the change designed to restore the existing stocks to the desired level by the end of the period. For example, if sales for the current period are expected to be $1,000,000 and stocks at the beginning of the period exceed the desired level by $100,000, current production for the period will be $900,000.[1] The *mpc* is assumed to be $\frac{3}{5}$. Finally, it is assumed that there are no production–income, or income–expenditure, lags in the economy.

Suppose that the economy is in equilibrium and that orders for fixed investment goods rise permanently by $100,000 per period. The impact of this on the level of real income and consumption expenditure, *relative to their values in the initial equilibrium position*, and on stocks is shown in table 10.5. The table also shows the change in planned investment expenditure per period (*relative to its level in the equilibrium position at the start of the analysis*). This change consists of two components: the permanent change in planned expenditure on fixed investment goods of $100,000 per period and the planned change in investment in stocks for each period. The accumulated stock deficiencies (the difference between the desired level of stocks and their actual level at the end of each period) are also shown.

In period 1 expenditure on fixed investment goods rises by $100,000, which is immediately matched by additional production and distributed income. Consumption expenditure therefore rises by $60,000, but businessmen in the consumption goods sector have not foreseen this. Their current production plans were based on the sales of the previous period, and so stocks of consumption goods will be run down by the amount by which demand exceeds their estimate, that

---

[1] An alternative assumption, perhaps more realistic, is that businessmen wish to hold stocks equal to a given *proportion* of expected current sales. A certain type of cyclical instability, 'the two-year inventory cycle', has been explained by a model based on this assumption. However, the analysis is complex and, as short-run analysis is the main concern of this book, this case is not discussed here.

TABLE 10.5. *Impact on real income of a permanent change in fixed investment expenditure with an expenditure–production lag of one period ($'000)*

(1) Period	(2) Planned fixed investment	(3) Planned production of consumption goods to make up stock deficiency (planned investment in stocks) [Col. (8) of previous period]	(4) Planned production of consumption goods to meet higher consumption expenditure of last period [Col. (6) of previous period]	(5) Income (= production) [(2)+(3)+(4)]	(6) Consumption expenditure [$\frac{3}{5}$ of col. (5)]	(7) Actual investment in stocks [(3)+(4)−(6)]	(8) Accumulated stock deficiency [−Σ col. (7)]	(9) Actual investment [(2)+(7)]	(10) Actual saving [(5)−(6)]
1	100	—	—	100	60	−60	60	40	40
2	100	60	60	220	132	−12	72	88	88
3	100	72	132	304	182	22	50	122	122
4	100	50	182	332	199	33	17	133	133
5	100	17	199	316	190	26	−9	126	126
6	100	−9	190	281	169	12	−21	112	112
7	100	−21	169	248	149	−1	−20	99	99
8	100	−20	149	229	137	−8	−12	92	92
9	100	−12	137	225	135	−10	−2	90	90
10	100	−2	135	233	140	−7	5	93	93
11	100	5	140	245	147	−2	7	98	98
12	100	7	147	254	152	2	5	102	102
13	100	5	152	257	154	3	2	103	103
14	100	2	154	256	154	2	0	102	102
15	100	0	154	254	152	2	−2	102	102
16	100	−2	152	250	150	0	−2	100	100
17	100	−2	150	248	149	−1	−1	99	99
18	100	−1	149	248	149	−1	0	99	99
Ultimately	100	0	150	250	150	0	0	100	100

is, by $60,000. Therefore, at the end of the first period, stocks are $60,000 below the desired level, and actual investment has risen by only $40,000 ($100,000 less $60,000 disinvestment in stocks); real income has risen by $100,000, consumption by $60,000, and actual and planned savings by $40,000.

In period 2, businessmen in the consumption goods sector will increase the rate of production by $120,000—of which $60,000 is related to the increase in the sales of the previous period and the other $60,000 is intended to restore stocks to the desired level. Planned investment expenditure in this period is therefore $160,000 greater than in the initial situation. However, this results in increased income and consumers' expenditure not anticipated by producers. Stocks are therefore further run down, and at the end of period 2, the stock deficiency is $12,000 greater than at the end of period 1. In period 3, this stock deficiency is not completely wiped out; but the rise in production of consumption goods is great enough to meet both the increase in current demand and to allow some stocks to accumulate.

The general pattern that emerges is that the deficiency in stocks is made up, and then more than made up so that an unintended accumulation of stocks occurs. This acts upon the production plans of businessmen to produce damped cycles of real income around the ultimate equilibrium level of income as predicted by the instantaneous multiplier. Eventually, the economy reaches this level where income is greater by $250,000 ($= \Delta I[1/(1-c)]$); stocks are at their desired level, investment in fixed investment goods is greater by $100,000, and consumption expenditure is greater by $150,000. At this level of income the additional consumption expenditure of $60,000 by income-earners in the investment goods sector is just great enough to take off the market the consumption goods not bought by the additional income-earners in the consumption goods sector; the latter produce extra consumption goods of $150,000 and buy $90,000 themselves. Schematically, the process is as shown in figure 10.6.

In this section businessmen have been assumed to behave in a mechanical manner. The analysis is not meant to apply directly to an actual situation, but merely to illustrate some of the complications which can arise when production is in anticipation of demand which cannot be foreseen with accuracy. In actual situations, businessmen base production plans on many other factors besides the previous month's sales. Many larger firms, for example, frequently have market research sections which attempt to forecast sales by using methods more sophisticated than the projection of the immediate past into the future.

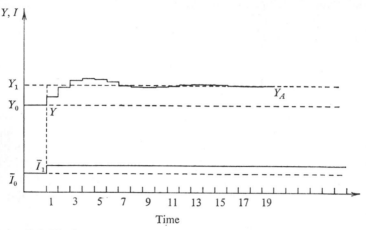

Figure 10.6. The impact on real income of a permanent rise in expenditure on fixed investment goods, with an expenditure–production lag. [*Note*: I_0 and I_1 refer to planned expenditure on fixed investment goods, Y_0 and Y_1 to equilibrium levels of real income; $Y_0 Y_A$ depicts the path of actual income.]

3. The multiplier and autonomous shifts in the consumption function

In the examples considered so far, the primary 'round' in the multiplier process has been due to the response of production to a change in planned investment. But autonomous changes in any of the components of income-creating expenditure can start a similar process. In this section, the consequences of a shift in the consumption function are analysed; the consequences of autonomous changes in government expenditure and taxation, and in exports and imports, are discussed in chapters 11 and 12 respectively.

Consider the case of a unit increase in consumption expenditure at each level of personal disposable income, that is, an *autonomous* rise in the consumption function of one unit. The resulting 'rounds' for the instantaneous multiplier are shown in table 10.6.

The autonomous increase in consumption expenditure means that at all former levels of disposable income, households now wish to buy more goods than previously, in this instance, to the value of one unit more; that is, they wish to save less. The primary increase in production of one unit is to accommodate this autonomous increase. But as a result of the primary increase in production and disposable income there will be induced increments of consumption expenditure, and these induced increments will, for any given value of the *mpc*, be of the same order of magnitude as in the case where the initial increment of disposable income arose from an expansion of production of investment goods.

TABLE 10.6

Round	ΔY	ΔC	ΔS	
			Autonomous	Induced
		1 ⟵ −1		
1	1	c		$1-c$
2	c	c^2		$c(1-c)$
3	c^2	c^3		$c^2(1-c)$
⋮	⋮	⋮	⋮	⋮
Total	$\dfrac{1}{1-c}$	$\dfrac{1}{1-c}$	-1	$+\dfrac{1-c}{1-c}(=1)$

The total rise in real income for *any* autonomous increment of income-creating expenditure of an amount, ΔE, is $\Delta Y = [1/(1-c)]\Delta E$, which can also be written as: $\Delta Y = \Delta E + [c/(1-c)]\Delta E$. It can be seen from the right-hand side that the rise in real income is the sum of the autonomous increment, ΔE, and the induced expansion of consumption expenditure, $[c/(1-c)]\Delta E$. When the consumption function rises, total saving remains unaltered, even though disposable income has increased. The increment of saving *induced* by the income expansion,

$$s\Delta Y = (1-c)\frac{1}{1-c}\Delta E,$$

just offsets the initial *autonomous* reduction in saving (the obverse of the autonomous increase in consumption expenditure).

This analysis shows that although *planned* saving has changed there is no change in *actual* saving at the new equilibrium level of income. This proposition is known as *the paradox of thrift*; it is illustrated in

183

figure 10.7. An economy is in equilibrium at a level of income, OY_0, which corresponds to the intersection of the saving function, S_0, with the investment function, $\bar{I}_0$. Suppose that people in total decide to save more *at each level of income*, so that a new saving function, S_1, results. Because a rise in planned saving from a given level of income does not lead automatically to a corresponding rise in planned investment, a contractionary process follows the rise in the saving function. The initial reduction in sales and production is followed by further, induced, falls in expenditure, production, employment and income until, at a lower level of income, OY_1, planned saving is again

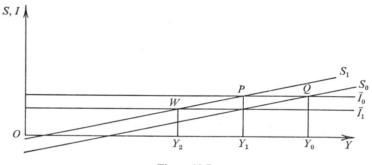

Figure 10.7.

just offset by investment expenditure. Persons have succeeded in raising their aggregate $aps(Y_1P/OY_1 > Y_0Q/OY_0)$ but not the amount saved $(Y_1P = Y_0Q)$.

Furthermore, if the fall in sales has an adverse effect on planned investment, this may be reduced, and a new, lower equilibrium level of income will result. For example, if planned investment expenditure is reduced to $\bar{I}_1$, the new, lower equilibrium level of real income will be OY_2 and the attempt to save more will result in a *fall* in actual saving. A rise in propensity to save will, through its effect on sales, have a depressing effect on expected rates of profit, and therefore on planned investment expenditure (see chapter 9). It is a common reaction to think of a rise in saving as likely to give rise to an increase in investment; but if it is assumed that ample funds are available to firms at the current rates of interest, it cannot be argued that a rise in the propensity to save will cause an increase in investment at these current rates of interest.

184

The analysis of this section can be used to illustrate the logical error known as the *fallacy of composition*. The above illustration shows that what may be true of any one individual is not necessarily true of all individuals taken together. One individual can effectively alter his rate of saving, and the impact of this on the level of economic activity may be ignored; but this is not possible if all individuals attempt to increase their saving.

In a situation where aggregate planned expenditure exceeds full employment supplies, an autonomous increase in planned saving would reduce aggregate excess demand and *could* result in the spending plans of investors (previously thwarted by lack of supplies) being fulfilled.

4. The multiplier and company saving

The discussion of the multiplier process in the previous sections was in the context of a two-sector model in which companies distributed all of their income to the personal sector. The case where company saving is positive will now be considered. The nature of company saving was discussed in chapter 3, section $1(e)$, and chapter 9, section $6(a)$. It was explained that retained company income may be in the form of depreciation allowances, D, or undistributed company profits, U.

If companies decide to retain a *given* amount of their gross income as depreciation allowances, $\bar{D}$, the disposable income of the personal sector will be $Y_p = Y - \bar{D}$. The existence of retained company income does not alter the nature of the consumption function:

$$C = A + cY_p.$$

But now at each level of real income, Y, personal disposable income, Y_p, will be less by the amount $\bar{D}$; consequently planned consumption expenditure and planned personal saving will be less by the amounts $c\bar{D}$ and $s\bar{D}$ respectively. This is illustrated by figure 10.8.

At each level of Y, Y_p lies below Y by $\bar{D} = KM$ and $C = A + c(Y - \bar{D})$ lies below $C = A + c(Y)$ by $c\bar{D} = LM$. At each level of Y, personal saving is less by $s\bar{D}$ $(= KL)$ than in the case where $Y_p = Y$.

The aggregate demand function is now given by:

$$E_1 = A + c(Y - \bar{D}) + \bar{I}$$

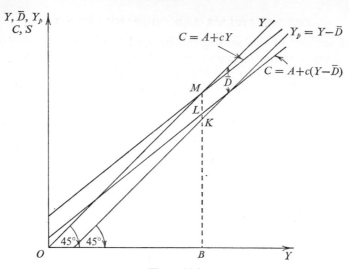

Figure 10.8.

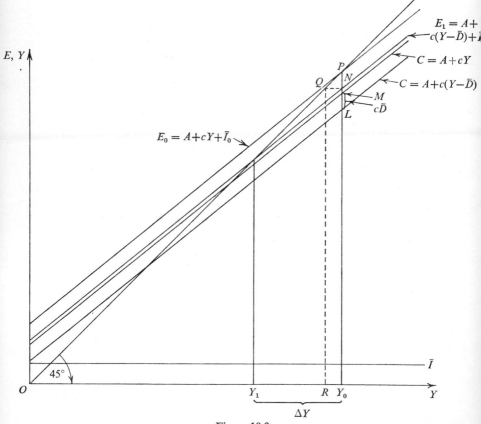

Figure 10.9.

compared with that where there was no retained company income:

$$E_0 = A + c(Y) + \bar{I}.$$

The respective equilibrium levels of income are given by solving for Y in:

$$Y = A + c(Y - \bar{D}) + \bar{I},$$

that is
$$Y_1 = \frac{1}{1-c}(A - c\bar{D} + \bar{I})$$

and
$$Y_0 = \frac{1}{1-c}(A + \bar{I}).$$

This is illustrated by figure 10.9.

The effect of the decision by companies to retain the depreciation allowances $\bar{D}$, is to cause a fall in the level of real income of

$$\Delta Y (= OY_0 - OY_1) = \frac{1}{1-c} c\bar{D}.$$

This change can be regarded as comprising a primary reduction in planned consumption expenditure at OY_0 of $c\bar{D}(= LM = NP)$, together with a further induced fall in income and consumption expenditure of $(c/[1-c])c\bar{D} (= RY_1)$. Viewed as a series of rounds the total change in income is

$$c\bar{D} + c(c\bar{D}) + c^2(c\bar{D}) + \ldots.$$

The sum of this geometric progression is $c\bar{D}/(1-c) = \Delta Y$. The change in output is in the consumption goods sector, since it is only consumption expenditure which has changed.

It should be noted that, if instead of companies retaining income of $\bar{D}$, personal saving had increased autonomously by the amount $\bar{D}$, the total change in income would have been $[1/(1-c)]\bar{D}$ (see section 3 above), which exceeds $[1/(1-c)]c\bar{D}$ by the amount

$$[1/(1-c)](1-c)\bar{D} = \bar{D}.$$

This difference is explained by the fact that an autonomous increase in total gross saving (personal saving plus retained company income) in the form of retained company income makes its impact upon expenditure through its effect upon personal disposable income. The initial effect on consumption expenditure in this case is $c\bar{D}$, whereas in the case of an autonomous change in personal saving, the initial increment of consumption expenditure is equal to $\bar{D}$.

The existence of gross saving in the form of given depreciation allowances does not affect the value of the income multipliers for autonomous changes in investment expenditure and/or movements of the consumption function, $C = A + cY_p$. The equilibrium level of income was shown above to be

$$Y = \frac{1}{1-c}(A - c\bar{D} + \bar{I})$$

from which it follows that:

$$\Delta Y = \frac{1}{1-c}(\Delta A, \Delta I).$$

Because the depreciation allowances are independent of the level of real income all *increments* of real income are distributed to the personal sector, and the marginal propensity to save of the personal sector determines the value of the multiplier.

Companies may also retain part of their income in the form of undistributed profits, U. If these are determined independently of income, that is, if $U = \bar{U}$, their effect would be as for depreciation allowances. In fact, as was explained in section 6(a) of chapter 9, undistributed profits are related to the level of company profits, and in turn these are related to the level of real income. In order to simplify the exposition it will be assumed that the relationship between undistributed profits and real income is $U = uY$.[1]

If retained company income is only in the form of undistributed profits, then $Y_p = Y - uY$, and the relationship between consumption expenditure and real income is:

$$C = A + c(1-u)Y.$$

The equilibrium level of income is obtained by solving for Y the equation:

$$Y = A + c(1-u)Y + \bar{I}.$$

The effect of undistributed profits $U = uY$ upon the relationship between Y and Y_p, and between C and Y is illustrated in figure 10.10.

[1] In chapter 9 it was argued (see p. 157) that undistributed profits are likely to be an increasing proportion of real income. For the reasons given on pp. 171–2 above, linear relationships are used throughout the book. For the purpose of analysing the multiplier effect in situations where $U = U(Y)$ is non-linear, the appropriate value of u used in the multiplier $1/[1 - c(1-u)]$ developed below is $u = \Delta U/\Delta Y$.

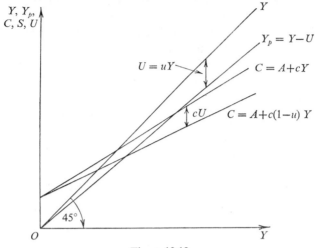

Figure 10.10.

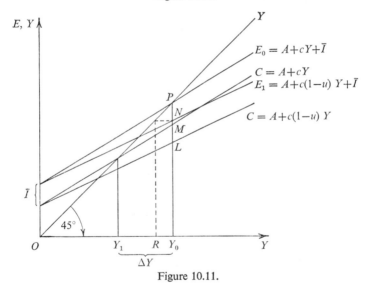

Figure 10.11.

At each level of income, personal disposable income is reduced by uY; as a result consumption expenditure and personal saving at each level of income are less, by $c(uY)$ and $s(uY)$ respectively.

The equilibrium levels of income for two economies, which differ only in that in one there are undistributed profits of $U = uY$, are

189

illustrated in figure 10.11 by OY_0 and OY_1. The aggregate demand function and equilibrium income for the economy where there is no retained company income are depicted by E_0 and OY_0 respectively.

The retention of company income in the form of undistributed profits causes a reduction in planned consumption expenditure at each level of real income, and as a result the equilibrium level of income is reduced. Because undistributed profits are related to the level of income they operate to reduce the value of the multiplier. If, for example, there is an increase in investment expenditure by an amount, ΔI, the initial increment of Y_p is $(1-u)\Delta I$, and the series of increments of induced consumption expenditure are

$$c(1-u)\Delta I + c^2(1-u)^2 \Delta I + c^3(1-u)^3 \Delta I + \ldots;$$

the sum of this series is $c(1-u)\Delta I/[1-c(1-u)]$, and the *total* increment of income is $\{1/[1-c(1-u)]\}\Delta I$. The multiplier process for a unit increment of investment expenditure viewed as a series of rounds is illustrated by Table 10.7. It should be noted that the increment of income, $1/[1-c(1-u)]$, is such that the increment of total gross saving, $\Delta U + \Delta S$, is equal to ΔI. In this particular case where $\Delta I = 1$,

$$\frac{u}{1-c(1-u)} + \frac{(1-c)(1-u)}{1-c(1-u)} = 1.$$

TABLE 10.7. *The effect of a unit change in*
investment expenditure

Round	ΔI	ΔY	ΔU	ΔY_p	ΔC	ΔS
1	1	1	u	$(1-u)$	$c(1-u)$	$s(1-u)$
2	—	$c(1-u)$	$uc(1-u)$	$c(1-u)^2$	$c^2(1-u)^2$	$sc(1-u)^2$
3	—	$c^2(1-u)^2$	$uc^2(1-u)^2$	$c^2(1-u)^3$	$c^3(1-u)^3$	$sc^2(1-u)^3$
$\vdots$	$\vdots$	$\vdots$	$\vdots$	$\vdots$	$\vdots$	$\vdots$
Total	1	$\dfrac{1}{1-c(1-u)}$	$\dfrac{u}{1-c(1-u)}$	$\dfrac{1-u}{1-c(1-u)}$	$\dfrac{c(1-u)}{1-c(1-u)}$	$\dfrac{s(1-u)}{1-c(1-u)}$

Alternatively, the multiplier can be derived as follows. The condition for equilibrium in the level of income may be written as:

$$Y = E,$$

that is $\qquad Y = A + c(1-u)Y + \bar{I},$

that is
$$Y = \frac{1}{1-c(1-u)}(A+\bar{I}),$$

from which it follows that

$$\Delta Y = \frac{1}{1-c(1-u)}(\Delta A, \Delta \bar{I}).$$

The difference between the levels of income in the two economies illustrated by figure 10.11 can be regarded as arising from the bodily downward movement of aggregate demand at the initial equilibrium level of income, Y_0, by the amount $c(u Y_0)$ represented in figure 10.11 by $NP\,(= LM)$, together with the consequent induced change in consumption expenditure

$$\frac{c(1-u)}{1-c(1-u)}(Y_0)$$

(which is equal to RY_1 in figure 10.11). The total change in income, ΔY, is equal to

$$\frac{1}{1-c(1-u)}c(u Y_0).$$

It can be demonstrated that the 'paradox of thrift' holds for an increase in company saving, equally as for an increase in personal saving. Consider the case where initially company retained income comprises both depreciation allowances, $\bar{D}$, and undistributed profits, $U = uY$. Then the consumption function, $C = A+cY_p$, may be written as

$$C = A+c(1-u)Y-c\bar{D}.$$

The equilibrium level of income, Y, is found by solving for Y:

$$Y = E,$$

that is
$$Y = A+c(1-u)Y-c\bar{D}+\bar{I},$$

that is
$$Y = \frac{1}{1-c(1-u)}(A-c\bar{D}+\bar{I}).$$

Assume now that companies decide to increase their depreciation allowances (perhaps because of some change in the system of taxation) by an amount, $\Delta \bar{D}$. The consequent change in income is

$$\Delta Y = \frac{1}{1-c(1-u)}c\Delta \bar{D}.$$

The multiplier process viewed as a series of rounds for an increment $\Delta\bar{D} = 1$ is shown in table 10.8.

TABLE 10.8. *The effect of a unit change in depreciation allowances*

Round	$\Delta\bar{D}$	ΔY	ΔU	ΔY_p	ΔC	ΔS
1	1			-1	$-c$	$-s$
2	—	$-c$	$-uc$	$c(1-u)$	$-c^2(1-u)$	$sc(1-u)$
3	—	$-c^2(1-u)$	$-uc^2(1-u)$	$c^2(1-u)^2$	$-c^3(1-u)^2$	$-sc^2(1-u)^2$
$\vdots$	$\vdots$	$\vdots$	$\vdots$	$\vdots$	$\vdots$	$\vdots$
Total	1	$\dfrac{-c}{1-c(1-u)}$	$\dfrac{-uc}{1-c(1-u)}$	$\dfrac{-1}{1-c(1-u)}$	$\dfrac{-c}{1-c(1-u)}$	$\dfrac{-s}{1-c(1-u)}$

It can be seen that as a result of the fall in income there are induced *falls* in undistributed company profits and personal saving of

$$\frac{-uc}{1-c(1-u)} \quad \text{and} \quad \frac{-(1-c)}{1-c(1-u)}]$$

respectively. The sum of these two items is unity. There is a net increase in company retained income of

$$\Delta\bar{D}+\Delta U = 1 + \frac{-uc}{1-c(1-u)}$$

and this is equal to the reduction in personal saving. That is, total gross saving is unchanged; the increased propensity to save by one sector does result in an increase in the saving of that sector, but only at the expense of the saving of the other sector.[1]

---

[1] An interesting further proposition is that if the increased depreciation allowances were matched by increased investment expenditure (as would be the case if, say, the taxation legislation was changed to permit companies to increase their depreciation provisions by 100 per cent of their additional investment expenditures) so that $\Delta\bar{D} = \Delta I$, the consequent change in income in the case where $u = 0$ would be

$$\Delta Y = \frac{1}{1-c}(-c\Delta\bar{D}+\Delta I) = \Delta I.$$

The unit multiplier in this case is akin to the balanced budget multiplier discussed in chapter 11 (see pp. 204–6). The unit change in output is of investment goods. Personal disposable income (and hence consumption expenditure) remains unchanged. The increased incomes earned by those producing investment goods are matched by $\Delta\bar{D}$, the reduction in personal disposable income, because of the increased depreciation allowances. Where u is positive the increment of income is less than unity because only $(1-u)$ of the income generated by the increased output of investment goods is distributed to the personal sector.

5. The multiplier and gap analysis

The multiplier analysis enables a figure to be given to the amount by which the aggregate demand schedule must be raised in order to close a given deflationary gap (see chapter 5). Suppose that the equilibrium level of real income in a two-sector economy where there is no retained company income falls short of the full employment level by an amount $\Delta Y = Y_e\,Y_f$, as in figure 10.12. It was shown in

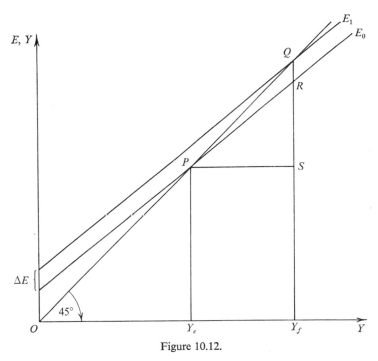

Figure 10.12.

chapter 5 that the aggregate demand schedule must be raised by an amount, ΔE, such that the aggregate demand schedule intercepts the 45° line at the full employment level of real income, $O\,Y_f$. In this case ΔE must be such that

$$\Delta E \frac{1}{1-c} = Y_e\,Y_f,$$

that is

$$\Delta E = (1-c)\,Y_e\,Y_f.$$

The autonomous rise of ΔE will give rise to a multiplier process;

the induced expenditures of $c\Delta Y$ together with ΔE, will raise the level of income to its full employment position.

In other words, it can be said that the achievement of full employment requires at the level of production OY_f that planned expenditures be Y_fQ. The increase in production from OY_e to OY_f would induce a rise in consumption expenditure of an amount, SR, but a further autonomous element of expenditure, RQ $(= \Delta E)$, would be necessary; for, without this, the production of a real income of OY_f would not be self-sustaining.

This chapter has been concerned with the multiplier process in the two-sector economy. It has been shown that the amount by which ΔY exceeds ΔE depends upon the magnitude of the induced consumption expenditure. This, in turn, depends (inversely) upon the size of the leakages to saving. In subsequent chapters it will be shown that other leakages—taxation payments and the purchase of imports—operate as additional factors limiting the induced expansion in the domestic production of consumer goods; but the multiplier process operates for the full economy as well as in the two-sector economy. The essence of the multiplier process is that the total increment of output is not limited to the production change in response to the primary increment in planned expenditure, but includes an induced expansion of the domestic consumer goods industries.

11

THE GOVERNMENT SECTOR AND THE DETERMINATION OF REAL INCOME

1. Introduction

The analysis of the process of the determination of real income in the simplified economy comprising only households and trading enterprises has been used to establish two basic propositions. First, that in the short run, the level of economic activity (and the extent of unemployed resources) are determined by the level of aggregate demand. And, secondly, that an autonomous increase in aggregate demand causes a change in real income which exceeds the autonomous increase by the amount of induced consumption expenditure. This latter is in turn limited by the proportion of the increased income allocated for saving, that is, the *leakage* from the income–expenditure circuit.

In this and the following chapter the role of the government and the oversea sectors is considered. The basic approach remains the same. The level of income is shown to be determined by aggregate demand, which, in the full economy, comprises planned expenditure upon domestically produced goods, net of their import content, by the public sector and oversea buyers, as well as by the private domestic sectors. It is shown that because taxation and purchases of goods from overseas do not give rise to demand for domestic production, they are leakages in the same sense as is saving.

Initially the argument assumes that the marginal propensity to consume is constant and identical for each income group. This means that it is not necessary to consider the distribution of personal disposable income as a specific factor determining aggregate demand. As in previous chapters it is assumed that the economy is operating below the full employment level of output. The analysis is concerned only with comparisons of positions of equilibrium; the path of real income from one equilibrium level to another is not discussed. For the present, the assumption that the cost and availability of finance are constant is maintained. It is also assumed that changes in the taxation system do not affect the productivity of the work force.

2. The Government sector

(a) Public enterprises and the government sector

In chapter 2 it was explained that the trading and financial enterprises sectors include all enterprises producing for the market regardless of the legal status of their owners. The *Australian National Accounts* does not distinguish the value added generated by government and privately owned enterprises. It does, however, show the income flowing to the public sector in the form of the surplus earned by the government-owned enterprises; and it does show the capital expenditure of public enterprises separately from that of private enterprises and governments. This is useful information since the pricing policies and uses of the surpluses of public enterprises, and the criteria for their investment decisions may differ significantly from those of private enterprises. To promote their overall economic policies governments may require the controllers of public enterprises to adopt policies which, to some extent, run counter to normal commercial practices.

For example, the pattern of the prices set by a public enterprise may be designed to give favoured treatment to particular sections of the community. The railways may set freight rates which favour the farm sector. The government-owned banks may offer certain borrowers, such as home-purchasers and exporters, favourable borrowing terms. Alternatively, an increase in the general level of the charges made by a public enterprise may be inspired by fiscal, rather than commercial, motives. For example, a State government may instruct the water supply authority to increase its charges in order to obtain additional government revenue. The Commonwealth Government may increase the charges made by the Postmaster-General's Department (postal and telephone charges, radio and television licences) in order to reduce the disposable real income of the private sector. In such cases the increase in charges is akin to an increase in sales taxation. Finally, the investment expenditures of public enterprises may be influenced by government policy. For example, in a period when there is substantial unemployment a State government may implement a programme of railway construction.

It is important to keep in mind that while the public enterprises are not a part of the government sector as defined, they frequently have access to finance from outside the private capital market, they may be able to operate with deficits which are met from government revenue, and their pricing and investment decisions may be influenced by governments. For these reasons their economic role is not exactly comparable with that of privately owned enterprises.

(b) The government sector and the national accounting identities

The Australian government sector comprises three groups of public authorities, the Commonwealth, State and local governments. The formal analysis of the process of income-determination is much simplified by treating the public sector as if it were one authority.

The economic functions of the government include the provision of collective goods and services, and the redistribution of money income through taxation and social service payments. These involve decisions as to how, and for whose benefit, the GNP is to be used. The role of economic analysis in this type of decision is that of clarifying the choices;[1] the actual choices are political decisions. A second major function of the government is to manipulate aggregate demand to achieve the desired level of economic activity. This is the function that is stressed in this book.

The government purchases currently produced goods and services in order to provide communal goods and services. Its expenditure comprises outlays in the nature of current consumption, for example, the salaries of politicians, 'free milk' for school children, and electricity for public buildings, and also expenditure of a capital nature, for example, road construction and new school buildings.

All of the *purchases* of the public sector are included in government expenditure, G. But government expenditure does not include all the *cash payments* of the government sector; in particular it should be noted that transfer payments in the form of cash social service benefits are not included in government expenditure. Such payments do not represent the exercise of effective demand by the public sector upon current production. However, they increase personal disposable income, and thus influence the households' effective demand, that is, consumption expenditure, C.

The accounts of the government sectors are presented in two forms. One form shows all the payments made by, and receipts of, the government, and includes the borrowing and debt redemption of the government. This type of account is necessary so that parliaments

---

[1] This cryptic statement is not meant to give the impression that economic analysis, can, in its present state, do any more than suggest rough approximations of the consequences for the various social groups of any major policy change.

can ensure that all government funds are properly accounted for. The other form, which is the one given in the *Australian National Accounts*, shows the current income flows between the government and other sectors, and the government sector's purchases of goods and services. It is this latter form which lies behind the present analysis.

The national accounting identities for the three-sector economy in which there is no company saving are

$$Y \equiv C+I+G; \tag{11.1}$$

that is, gross national product is equal to the expenditure made by the three sectors.

$$Y_p \equiv Y-T; \tag{11.2}$$

that is, personal disposable income is equal to the national income less the net withdrawal of income by the government.

$$Y_p \equiv C+S; \tag{11.3}$$

that is, personal income is divided between consumption expenditure and personal saving

$$G \equiv T+B; \tag{11.4}$$

that is, government expenditure is equal to the net withdrawal of incom efrom the private sector plus the budget deficit, B, (the funds obtained by borrowing). From identities (11.1) to (11.3), it follows that

$$I+G \equiv S+T. \tag{11.5}$$

The above identities are in terms of *ex post* quantities. Identity (11.5) expresses the truism that the gross national income allocated for purposes other than consumption expenditure, $S+T$, is equal to the value of the national output absorbed in uses other than consumption, $I+G$.

It was shown in chapter 4 that in the two-sector model, the condition for equilibrium is that planned saving equals planned investment expenditure. The remainder of this chapter is concerned with the analysis of equilibrium situations, and the quantities referred to are *ex ante*. It is shown in the following section that in the three-sector economy, the corresponding condition for equilibrium is that the sum of planned saving and taxation equals the sum of planned investment expenditure and government expenditure.

3. The equilibrium level of income

(a) Government expenditure as a component of aggregate demand

It was shown in chapter 4 that income is at its equilibrium level when aggregate demand is equal to the planned level of production. In the three-sector economy aggregate demand comprises planned consumption and investment expenditures together with government expenditure.

Government expenditure is not dependent upon government income in the sense that consumption expenditure is dependent upon personal disposable income. In chapter 7 it was shown that the Commonwealth Government (which is able to exercise considerable control over the finance available to the State governments) has unlimited financial resources. Unlike the other economic entities, the spending of the government sector need not be restrained because it lacks finance. Rather, the extent of government expenditure is limited by the competing demands of the other sectors upon physical resources. It is shown in the following sections that the level of government expenditure, and the level and structure of taxation are independent policy instruments which the government can use in order to achieve a desired level and composition of aggregate demand.

Discussion of the factors which determine the government's expenditure and taxation decisions is deferred to section 4 below. These decisions are incorporated in the budget. In the period between budgets, government expenditure represents a constant component of aggregate demand and is written as $G = \overline{G}$; it is independent of both the level of economic activity and the actual level of government revenue.

If the government spent, but did not withdraw income from the other sectors (an unrealistic situation in practice), the short-run aggregate demand schedule would be

$$E = C(Y) + \overline{I} + \overline{G}.$$

In the case where the consumption function is of the form

$$C = A + cY_p,$$

and where all the national income is distributed to households, the equilibrium condition that aggregate supply equals aggregate demand will be

$$Y = E,$$

199

that is, $$Y = E = A + cY + \bar{I} + \bar{G},$$

that is, $$Y = \frac{1}{1-c}(A + \bar{I} + \bar{G}).$$

The total change in income associated with a change in government expenditure, ΔG, would be

$$\Delta Y = \frac{1}{1-c}\Delta G.$$

That is, the value of the income multiplier is the same for ΔG as for ΔA, or ΔI.[1]

The government's purchases represent an injection into the income–expenditure circuit. In practice the government imposes *net taxation, T*, which is taxation less cash social service payments.[2] This represents a withdrawal of income from the other sectors. The effects of this withdrawal are considered in the following section.

(b) Taxation and the equilibrium income

The Australian tax system comprises three major types of taxes: those based on earnings—income taxes; those based on purchases, for example, sales taxes, excise and customs duties and payroll tax; and those based on asset ownership, for example, land taxes, rates paid to local governments, motor registration fees and dog licences. Given the existing system of taxation, the revenue collected by the first two types of taxation (which will be described as *income* and *sales* taxes respectively) is clearly dependent upon the level of national income. Taxes based on property ownership are not dependent upon national income, and will be included in the category of *lump sum* transfers. As well as collecting taxation the government pays cash social service benefits to persons, and in the short run (with the exception of unemployment benefits), these are also mainly independent of national income. These benefits (which in Australia in

---

[1] An example may make this algebra more meaningful. The income-, production-, and employment-creating effects of a specific road or school construction programme will be the same whether they are built for private entities or the government.

[2] This is a slightly simplified treatment in that it ignores the net surplus of public enterprises and the interest paid on the government debt. The former is a minor source of government revenue; it was pointed out above that an increase in the charges of public enterprises is akin to an increase in sales taxation. Payment of interest on the government debt is treated in *Australian National Accounts* as a transfer payment and not as a payment for a current service.

recent years have comprised about 9 per cent of personal disposable income and are equal to about 80 per cent of personal income taxation) are also lump sum transfers. For the present purposes it is convenient to speak of the balance between lump sum taxes and social service benefits as *lump sum taxation*, $\bar{T}$, and to speak as if it were positive. The principles developed apply equally to situations where the balance is negative.

The existence of net taxation means that at any level of real income, personal disposable income, and therefore consumption expenditure, will be less. That is, net taxation operates to shift the position of the aggregate demand schedule. As each of the three forms of taxation has a unique impact upon aggregate demand they will be considered separately. Several important propositions valid in any tax system can be established by using the example of lump sum taxation. As it is the simplest case to comprehend (and to explain) it is discussed first.

(i) *Lump sum taxation*. Consider an economy which originally has two sectors. Assume that a government is established and that it imposes a system of lump sum taxation which raises revenue of $\bar{T}$. At each level of real income, personal disposable income will be reduced by $\bar{T}$, as illustrated in figure 11.1a.

Where the consumption function is of the form $C = A + cY_p$, the imposition of taxation does not lead to a change in consumers' behaviour. This is still described by the same consumption function. But it does cause a change in the relationship between consumption expenditure and real income. Because Y_p is related to Y in a specified manner (in this case, $Y_p = Y - \bar{T}$), it is possible to derive a relationship showing the level of C associated with any given level of Y. This function, $C = C(Y)$, is designated the *consumption–national income relationship*. In figure 11.1b, C is shown as a function of Y, not Y_p. The tax reduces Y_p by $\bar{T}$ so, at each level of Y, C is now $c\bar{T}$ less than before the tax. That is, the effect of the tax upon aggregate demand is exactly the same as in the case where households decide to save an amount, $c\bar{T}$, more at each level of real income.

In figure 11.1b, $E_0 (= A + cY + \bar{I})$ represents the aggregate demand function in the original situation. The imposition of the tax causes the consumption–national income relationship to change from $C_0 = A + cY$ to $C_1 = A + c(Y - \bar{T})$, and the aggregate demand function is shifted bodily downwards by $c\bar{T}$ to $E_1 (= A + c(Y - \bar{T}) + \bar{I})$. The initial reduction in expenditure upon consumer goods of $c\bar{T}$

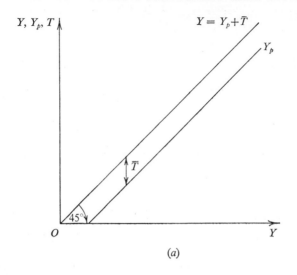

(a)

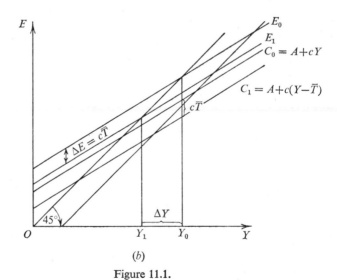

(b)

Figure 11.1.

causes a reduction in production and hence income, and results in a further (induced) fall in consumption expenditure. The total change in income, ($Y_0 Y_1$, in figure 11.1 b), is

$$\Delta Y = c\overline{T} + \frac{c}{1-c}c\overline{T} = \frac{1}{1-c}c\overline{T}.^1$$

If the government were to pay cash social service benefits which exceeded the taxation collected, net taxation, $\overline{T}$, would be negative, and the equilibrium level of income would lie above the original level by an amount $[1/(1-c)]c\overline{T}$.

If the government ceased raising taxation and paying social service benefits, but spent an amount G on, say, the construction of homes for the aged, the equilibrium level of income would lie above the original level by an amount $[1/(1-c)]G$. The change in real income consequent upon a change in expenditure, ΔG, is greater than that consequent upon the payment of an equal amount of social service benefits, $-\Delta\overline{T}$. The spending of ΔG represents a demand for currently produced goods, whereas the payment of the social service benefits is not an act of expenditure upon current production. It is an income transfer to persons, who respond to this change in their disposable income by allocating $c(-\Delta\overline{T})$ to consumption expenditure, and $s(-\Delta\overline{T})$ to saving. The initial increase in spending associated with $-\Delta\overline{T}$ falls short of ΔG by the portion which is saved, $s(-\Delta\overline{T})$; consequently the induced consumption expenditure in the case of the social service benefits is also less than that in the case of the government expenditure $\{[c/(1-c)]\,c\Delta\overline{T} < [c/(1-c)]\}\,\Delta G$. The change in income associated with the payment of increased lump sum taxation of $\Delta\overline{T}$ is $[c/(1-c)]c\Delta\overline{T}$, but is, of course, negative.

It should not be thought that the income-determination (or multiplier) process is in some way different for tax withdrawals and social service payments. The general principle, that the increase in income comprises the production response to the initial shift in aggregate demand, together with the consequent induced consumption expenditures, holds in this case as it did for a shift in the investment, government expenditure or consumption functions.

This example illustrates an important general principle, namely,

---

[1] This expression follows the form used in chapter 10; there the income multiplier is shown to be the sum of the initial increment of production consequent upon the movement in the aggregate demand curve at the initial equilibrium level of income (in this case $c\overline{T}$) together with the consequent induced increment of production in the consumer-goods sector (in this case, $[c/(1-c)]c\overline{T}$).

that the impact of budgetary actions upon national income cannot be gauged by comparing the expenditure, G, with the net taxation, T. The former directly influences aggregate demand, whereas the latter makes its immediate impact upon the disposable income of the households sector. The raising of T causes a change in the expenditure of the households sector of cT, and it is this change which should be compared with G. It would not then be correct to assess the impact of the budget upon economic activity by considering the budget deficit, B. If, for example, the government raised a lump sum tax, $\bar{T}$, and used the proceeds to build homes for the aged of value $\bar{G} = \bar{T}$, there would be a primary net increase in aggregate demand of $\bar{G} - c\bar{T}$, and an increase in real income of $[1/(1-c)]\,(\bar{G} - c\bar{T}) = \bar{G}$.

The balanced budget multiplier. This latter example is an illustration of what is usually described as the 'balanced budget multiplier'. The argument is illustrated by figure 11.2. Initially there is no government sector; the aggregate demand function is $E_0 = A + cY + \bar{I}$ and the equilibrium level of income is OM. The imposition of the tax, $\bar{T}\,(= PQ)$, reduces personal disposable income to $Y - \bar{T}$, and as a result of the tax the aggregate demand curve shifts bodily downwards by $c\bar{T}$ and passes through Q. However, the government expenditure of $\bar{G} = \bar{T}\,(= PQ = QP')$ causes the demand curve to shift bodily upwards and to pass through P'. The new aggregate demand curve is

$$E_1 = A + c(Y - \bar{T}) + \bar{I} + \bar{G},$$

and the new equilibrium level of income OM' exceeds the original level by $MM'\,(= PQ)$, that is, by the amount of government expenditure.

In a closed economy a budgetary change which comprises an increase (or decrease) in government expenditure of ΔG, together with changes in the structure of taxation such that tax revenues at the new equilibrium level of income[1] are also raised (or lowered) by the same amount, results in a change in national income equal to that amount; that is, the multiplier, $\Delta Y/\Delta G$, is unity.

There are various ways of looking at this unitary balanced budget

---

[1] In the present case of lump sum taxation, tax revenues would be changed by $\Delta\bar{T}$ at each income level. But when taxation revenues depend in part upon the level of national income, the balanced budget change implies that the *net* change in taxation revenue should equal ΔG. This net change comprises both the revenue change at the original income level resulting from the (autonomous) change in the structure of taxation, together with the (induced) change consequent upon the change of real income.

multiplier. First, the impact of ΔG and $\Delta \bar{T}$ may be considered separately, and the two changes netted out. Thus, in the case above:

ΔG gives rise to

$$\Delta Y_1 = \Delta G + \frac{c}{1-c} \Delta G$$

and $\Delta \bar{T}$ gives rise to

$$\Delta Y_2 = c\Delta \bar{T} + \frac{c}{1-c} c\Delta \bar{T}.$$

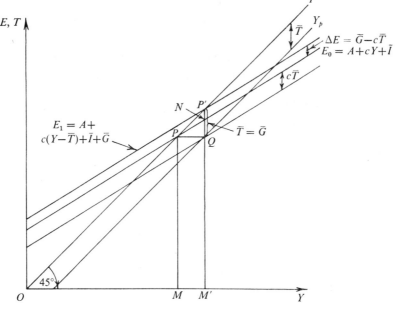

Figure 11.2.

Since $\Delta \bar{T} = \Delta G$ the net change, $\Delta Y_1 - \Delta Y_2$, can be expressed as

$$\Delta Y = \left(\Delta G + \frac{c}{1-c}\Delta G\right) - \left(c\Delta G + \frac{c}{1-c}c\Delta G\right) = \Delta G.$$

Alternatively, ΔY may be considered as the resultant of the net upward movement in aggregate demand, $\Delta G - c\Delta \bar{T}$, $(= (1-c)\Delta G)$, together with the induced consumption effects, $[c/(1-c)](1-c)\Delta G$, that is,

$$\Delta Y = (1-c)\Delta G + \frac{c}{1-c}(1-c)\Delta G = \Delta G.$$

205

A third approach is as follows: when the government spends ΔG, this calls forth an increase in real income in the form of the newly produced output for the government, for example, homes built for the aged. This production gives rise to an increase in personal disposable income of the same amount; but, as the government is withdrawing a matching amount of income by its tax change, overall, personal disposable income (and hence consumption expenditure) is unchanged. The increase in output comprises only the increased production demanded by the government.

The impact of taxation upon saving. The lump sum tax example can be used to demonstrate another proposition valid for any tax system, namely, that in a closed economy the equilibrium level of income is that at which the sum of the leakages (planned saving and taxation revenue) is equal to the sum of the autonomous expenditures (planned investment and government expenditures). It follows that, given the autonomous expenditures, an increase in taxation revenue will be matched by a corresponding decline in *ex post* saving.

These propositions can be demonstrated as follows: the distinguishing characteristic of the equilibrium level of real income is that the planned expenditure to which it gives rise equals the planned output. That is, if any actual income is to be an equilibrium level of real income it must satisfy the condition that

$$Y = E,$$
that is, $$Y = C(Y) + \bar{I} + \bar{G}.$$

Planned consumption expenditure equals real income less taxation and less planned saving, so the equilibrium condition may be written as:

$$Y - (\bar{I} + \bar{G}) = Y - (T + S)$$
that is, $$\bar{I} + \bar{G} = T + S.$$

Given $\bar{I}$ and $\bar{G}$, in equilibrium, $(T + S)$ is given, and an increase in T must therefore be matched by a decrease in S.

The same propositions can be demonstrated with the aid of geometry. Figures 11.3a and 11.3b illustrate an economy where lump sum taxes are imposed. The levels of planned investment and government expenditures are given, and their total is indicated by OH in both diagrams. Figure 11.3a depicts an initial position where a lump sum tax raising revenue of $\bar{T}_0$ is in operation.

Personal saving is shown as a function of national income, and in

206

the initial situation is indicated by $S_0 = S_0(Y)$. $\overline{T}_0$ is added to the saving-national income relationship to give the total leakages, $S_0(Y) + \overline{T}_0$. At any level of real income, say OB, personal disposable income is OB less the tax NM ($= ED$), that is, $Y_p = MK + BN$.

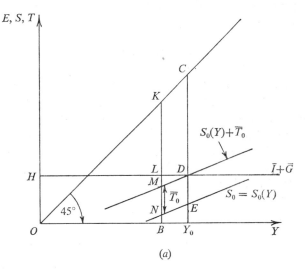

(a)

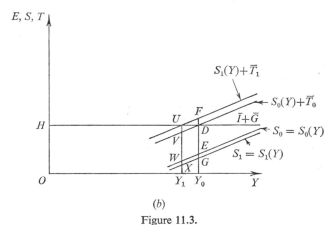

(b)

Figure 11.3.

Personal disposable income is allocated between saving, BN, and consumption expenditure, MK, ($= Y - T - S$). Aggregate planned expenditure at OB is then $MK + BL$, ($= C + \overline{I} + \overline{G}$), which exceeds the output OB by ML. Because current aggregate demand exceeds

207

output, there will be an increase in output to the equilibrium level of OY_0, at which the condition,

$$Y-(\bar{I}+\bar{G}) = C = Y-(S+T),$$

is satisfied. The difference between $\bar{I}+\bar{G}$ and $S_0(Y)+\bar{T}$ indicates the unplanned change in stocks which would occur at any non-equilibrium levels of income.[1]

Suppose that the lump sum tax is now increased from $\bar{T}_0$ to $\bar{T}_1$. The consequences of this are illustrated in figure 11.3b. The new tax is of amount GF ($= XU$), which exceeds $\bar{T}_0$ by $DF+GE$. Saving as a function of Y_p is unaltered, but as a function of Y shifts downwards bodily by $s(T_1-T_0)$, that is, by GE. The increased taxation causes a fall in national income of $Y_0 Y_1$, and this gives rise to a matching fall in personal disposable income. As a consequence of this fall in income there is an induced fall in saving of DF ($= VU$). The two components of the decrement of (personal) saving match the increment of taxation, $DF+GE$. At the new equilibrium level of income, OY_1, the sum of planned saving, $Y_1 X$, and taxation, XU, is again equal to OH.

There is a second, quite different, sense in which taxation may be 'paid out of' saving. This applies when the tax leads to a change in consumer behaviour in the sense that the previous consumption function no longer applies. If, for example, consumers in the short run continue to consume at the same rate after an increase in lump sum taxation of $\Delta \bar{T}$ (for reasons given in chapter 8), then, temporarily, $C = A+cY_p$ will be shifted bodily upward by $c\Delta\bar{T}$; the equilibrium level of income would not change, but *ex post* saving would fall by the increase in taxation revenue.

The proposition that, given the levels of planned investment expenditure and government expenditures, changes in the propensity to save and in the structure of taxation cause the level of income to change, but that, at each equilibrium level of income, the sum of saving and taxation revenue are unchanged is not to be confused with the national accounting identity, $S+T \equiv I+G$. This *ex post* equality holds at any level of income. If the change in production consequent upon a change in demand occurred only after a time lag, there would temporarily be disequilibrium levels of income. For example, if after the increase in taxation illustrated by figure 11.3b,

[1] The argument is an extension of that developed in chapter 4. See, in particular, pp. 57–9.

businessmen temporarily continued to produce the output OY_0, actual saving (which would temporarily be Y_0G) together with taxation would be Y_0F; this exceeds their value at the equilibrium level of income, by DF. This excess matches the unplanned investment in stocks arising from the failure of businessmen to anticipate the initial decline in consumption spending of $c(\overline{T}_1 - \overline{T}_0)$ which occurs as a consequence of the increased taxation.

(ii) *Income taxation.* The taxation raised by the taxes on earnings can be expressed as a function of national income thus, $T = T(Y)$. It should not be thought that the national income is the tax base. The taxable income of an individual entity is not identical with the entity's contribution to value added. In calculating its taxable income an entity may deduct from its income such items as medical, dental, and educational expenses, and contributions to charitable institutions. The taxable income is also reduced by 'allowances' made for dependants. The taxable income of an entity includes items other than income earned by contributions to current production; for example, capital gains made by a professed speculator are subject to the income tax. Although the sum of the individual entities' taxable receipts is not identical with the national income it is clearly closely geared to the national income, and so the receipts from 'taxation based upon taxable earnings' (which is a more accurate title than the 'income tax') may be expressed as a function of national income.

In some countries (including Australia), the earnings of companies are subject to income tax.[1] Company income is related to national income, so company taxation like personal taxation can be regarded as a function of national income. In this chapter it is assumed that companies distribute all their income; accordingly increases in income taxation, whether of persons or of companies, reduce personal disposable income.[2]

---

[1] In Australia in recent years the revenue from company income tax has been equal to about half that of personal income tax.

[2] The role of company saving in a two-sector economy was discussed in chapter 10, section 4. In the real world companies do retain some portion of their income. An increase in the rate of tax on company income is likely to fall mainly upon this retained income, and will reduce the internal funds available to enterprises (see section 6(a), chapter 9). The level of company taxation will also make a direct impact upon investment expenditure, because it is the expected rate of profit *post-tax* which is relevant to the investment decision. In so far as companies cut their dividend rates because of increased company taxation, the effect will be to reduce personal disposable income, and to cause a bodily downward movement of the consumption–national income relationship.

Where taxation is a function of national income, the condition for the equilibrium level of income, discussed in the previous section, that the sum of planned investment and government expenditures equals the sum of planned saving and taxation holds. But an economy in which taxation is related to national income has some interesting characteristics not present in the economy which raises only lump sum taxes.

Consider an economy which originally raised lump sum tax, $\bar{T}$, and had achieved an initial equilibrium level of income, $O Y_0$; for example, the economy depicted in figure 11.4a. It now replaces this tax with an income tax of the form $T = t Y$, where the *marginal rate of tax*, $t (= \Delta T / \Delta Y)$, is the ratio of the change in taxation revenue to the small change in income which gave rise to it and is a positive fraction less than one. In the particular case considered below the marginal rate of tax is constant. The income tax is designed to raise the same revenue as the lump sum tax *at* the initial equilibrium level of income $O Y_0$. The initial situation with the lump sum tax is referred to as Economy A, and is illustrated by figure 11.4a. Economy B, illustrated by figure 11.4b, is identical except that the income tax is substituted for the lump sum tax.

The same consumption function, $C = A + c Y_p$, describes consumer behaviour in both economies, but the consumption–national income relationship in Economy A is $C = A + c(Y - \bar{T})$ or $C = A + c Y - c \bar{T}$, and in Economy B is $C' = A + c(Y - t Y)$ or $C' = A + c(1 - t) Y$. The relationships between personal disposable income and national income on the one hand and the corresponding consumption–national income relationships on the other for the two economies are shown in figures 11.5a and 11.5b respectively. The saving–national income relationships, $S = -A + s(Y - \bar{T})$ for Economy A and $S' = -A + s(1 - t) Y$ for Economy B, are shown by $S = S(Y)$ and $S' = S'(Y)$ in figures 11.4a and 11.4b respectively.

Because the income tax is designed to raise the same revenue at the initial level of income, $O Y_0$, (that is, ML in figure 11.4a equals $M'L'$ of figure 11.4b), personal disposable income and, consequently, consumption expenditure at $O Y_0$ will be unchanged (LK of figure 11.4a equals $L'K'$ of figure 11.4b). Planned investment and government expenditures are the same, so that at $O Y_0$ aggregate demand in Economy A ($Y_0 K$ in figure 11.4a), is equal to that in Economy B ($Y_0 K'$ in figure 11.4b). However, the slopes of the respective aggregate demand functions EE ($= A + c(Y - \bar{T}) + \bar{I} + \bar{G}$) in figure 11.4$a$,

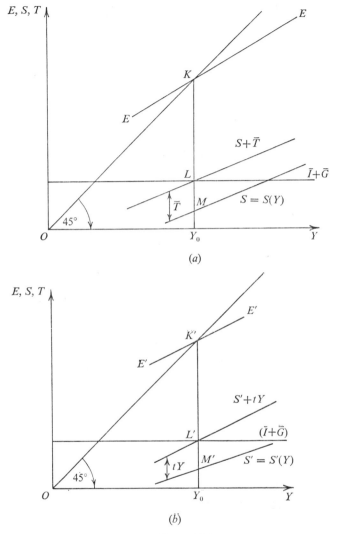

Figure 11.4.

and $E'E'$ ($= A + c(1-t)Y + \bar{I} + \bar{G}$) in figure 11.4$b$ differ. These slopes reflect the marginal increment of planned expenditure associated with a small increment of national income. As planned investment and government expenditures are independent of national income, the slopes of the respective aggregate demand curves are c and $c(1-t)$.

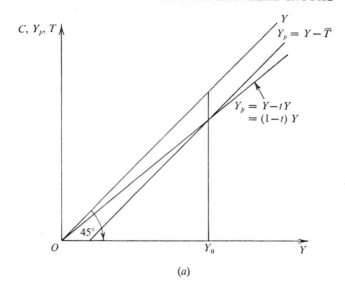

(a)

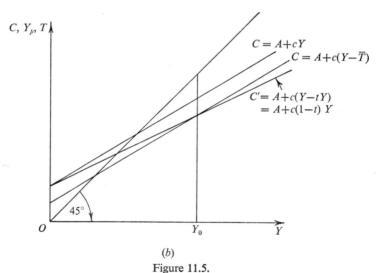

(b)

Figure 11.5.

The dampening effect of the marginal rate of tax. The relationship between the slope of the aggregate expenditure function and the value of the income multiplier was discussed fully in the previous chapter. Clearly the greater is t, the less is the slope of $E'E'$ in figure

212

11.4b and the less is the multiplier. An example will illustrate the dampening effect of t upon the multiplier.

Assume that in both Economy A and Economy B there is an increase in planned private investment of amount ΔI. In each economy this gives rise to a primary increase in output of ΔI. In Economy A the primary increase in personal disposable income is also equal to ΔI, and the series of induced consumption expenditures is

$$c\Delta I, \quad c^2\Delta I, \quad c^3\Delta I....$$

The sum of this series is $(c\Delta I)/(1-c)$, and so the total increment of income in Economy A is

$$\Delta I + \frac{c\Delta I}{1-c} = \frac{1}{1-c}\Delta I.$$

In Economy B, the primary increase in personal disposable income is only $(1-t)\Delta I$, for the government takes $t\Delta I$ in taxation. The series of induced consumption expenditure is then

$$c(1-t)\Delta I, \quad c^2(1-t)^2\Delta I, \quad c^3(1-t)^3\Delta I...,$$

the sum of which is $[c(1-t)\Delta I]/[1-c(1-t)]$. The total increase in income is then:

$$\Delta Y = \Delta I + \frac{c(1-t)}{1-c(1-t)}\Delta I = \frac{1}{1-c(1-t)}\Delta I.$$

An alternative method of deducing the respective multipliers is as follows:

Economy A	Economy B
$E = A + cY - c\overline{T} + \overline{I} + \overline{G}$	$E' = A + c(1-t)Y + \overline{I} + \overline{G}$
For equilibrium, $Y = E$	For equilibrium, $Y = E'$
so in equilibrium	so in equilibrium
$Y - cY = A - c\overline{T} + \overline{I} + \overline{G}$	$Y - c(1-t)Y = A + \overline{I} + \overline{G}$
i.e. $Y = \dfrac{1}{1-c}(A - c\overline{T} + \overline{I} + \overline{G})$	i.e. $Y = \dfrac{1}{1-c(1-t)}(A + \overline{I} + \overline{G})$
and $\Delta Y = \dfrac{1}{1-c}(\Delta A, \Delta I, \Delta G)$	and $\Delta Y = \dfrac{1}{1-c(1-t)}(\Delta A, \Delta I, \Delta G)$

The following arithmetical example shows that the existence of a tax leakage which is an increasing function of real income has a substantial dampening effect upon the income multiplier. Assume that in both Economy A and B, $C = 100 + \frac{4}{5}Y_p$, $\overline{I} = 200$ and $\overline{G} = 300$, where the unit of measurement is $m. In Economy A,

213

$\bar{T} = 250$, and in Economy B, $T = \frac{1}{8}Y$. Initially in both economies the equilibrium level of income will be 2,000, T will be 250, Y_p will be 1,750, and C will be 1,500. If private investment expenditure increases by 100, in Economy A,

$$\Delta Y = \Delta I + \frac{c}{1-c}\Delta I = 100 + 400 = 500.$$

In Economy B,

$$\Delta Y = \Delta I + \frac{c(1-t)}{1-c(1-t)}\Delta I = 100 + 233\frac{1}{3} = 333\frac{1}{3}.$$

That is, the marginal rate of tax of $\frac{1}{8}$ reduces the induced consumption expenditure by 42 per cent.

Linear functions are used above for expositional purposes.[1] However, in practice, the marginal rate of tax, $t = \Delta T/\Delta Y$, increases with the level of national income, and exceeds the average rate of tax, T/Y. Consequently, the dampening effects of the tax system upon the income multiplier may be quite substantial even though taxation revenues collected may not be a large fraction of national income.[2]

The above analysis shows that the income tax system works to dampen the multiplier effect; and it is sometimes said that a progressive income tax system works as a 'built-in stabilizer' of economic activity. The term, 'stabilizer', is an unfortunate one. A mechanical stabilizer operates by exerting a positive counterforce to offset an outside force which has pushed the machine from a desired path. The tax structure does not operate as a stabilizer in this sense; rather it operates to reduce the total displacement resulting from any given initial change.

The payment of unemployment benefits by the government also

---

[1] It was explained in chapter 4 (see p. 60) that the non-linear case does not raise any additional conceptual problems, but it is more difficult to illustrate in arithmetic and algebraic terms.

[2] In Australia total income taxes have in recent years been about 1/8 of national income, but the marginal rate is greater than this. The argument in the text that $\Delta T/\Delta Y$ rises with Y assumes that income per head rises with Y. If an increase in Y were associated only with an increase in the employment of less skilled workers, $\Delta T/\Delta Y$ would fall as Y increased. In fact, the average income per employed worker rises with an increase in economic activity because, for example, more overtime is worked. Consequently, because the personal income tax rate is progressive (that is, an individual's tax liability rises more than proportionately to his income), the value of t increases with Y. Also, as Y increases the share of company income is likely to increase, and the rate of company income tax is high relative to the marginal rate of personal income tax.

operates to dampen the multiplier effect. It might at first be thought that such benefits do involve a true stabilizing effect, for they cause an actual increase in the transfer payments to the private sector when economic activity falls; whereas in the case of taxation there is only a lesser tax-withdrawal from the private sector. An illustration will, however, show that the unemployment benefit has only a dampening effect.

Suppose that in a particular economy the current equilibrium level of income (measured in terms of a currency unit with constant value) is 2,000. The relationship between output and employment is such that one worker is employed for each 20 of output, so that initially 100 workers are employed. The value of c is $\frac{4}{5}$, and of t, $\frac{1}{8}$. If there is an autonomous decline in planned investment expenditure of 100, then, in the absence of any unemployment benefit

$$\Delta Y = \frac{1}{1 - c(1-t)} \Delta I = 333\frac{1}{3},$$

and $16\frac{2}{3}$ workers will become unemployed.

If, however, there were an unemployment benefit of 5 paid to each unemployed worker, then for each decline in Y of 20 there is an unemployment benefit transfer payment to the personal sector of 5. If the ratio between the change in the benefit payments and national income is designated by b, then in this particular case $b = \frac{1}{4}$. For $\Delta Y = 1$, $\Delta Y_p = 1 - t - b$[1] and $\Delta C = c(1 - t - b)$. The slope of the aggregate demand curve would be $c(1-t-b)$ and the total change in income consequent upon an autonomous shift in aggregate demand of ΔE would be: $\{1/[1 - c(1-t-b)]\}\Delta E$. For the particular values of this example, ΔI of -100 leads to ΔY of -200, which comprises the induced decline in the output of consumption goods of 100, and the decline in the investment goods sector of 100.

The unemployment benefit can operate only to dampen the induced fall in personal disposable income which follows from the primary fall in national income. Even in the case where the induced fall in personal disposable income is completely prevented, this would

---

[1] If Y increases by 1, taxes collected rise by t, but the unemployment benefit transfer payment falls by b because of reduced unemployment consequent upon the increase in output. b is the ratio between the increment (decrement) in the amount of unemployment benefit paid, and the small decrement (increment) of income (and employment) which gave rise to it. If, for example, the share of wages in an increment of national income is one half, and the rate of the benefit paid is one half of the wage rate, then $b = \frac{1}{4}$.

prevent only the induced decline in demand for consumer goods—it could not prevent (or offset) the primary fall in real income. Thus, if in the above example the value of $(t+b)$ had been 1 the reduction in taxation and the increase in the benefit payments would be such that personal disposable income would not change, and consumption expenditure would not fall; the consumption expenditure–national income relationship would be a horizontal line. But national income would still have fallen by 100 because of the reduced demand for investment goods.

In the particular example above, in the absence of the benefit a fall in investment expenditure of 100 led to a fall in income of $333\frac{1}{3}$, and to the unemployment of $16\frac{2}{3}$ workers; whereas where the benefit is paid, the fall in income is only 200, and 10 workers are unemployed. In the former case, there would be an induced budget deficit, equal to the fall in government revenue, of $t\Delta Y = 41\frac{2}{3}$; whereas in the latter case, the induced change in the budgetary position comprises a lesser fall in tax receipts of $t\Delta Y = 25$ *plus* the payment of benefits of $50 = b\Delta Y$. That is, the *further* increase in the deficit consequent upon the payment of the benefit is $33\frac{1}{3}$. It is explained below that the deficit is not a particularly important economic quantity. The most important difference between the two situations is that the level of real income and employment is significantly greater where the benefit is paid. The unemployed receive as benefits only a fraction of the greater national income—in this case 50 of $133\frac{1}{3}$.[1]

It was shown in the previous section that the income change consequent upon an increase in a lump sum tax, $\Delta\overline{T}$, is

$$\Delta Y = \frac{1}{1-c}\, c\Delta\overline{T}.$$

In a system where an income tax of the form $T = tY$ is collected, a change in the rate of tax from t_0 to t_1 causes an income change of

$$\Delta Y = \frac{1}{1-c(1-t_1)}\, c(t_0 - t_1)\, Y_0,$$

where Y_0 is the equilibrium level of income when t_0 applies. The tax change means that at the income level Y_0, Y_p changes by $(t_0 - t_1)\, Y_0$,

---

[1] The assumptions of a closed economy with a constant price level eliminate some elements which complicate the politics of unemployment benefits. In an open economy operating close to full employment, the greater is the unemployment benefit, the greater will be the positive fiscal or monetary action which the government must take to achieve a particular check to price inflation and/or to improve the balance of trade.

and this causes a change in consumption expenditure *at* Y_0 of $c(t_0 - t_1)Y_0$. This latter term is the bodily shift in the aggregate demand function; the slope of the function becomes $c(1 - t_1)$. The total change in income comprises the bodily shift in the aggregate demand schedule, plus the induced change in consumption expenditure; that is:

$$\Delta Y = c(t_0 - t_1)Y_0 + c(1 - t_1)c(t_0 - t_1)Y_0 + c^2(1 - t_1)^2 c(t_0 - t_1)Y_0 \ldots$$
$$= \frac{1}{1 - c(1 - t_1)}c(t_0 - t_1)Y_0.$$

As for any change in taxation which affects personal disposable income, the change in output is in the consumer goods sector.

(iii) *Sales taxation.* The imposition of a general sales tax will cause an increase in the money valuation of a given real income because it will cause the price level to rise. If the money income of households were to rise in proportion to the sales tax, then the real demand for consumer goods would be constant. But, if it is assumed that money-wage rates in the current short period are determined independently of the current price level, the money income received by households from any level of production will not increase in proportion to the price level; consequently the real income of households, and hence real consumption expenditure, will be reduced.

Consider an economy where initially there was no taxation and the level of real income was Y_0. Assume that the government now imposes a sales tax, at a rate of g, upon all *final* goods and this leads entrepreneurs to set market prices of $(1 + g)$ times their former level. Then, if in the absence of the tax the index of market prices was P_0, after the tax the index will be $P_1 = (1 + g)P_0$.

Throughout this book GNP measured in constant base period prices has been referred to as real income, Y.[1] The symbol, Y_m, will be used to represent *GNP measured in current market prices*. The price level, prior to the imposition of the sales tax, will be used as the base period price level.[2] After the imposition of the tax it will be necessary to divide Y_m by $1 + g$ in order to obtain the value of Y. That is, $Y = Y_m/(1 + g)$, which may also be written as $Y = Y_m - gY$. *In terms of current prices* the revenue from the sales tax will be $T = gY$; the value of this revenue *in terms of constant prices* will be $T/(1 + g)$.

[1] See chapter 4, p. 42. [2] See chapter 3, section 4.

After the tax is imposed, Y_m is divided between the government revenue, T, and the disposable money income of the personal sector, $Y_m - T$. The real disposable income of the personal sector is

$$Y_p = \frac{Y_m - T}{1+g} = \frac{1}{1+g} Y.^1$$

The consumption function, $C = A + cY_p$, is itself expressed in real terms; accordingly, the post-tax relationship between consumption expenditure and income, where both are expressed in real terms, is

$$C = A + c\left(\frac{1}{1+g}\right) Y.^2$$

For a three-sector economy where a general sales tax is imposed the aggregate demand function expressed in real terms is therefore

$$E = A + c\frac{1}{1+g} Y + I + G.$$

For equilibrium, Y must equal E. It follows that in equilibrium:

$$Y = \frac{1+g}{1+g-c} (A + I + G),^3$$

and

$$\Delta Y = \frac{1+g}{1+g-c} (\Delta A, \Delta I, \Delta G).$$

[1] Personal disposable income in terms of current prices is $Y_m - gY$, or since $Y_m = (1+g)Y$, it may be written $(1+g)Y - gY$. This is converted to real terms by dividing by $1+g$; thus

$$Y_p = \frac{Y_m - T}{1+g} = \frac{1}{1+g} Y.$$

[2] This implies that A is a constant component of planned consumption expenditure in real terms, that is, it is independent of the current level of prices. However, it may be that a change in the price level could cause a change in the value of A. For example, if A is consumption expenditure financed from wealth rather than income, a rise in the price level, by reducing the real value of past savings, could lead to a fall in the value of A. (See chapter 8, section 4, especially pp. 125–6.) The analysis can be adapted to take account of such an effect.

[3]
$$Y = E = A + c\frac{1}{1+g} Y + I + G,$$

that is,
$$Y - c\frac{1}{1+g} Y = A + I + G;$$

and so
$$Y = \frac{1+g}{1+g-c} (A + I + G).$$

This expression can also be written as

$$\Delta Y = \frac{1}{1-c(1-[g/(1+g)])} (\Delta A, \Delta I, \Delta G).$$

It can be seen that the value of the real income multiplier,

$$1 \Big/ \left[1 - c\left(1 - \frac{g}{1+g}\right)\right],$$

parallels the multiplier deduced above for the income tax, viz. $1/[1 - c(1 - t)]$; however, for equal values of g and t, the multiplier in the case of the sales tax is greater than in the case of the income tax.

The difference may be explained as follows: both g and t represent leakages from the income–expenditure–production circuit, but for equal values of g and t the leakage of real income to sales taxation consequent upon any given increment of real income, ΔY, is less. In the case of the income tax, the leakage of real income from ΔY to government revenue is $t\Delta Y$; whereas in the case of the sales tax, the increment of revenue to the government consequent upon the increment of real output, ΔY, is $g\Delta Y$ in terms of actual current dollars. Because of the increase in the price level consequent upon the imposition of the sales tax, the value of this money revenue expressed in real terms is only $[g/(1+g)]\Delta Y$, which is less than $t\Delta Y$. Thus, the magnitude of the sales tax leakage, when expressed in real terms, is less than the income tax leakage.

The effect upon the level of economic activity of the imposition of the sales tax depends upon the primary effect—its impact upon aggregate demand in real terms at the initial equilibrium level of real income, Y_0—together with the induced effect upon consumption expenditure.

It has been demonstrated above (see chapter 4, section 4) that the induced consumption expenditure depends upon the slope of the aggregate demand function; where planned investment and government expenditures are independent of income, the slope of the aggregate demand function is equal to that of the consumption–income relationship, that is, its slope equals $\Delta C/\Delta Y = c(1-t)$. In the case where there is a sales tax, the relationship between consumption expenditure and income in real terms is

$$C = A + c\left(\frac{1}{1+g}\right)Y.$$

219

That is, the slope of the aggregate demand function is $c[1/(1+g)]$. The real income multiplier derived above, $(1+g)/(1+g-c)$, may be written as

$$1 \Big/ \left[1 - c\left(\frac{1}{1+g}\right) \right].$$

In this latter form, its value is seen to be the reciprocal of one minus the value of the slope of the aggregate demand function.

The imposition of the sales tax initially reduces personal disposable real income from Y_0 to $[1/(1+g)]Y_0$,[1] that is, by $[g/(1+g)]Y_0$. Consequently real consumption expenditure at Y_0 is reduced by $c[g/(1+g)]Y_0$; there will also be an induced fall in consumption expenditure, and the resultant total change in real income will be

$$\Delta Y = \frac{1+g}{1+g-c}\, c\, \frac{g}{1+g} Y_0.$$

The imposition of the sales tax may also cause a reduction in investment and government expenditures measured in real terms. In the extreme case where investment and government expenditures are constant in money terms, then in real terms the sales tax will cause a *pro rata* fall in real expenditures. Unless firms have no access to additional finance it is more plausible to think of investment plans as being made in terms of real factors, that is, the decision will be to install x new machines rather than to spend $\$y$. However, the increased price of investment goods and the reduced demand for consumer goods will cause a fall in the expected rate of profit (see chapter 9), and so demand for investment goods in real terms may be revised downwards. The money expenditure on investment goods may then rise or fall. On the other hand, as the government's spending and tax-raising decisions are assumed to be independently determined, it follows that government expenditure will be constant in real terms.[2] If the sales tax results in reductions of ΔI and ΔG, in investment and government expenditures (measured in real terms) respectively, this will give rise to an additional change in real income of

$$\frac{1+g}{1+g-c}\,(\Delta I + \Delta G).$$

[1] See footnote 1 on p. 218.
[2] In fact Australian local and state governments and the semi-governmental authorities cannot make their expenditure decisions independently of their revenues. The argument could be modified to allow for this.

An arithmetical illustration. The following arithmetical example illustrates the argument. Assume that prior to the imposition of the sales tax the aggregate demand function was of the form

$$E = C+I+G,$$

and that $C = 60+\frac{4}{5}Y$, $I = 80$, $G = 60$ (financed by borrowing) where all quantities are in terms of $m. The initial equilibrium level of real income is $Y_0 = 1,000$.

Suppose that a sales tax at a rate $g = \frac{1}{5}$ is imposed, and that it causes a reduction in planned investment expenditure measured in terms of the initial price level of $\Delta I = -5$ to $I' (= 75)$; but that government expenditure in real terms remains unchanged.

The aggregate demand function in real terms after the imposition of the tax is

$$E' = A+c\left(\frac{1}{1+g}\right)Y+I'+G,$$

and the new equilibrium level of real income, $Y_1 = 585$.

The change in the level of real income is

$$\Delta Y = \frac{1+g}{1+g-c}\left\{-\left[c\left(\frac{g}{1+g}\right)Y_0+\Delta I\right]\right\}$$

$$= \frac{1+\frac{1}{5}}{1+\frac{1}{5}-\frac{4}{5}}\left\{-\left[\frac{4}{5}\left(\frac{\frac{1}{5}}{1+\frac{1}{5}}\right)1,000+5\right]\right\} = -415.$$

The term $-\{c[g/(1+g)]Y_0+\Delta I\}$ is the multiplicand; it is the amount by which the aggregate demand function in real terms shifts downwards at Y_0; $(1+g)/(1+g-c)$ is the value of the real income multiplier.

The effect of the imposition of the sales tax is illustrated by figure 11.6, in which the pre-tax aggregate demand function is indicated by $E = C(Y)+I+G$ and that of the post-tax situation by $E' = C'(Y)+I'+G$.

The analysis in terms of market prices. The use of the pre-tax price level as the base period price level was an arbitrary choice. The analysis may be made in terms of the prices ruling in any particular period. For example, the analysis may be made in terms of current market prices as follows:

The consumption function, $C = A+cY_p$, is defined in terms of the pre-tax price level. The disposable money income of households is Y_m-T. Now $T = gY_m/(1+g)$; accordingly the disposable money

221

...come of households is $[Y_m - gY_m/(1+g)]$; the value of this in terms of pre-tax prices is $[1/(1+g)][Y_m - gY_m/(1+g)]$. Thus, in pre-tax prices the relationship between C and Y is

$$C = A + cY_p$$

$$= A + \frac{c}{1+g}\left(Y_m - \frac{gY_m}{1+g}\right)$$

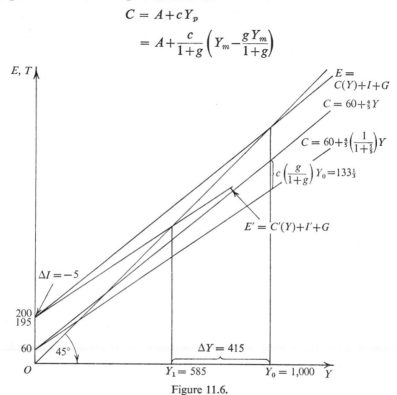

Figure 11.6.

In terms of post-tax prices this becomes

$$C_m = A(1+g) + c\left(\frac{1}{1+g}\right)Y_m.$$

The other components of aggregate demand expressed in market prices, government expenditure, G_m, and planned investment expenditure, I_m, are equal to $(1+g)$ times their value measured in pre-tax prices.

Thus, the aggregate demand function in the post-tax situation, E_m, is described by

$$A(1+g) + c\left(\frac{1}{1+g}\right)Y_m + I_m + G_m;$$

222

the condition for equilibrium is that aggregate demand equal aggregate supply, that is

$$Y_m = E_m,$$

which may be written as

$$Y_m = \frac{1+g}{1+g-c}\,[A(1+g)+I_m+G_m].$$

It follows that

$$\Delta Y_m = \frac{1+g}{1+g-c}\,[\Delta A(1+g),\quad \Delta I_m,\quad \Delta G_m].$$

That is, the numerical value of the multiplier,

$$\frac{1+g}{1+g-c}\left\{= \frac{1}{1-c[1-g/(1+g)]}\right\},$$

is not influenced by the particular set of prices used.

TABLE 11.1

	In terms of base period prices, P_0	In terms of post-tax market prices, P_1
1. Initial aggregate demand		
(a) Planned consumption expenditure	$C = A+cY_p = 60+\tfrac{4}{5}Y$	$C_m = A_m+cY_{pm} = 72+\tfrac{4}{5}Y_m$
(b) Planned investment expenditure	80	96
(c) Government expenditure	60	72
2. Initial equilibrium income	$Y_0 = 1,000$	$Y_{0m} = 1,200$
3. Impact of tax		
(a) Planned consumption expenditure	$C = A+c\left(\dfrac{1}{1+g}\right)Y$ $= 60+\tfrac{2}{3}Y$	$C_m = A(1+g)+c\left(\dfrac{1}{1+g}\right)Y_m$ $= 72+\tfrac{2}{3}Y_m$
(b) Planned investment expenditure	75	90
(c) Multiplicand	$c\left(\dfrac{g}{1+g}\right)Y_0+I = -138\tfrac{1}{3}$	$c\left(\dfrac{g}{1+g}\right)Y_{0m}+I_m = -166$
(d) Multiplier	$\dfrac{1+g}{1+g-c} = 3$	$\dfrac{1+g}{1+g-c} = 3$
(e) Change in income $(= 3(d)\times 3(c))$	415	498
4. New equilibrium income $(= 2-3(e))$	585	702

The effect of the imposition of the sales tax calculated in terms of both the initial level of prices, P_0, and the post-tax price level, P_1 $(= (1+g)P_0)$, is set out in Table 11.1 above. The subscript, m, is used to denote that the quantity is expressed in terms of the post-tax price level.

If the sales tax is imposed at varying rates upon different goods this will lead purchasers to substitute less heavily taxed items for the more heavily taxed. The calculation of the impact of such a tax system upon real disposable income, and of the appropriate value for g is very complicated, and involves the use of index numbers. Conceptually, however, this case can be analysed in terms of the general approach developed above.[1]

(iv) *The three types of taxation.* In an economy where all three forms of taxation are imposed, the relationship between GNP in terms of current market prices, Y_m, and personal disposable income in terms of current market prices, Y_{pm}, will be

$$Y_{pm} = Y_m - \left[\bar{T}_m + \frac{g}{1+g} Y_m + t \left(Y_m - \frac{g}{1+g} Y_m \right) \right].$$

where $\bar{T}_m$ is net lump sum taxation in terms of market prices, $[g/(1+g)] Y_m$ is sales taxation revenue in terms of market prices, and $t(Y_m - [g/(1+g)] Y_m)$ is income taxation revenue in terms of current market prices.

Income taxation is written as a function of GNP at factor cost, not of market prices.[2] That is, t is a fraction of GNP *less* the revenue from sales taxation. This implies that at any given level of economic activity (as indicated by the level of real income and employment) the revenue raised by the income tax is independent of the rate of sales taxation. It is assumed that the imposition of a sales tax at a rate, g, causes the level of prices to rise by the factor $(1+g)$.

---

[1] The calculation of the new equilibrium level of income could be made in terms of current market prices, but the problem of interpreting the 'real' significance of the change from the initial equilibrium position, as measured in the initial market prices, would remain.

[2] It was explained in chapter 2 (see pp. 15–17) that factor costs are the gross incomes, including profits, paid to the factors of production. If a sales tax is imposed, GNP, measured at market prices, exceeds GNP at factor cost by the amount of the indirect taxation revenue. In the particular case considered in the text GNP measured in constant prices, Y, has the same value as the GNP at current prices measured in terms of factor cost. This latter quantity is defined as Y_m less the sales tax revenue, T. The sales tax is imposed at a rate g upon final goods measured at their factor cost; that is, $T = gY$. Consequently, $Y_m - T = Y_m - gY$.

The consumption function expressed in terms of the prices of a base period prior to the imposition of the sales tax, is $C = A + cY_p$. To convert GNP in current market prices, Y_m, to GNP in terms of base period prices, Y, it is necessary to divide Y_m by $1+g$.

The consumption–income relationship, $C = C(Y)$ is:

$$C = A + c(Y - T),$$

where T is the value of taxation revenue in terms of base period prices. $(Y-T)$ may also be written as $Y_{pm}/(1+g)$; substituting for Y_{pm} in the consumption–income relationship above gives

$$C = A + c\left(\frac{Y_m - \left[\overline{T}_m + \dfrac{g}{1+g}Y_m + tY_m - t\dfrac{g}{1+g}Y_m\right]}{1+g}\right),$$

which is consumption expenditure in terms of base year prices. Consumption expenditure in terms of current market prices, C_m, is $C(1+g)$, that is

$$C_m = A(1+g) - c\overline{T}_m + c\left(\frac{1-t}{1+g}\right)Y_m.$$

The aggregate demand function in terms of current market price is

$$E_m = A(1+g) - c\overline{T}_m + c\left(\frac{1-t}{1+g}\right)Y_m + I_m + G_m.$$

In equilibrium, $Y_m = E_m$, so that the equilibrium level of income in terms of current market prices is

$$Y_m = \frac{1+g}{1+g-c(1-t)}[A(1+g) - c\overline{T}_m + I_m + G_m].$$

It follows from this that

$$\Delta Y_m = \frac{1+g}{1+g-c(1-t)}[\Delta A(1+g), \quad c\Delta\overline{T}_m, \quad \Delta I_m, \quad \Delta G_m].$$

The multiplier, $[1+g]/[1+g-c(1-t)]$, may also be written as

$$\frac{1}{1-c\left(\dfrac{1-t}{1+g}\right)} = \frac{1}{1-c(1-t)\left(1-\dfrac{g}{1+g}\right)}.$$

In this latter form, the value of the multiplier is again seen to be equal to the reciprocal of one minus the slope of the aggregate demand function. The slope of the aggregate demand function is:

$$\frac{\Delta E_m}{\Delta Y_m} = \frac{\Delta C_m}{\Delta Y_m} = c\frac{(1-t)}{1+g}.$$

If the analysis is made in terms of base period prices, the aggregate demand function is $E_m/(1+g)$, and the equilibrium level of income in terms of constant base period prices is

$$Y = \frac{1+g}{1+g-c(1-t)}\,(A-cT+I+G).$$

It can again be seen that the numerical value of the multiplier is independent of the particular set of prices used. If base period prices are used, an increase in, say, government expenditure of ΔG will result in $\Delta Y = k\Delta G$. If current market prices are used the numerical values of ΔG_m and ΔY_m are $(1+g)$ times ΔG and ΔY respectively, and the expression for the change is $\Delta Y_m = k\Delta G_m$.

4. Fiscal policy

If the government had full information about the spending behaviour of the different economic sectors it could design a combined fiscal–monetary policy to achieve the level of economic activity desired by the policy makers. And this particular output, designated Y^*, could be divided between consumption, investment and government expenditures in a desired pattern, $C^*+I^*+G^* = Y^*$.

Given the profit expectations of businessmen, credit policy could be directed to achieve the level of investment expenditure, I^*. The government can directly determine G^*. Given that $C = A+cY_p$, it follows that to induce consumers to spend C^* when real income is Y^*, consumers must be left with that disposable real income, Y_p^*, which induces C^*. This could be done by use of any one of the many tax systems which reduce disposable real income at Y^* to Y_p^*, where $Y_p^* = Y^*-T^*$. Such a tax system could combine any system of lump sum, income and sales taxes, and social service benefits, as long as *net taxation* at Y^* is T^*. For each such tax system there will be a particular consumption–income relationship, but all will have the common property that $C = C^*$ when $Y = Y^*$; that is, each of these consumption–income relationships, when combined with I^* and G^*, will give an aggregate demand function such that the equilibrium level of income is Y^*.

It should be noted that once Y^*, I^* and G^* are chosen, the taxation which has to be collected is determined by the consumption function, $C = A+cY_p$, and this amount will increase with any upward shift in that function. That is, taxation is needed to reduce consumption expenditure to C^* at Y^*, and not to meet the 'financial needs' of the government. If, with given Y^*, either I^* or G^* is reduced, it would be necessary to reduce taxation.

This approach to budgetary policy follows once government manipulation of aggregate demand is accepted. The approach does not involve any *a priori* assumptions as to which components of aggregate demand should be stimulated or checked, or which social or income groups should be more favourably, and which less favourably, treated when the government intervenes to alter aggregate demand. That is, it is quite compatible with the simultaneous use of the fiscal techniques to bring about changes in the distribution of income. Conceptually the government can divide the national product between C^*, I^* and G^* as it desires.[1] Furthermore, through its taxation and social service system, it can allocate personal disposable income between the individual households to achieve any desired distribution of disposable income, consistent with the generation of C^*.

As long as it is assumed that the marginal propensity to consume of each income group is the same,[2] there is a unique value of Y_p^* corresponding to C^*; that is, aggregate consumption expenditure is independent of the distribution of income. If this condition does not hold, the required amount of taxation, T^*, at Y^*, to induce C^*, will depend upon the desired distribution of income.

For example, assume that initially a particular income distribution had been desired, and that the structure of net taxation had achieved this, and also that the resource use pattern $C^* + I^* + G^* = Y^*$ had been implemented. Now suppose the government desires to alter the distribution of income in favour of old age pensioners, whose marginal propensity to consume is c', at the expense of upper income

---

[1] The argument tacitly assumes that fiscal actions do not affect productivity. In practice they may do so; for example, high rates of income taxation may cause people to work more, or less, intensively. In principle, if the government had information about the effect of fiscal actions upon the potential full employment level of real income it would choose as its overall target one of the possible patterns of resource allocation of one of the possible levels of real income. It does not necessarily follow that it would adopt the tax system which gave the greatest value of Y^*; it may be considered more desirable to accept a lower level of the real national income in order to attain a particular distribution of income. Furthermore, the argument in the text refers to a closed economy. In an open economy, the use of fiscal policy to achieve a particular level of domestic economic activity may be inhibited by the balance of payments situation. This complexity is considered in the next chapter.

[2] There are, of course, differences in the consumption functions of individual households within any income group, but in macroeconomic analysis, only the consumption function of the group is relevant.

groups, whose marginal propensity to consume is c''. To achieve its aim, the government increases the progressiveness of personal income tax and the rate of the old age pension. If $c'' < c'$ then to keep C^* constant, the government could pay increased pensions of only $(c''/c')R$, where R is the increased amount of income tax. That is, such an income redistribution would require an increase in net taxation, and hence of the budget surplus.

Similar modifications would have to be made if the marginal propensity to consume of the recipients of a primary increase in income had a different marginal propensity to consume to other groups. If, for example, the government decided to increase G^* by expenditure upon public works using only unskilled, low income workers, appropriate allowance would have to be made if their marginal propensity to consume differed from that of those taxed.[1]

In the present analysis the budget balance is a quantity of little economic significance. The argument that the budget balance is an indicator of the economic impact of the budget was rejected above (see p. 204), where it was shown, for example, that the balanced budget multiplier is unity.[2] As the argument is based on the assumption that credit conditions are constant, the monetary effect of a budget deficit (which is to increase the quantity of money, as explained in chapter 7) is not considered here. Since changes in the quantity of money can be achieved by simpler alternative techniques it is unnecessary to use the budgetary technique for that particular purpose.

If, however, one end of government policy is to balance the budget without borrowing, this does not mean that budgetary policy cannot

---

[1] In this case if the *mpc* of the workers were c', then the income change for increased government expenditure of ΔG would be

$$\Delta Y = \Delta G + c'\Delta G + c(c'\Delta G) + c^2(c'\Delta G) + ..., \quad \text{or} \quad \Delta Y = \Delta G + \frac{1}{1-c}c'\Delta G,$$

where c is the marginal propensity to consume for the community as a whole. There is an implicit assumption underlying the multiplier analysis that either the *mpc* of different economic groups is identical, or that any expenditure results in an increment of income which is distributed to a typical cross-section of the different economic groups, so that $\Delta C/\Delta Y$ is the same for any increase in expenditure.

[2] The common argument that an increase in the budget surplus is contractionary is an approximate 'rule-of-thumb' as long as the surplus is achieved by either a reduction in government expenditure, or an increase in taxation, or a combination of both. If, however, there has been an increase in taxation and a lesser increase in government expenditure, the budget surplus may be associated with a net upward shift in aggregate demand.

be used to achieve Y^*. But it does limit the ability of the government to allocate Y^* between C^*, I^* and G^*, and it does involve much greater changes in taxation and government spending than if this (self-imposed) constraint is not accepted. An example will illustrate the point.

Suppose Y^* is 1,000, and, initially, $C = 50 + \frac{4}{5}Y_p$, $I^* = 100$, $G^* = 250$ and $T = \frac{1}{4}Y$, which, at $Y = Y^*$, gives $T^* = 250$, and the budget is balanced. If now there is an autonomous shift downwards in the consumption function of $\Delta A = 10$, the change in income will be

$$\Delta Y = \frac{1}{1 - c(1 - t)} \Delta A = 25,$$

and an (induced) deficit of $t\Delta Y = 6\cdot25$ will develop. If the government considers that the allocation of the desired output between C^*, I^*, and G^* should not be altered, then, in the absence of the balanced-budget constraint, the tax system would be altered so that the taxes collected at Y^* are 12·5 less than before. Given $Y^* = 1,000$, $G^* = 250$, and $I^* = 100$, to induce C^* of 650 with $C = 40 + \frac{4}{5}Y_p$ requires that Y_p^* be 762·5, and T^* be 237·5, which necessarily involves a deficit. Alternatively, if the government decided that, in the face of the reduced demand for consumption goods, the appropriate policy was to increase G^* by 10, this would involve a deficit of 10.

But if the budget is to be balanced, the government can either increase I^* by use of monetary policy, or increase G^* by 25, and increase t from $\frac{1}{4}$ to $\frac{11}{40}$.[1] That is, the balanced budget expansion requires that the size of the public sector (as measured by G/Y) and the severity of taxation (as measured by T/Y) should both be greater than they would be if budget deficits were acceptable.

In the next chapter it is explained that the government's use of fiscal policy to manipulate the domestic level of activity may be inhibited by considerations of its impact upon the external position. And in the final chapter monetary and fiscal policy are considered in the wider context of the real world situation where the government lacks the complete knowledge of economic behaviour assumed in this chapter.

[1] $Y^* = A + c(Y^* - T^*) + I^* + G^*$ and $G^* = T^*$. The only unknown is G^*, and solving for this gives $G^* = 275$. For a balanced budget $T^* = G^*$, so that if, say, the tax system was based on income, a tax rate, $t = G^*/Y^*$, should be imposed to achieve a balanced budget.

THE OPEN ECONOMY

The *closed economy*, by definition, has no trading relations with other countries; that is, all the supplies passing through the domestic market are entirely produced and absorbed by domestic entities. However, when an economy engages in international trade, imports provide an additional source of market supplies, and exports absorb a part of the domestic output. This chapter is concerned with such an *open economy*.

There is first a description of the national accounting and balance of payments identities. A second section is concerned with the determination of the domestic level of real income. The third and fourth sections discuss factors which cause changes in real income and in the balance of trade.

1. The national accounting and balance of payments identities

(*a*) *The national accounting identities*

In chapter 3, the following *ex post* national accounting identity was set out:

$$C + I + G + X - M \equiv Y.$$

That is, gross domestic expenditure (GNE *plus* export expenditure *less* expenditure on imports) equals gross national product. Before beginning an analysis of the determination of the level of real income in the open economy it is necessary to discuss in somewhat more detail the nature of this identity.

Suppose that in a specified period the domestic economy imported goods and services, M, from the rest of the world, and exported goods and services, X; domestic market supplies, $Y + M$, would be matched by the gross market expenditure, N, which is gross national expenditure plus exports. That is,

$$N (= Y + M) = C + I + G + X.$$

It would no longer be true that gross market expenditure equals the value of domestic production, for some part of the gross market expenditure represents the purchase of the products of the rest of the world.

If all the imports were 'completely finished goods' it would be possible to separate physically the final goods which make up domestic market supplies into two groups—those produced entirely within the domestic economy with no *import content*, and those produced entirely in the rest of the world economy. If this were the case, GNP could be calculated by summing the value of the final products of the domestic entities.

In fact, domestic trading enterprises invariably use some imported components; for example, almost all Australian enterprises use materials involving imported petroleum products. Thus, the selling prices of the products of domestic enterprises cannot be entirely resolved into factor payments to domestic productive factors, indirect taxes and depreciation allowances; and GNP falls short of the sum of the value of domestic products as they leave domestic enterprises in their final form by the amount of their import content. For example, assume that 20 per cent of the value of each final good and service represents the value of the import content. If, in a particular period, market expenditure is $100 m., this will be matched by market supplies of $100 m. But the value added as a result of domestic economic activity (that is, GNP) is $80 m. The balance of $20 m. represents the value of imports, which are intermediate goods and services from the viewpoint of the domestic economy.

All imported goods, even those commonly referred to as 'finished consumer goods' (such as packaged Dutch cheese and Swedish glassware) are further 'processed' to some degree within the domestic economy. In the limiting case the processing is confined to the value added by domestic retailers. It is appropriate to think of all the market supplies purchased by the various sectors as having passed through domestic trading enterprises and having generated domestic income to a degree depending (inversely) upon their respective import components. It is domestic economic activity which generates domestic real income; and the aggregate demand for domestic economic activity is the domestic market expenditure *less* that portion of it which represents a demand for economic activity in the rest of the world.

(b) *The balance of payments*

The transactions between the domestic economy and the rest of the world for a given period are recorded, in summary form, in the *balance of payments* account.[1] The credit items in this account comprise the transactions which are a *source* of foreign exchange for the domestic economy, and the debit items, the *uses* of this foreign exchange.

For most countries, and certainly for Australia, by far the most important single source of foreign exchange is the sale of portion of the output of the domestic economy to foreign purchasers. These sales are of goods, such as wool and wheat, and of services, such as transport and insurance; and the foreign buyers may be resident oversea, or, as in the case of tourists, temporary residents in the domestic economy. For simplicity all such sales will be described as *exports*, X. The corresponding purchases by domestic entities from oversea sellers will be described as *imports*, M. This latter item normally constitutes by far the largest single component of the uses of the foreign exchange in any given period. The difference between the value of exports and imports for a given period will be called the *balance of trade*.

A second flow of payments between the domestic and oversea economies arises from the income payments by domestic entities to foreign owners who have property holdings in the domestic economy; for example, the dividends paid to General Motors, the American parent company of General Motors–Holden. This item, less the corresponding income receipts by domestic entities from their owner-ship of foreign property, is the *net property income payable oversea*. The sum of the balance of trade and the net property income payable oversea is the *oversea balance on current account*, R. In the Australian case this item is positive, and hence constitutes a net use of foreign exchange.

As this book is mainly concerned with economic activity in the sense of the production of goods and services, it is the international trade transactions which are of primary relevance. The most obvious direct effect of the net payment of property income to foreign entities upon domestic economic activity is through its influence upon the

[1] Official statistics relating to the Australian balance of payments are contained in the publication, Commonwealth Bureau of Census and Statistics, *Balance of Payments*.

disposable incomes of domestic residents. However, to simplify the exposition, it will be assumed that the net payment is zero; that is, the balance of trade is equal to the oversea balance on current account, and it will also be represented by $R (= X - M)$.

The items discussed so far involve *current transactions*; that is, they comprise payments arising from the production and distribution of the domestic and oversea national incomes. They are summarized in the current account section of the balance of payments statement (see Table 12.1).

If the only source of purchasing power acceptable to oversea sellers were the proceeds of exports, the purchase of imports in any given period would be limited to the value of exports. However, in an advanced economy, the central bank holds a stock of *international reserves*—gold, balances of those currencies which are acceptable in foreign transactions (for example, sterling and U.S. dollars), and holdings of securities which can be readily converted to foreign currency. In addition, the member countries of the International Monetary Fund have the right to draw upon this organization for loans.[1] A reduction of a country's international reserves represents a source of foreign exchange for the given period. In effect, the country obtains foreign exchange for the financing of foreign transactions by surrendering part of its national wealth; for foreign reserves are, in effect, a store of value constituting a deferred claim on the output of the rest of the world.

A second non-current source of foreign exchange is from the net capital inflow[2] to the domestic economy. Transactions between domestic and foreign entities which involve the sale and purchase of existing assets, borrowing and lending, and debt redemption are recorded, along with changes in the economy's international reserves,

---

[1] These international drawing rights are somewhat akin to the overdraft limits negotiated between Australian trading banks and their domestic clients. The member nations know that they can rely upon drawings up to specified limits.

[2] The terms 'capital inflow' and 'foreign investment' are used in this chapter to describe financial transactions. Only in the case of one of the forms of direct foreign investment discussed below is this capital inflow directly associated with the addition to the stock of domestic (physical) capital goods. However, it should be noted that, unlike an increase in the size and ownership of stock of the financial assets created and held by domestic entities, international financial capital transactions do have direct *real* significance. For example, an increase in international reserves, other factors being equal, represents command over world output; foreign investment gives rise to income payments which increase the international reserves of the economy receiving the payments and reduce those of the economy which received the capital inflow.

in the *capital account* section of the balance of payments statement (see Table 12.1).

The capital transactions may involve the domestic government; the foreign loan raisings of the government net of repayments and any loans it extends to oversea entities comprise the net government oversea loans. Alternatively, if the capital transactions involve private domestic entities, they are part of the private capital flow. Three main items in the private capital flow arise from trade credit, portfolio investment and direct investment. Trade credit granted to a domestic importer is, in effect, a short-term loan granted by the seller (conditional, of course, upon its use to finance the purchase of the seller's goods). For example, a Japanese toy manufacturer may sell toys on three months' trade credit to an Australian importer; in principle at the time of the sale a current item—import of toys—will be recorded in the current account, and simultaneously, a capital item—receipt of trade credit—will be recorded. At the end of the three months when the importer pays for the goods there will be no transaction of an income (current) nature, but two capital transactions—a reduction in foreign indebtedness in the form of trade credit liabilities, and a matching reduction in the asset, international reserves.

Foreign entities may purchase the shares of domestic entities in order to further business interests; for example, an American soup manufacturer may make a take-over bid for the shares of a domestic soup manufacturer in order to gain entry to the Australian market. Alternatively, the foreign firm may enter the Australian market by the establishment of a new subsidiary enterprise in Australia. These are alternative forms of *direct foreign investment*, and they comprise part of the private capital inflow. In the case of a capital inflow into Australia, the foreign investors will either pay the Australian sellers with Australian currency purchased from the banking system in exchange for foreign currency, or will pay the sellers with cheques drawn against the purchasers' banks. In this latter case, the Australian sellers will exchange this foreign currency for Australian bank deposits. In both cases the Australian trading banks will exchange the foreign currency for reserves with the Reserve Bank, and the latter's holding of international reserves will increase (see chapter 7 above).

The purchase by foreigners of domestic securities may not be motivated by the desire to control the operations of domestic enterprises; the *portfolio investment* element of the private capital inflow is that part made for normal financial reasons, for example, by way of the purchase of shares through the stock exchange. It also causes an increase in the Reserve Bank's international reserves, and in the trading banks' reserves with the Reserve Bank (thus improving their liquidity position), and, of course, in the public's holding of bank deposits.[1]

It can be seen that there are a multitude of possible combinations of transactions which would permit an import surplus during any particular period. If, as is assumed in this chapter, the net property income payable overseas is zero, the import surplus will be matched by an increase in the indebtedness of the domestic economy to the oversea economy, or a decrease in its net claims against the oversea economy. An import surplus means that the domestic economy is absorbing more of the output of the rest of the world economy, than the rest of the world economy is absorbing of the domestic economy's output. In the alternate case of an export surplus, the net surplus of

TABLE 12.1. *The Australian balance of payments for the year to June 30, 1965*

(The items are rounded to the nearest $10m.)

Sources of funds	$m.		Uses of funds	$m.
		Current transactions		
Export proceeds	3,120		Import proceeds	3,600
Import surplus		480		
		3,600		3,600
Deficit on current account	780		Net property income payable oversea	300
		3,900		3,900
		Capital transactions		
Net government borrowing oversea	−40		Balance on current account	780
Net private capital inflow	520			
Reduction in international reserves	300			
		780		780

[1] A likely consequence of a marked increase in the portfolio capital inflow will be an increase in stock exchange prices and an easing of the rate of interest. As explained in chapters 6 and 9 this is likely to encourage the rate of investment expenditure planned by Australian enterprises.

the rest of the world's absorption of the output of the domestic economy, other things being equal, will be matched by an increase of the domestic economy's holding of foreign assets, or a reduction in its net indebtedness to the rest of the world. It should not be thought that an import (export) surplus will necessarily be associated with a decrease (increase) in the domestic economy's international reserves. For example, if foreign investors have been prepared to lend to domestic entities a net amount in excess of the import surplus, the domestic economy's international reserves will increase, although this increase will be less than the increase in the net foreign borrowing by the domestic economy. In the Australian case, in most of the post-war years there has been an import surplus and a net capital inflow.

Since there are many uses and sources of foreign exchange, it is normally not possible to regard any particular use as being financed by any particular source.[1] It would not be correct, for example, to think of an import surplus as being 'financed' by a contemporaneous net inflow of portfolio investment, in the sense that the former would not have been possible without the latter.

The balance of payments records what has happened; and in a market economy what has happened is the outcome of a multitude of decisions made by individual entities each pursuing its own particular ends. In the past these decisions in aggregate have given rise to painful consequences arising from severe deficits in the balance of payments which led to sharp changes in the domestic price level, rate of production and volume of imports. Consequently in modern mixed economies, international transactions are subject to a sub-stantial degree of conscious economic planning. For example, the Australian government has conferred upon its agent, the Reserve Bank, the right to acquire all of the foreign exchange received by Australians; it determines the foreign exchange rate; and the Australian Government has, with varying degrees of severity, controlled the flow of imports (both in total and composition), and certain forms of capital movements.

The primary purpose of this chapter is to study the implications for the level of domestic economic activity of the existence of foreign trade. It will be assumed (unless the contrary is specifically stated)

---

[1] One exception to this is the treatment in the Australian balance of payments of the undistributed profits of foreign-owned enterprises operating in the domestic economy. The undistributed profits are treated as a 'use' of foreign currency in the form of current property income payable overseas; the 'source' of this foreign currency is the 'reinvestment' of these undistributed funds.

that, for the short period considered, the level of international reserves and/or the capital inflow are such as to enable the financing of any import surplus which may occur. It is initially assumed that current economic policy is given; among other things this means that the exchange rate, the level of tariffs, and monetary and fiscal policy are unaltered in the short period. In practice, should an import (or export) surplus be unusually marked and sustained, a change in economic policy will be made; however, discussion of the design of overall economic policy is deferred to the final chapter.

2. The equilibrium level of income

To move from the *ex post* truisms of the balance of payments and national income statements to the process of income-determination it is necessary to explain the factors which determine *planned* expenditure.[1] The factors determining planned consumption, gross private investment, and government expenditures have been discussed in earlier chapters; a discussion of the determinants of planned expenditures upon imports and exports now follows.

(a) *Expenditure upon exports*

The level of exports of the domestic economy is obviously influenced by the level of economic activity in the rest of the world economy. And the level of exports influences the level of real income of the domestic economy. This in turn influences the level of imports of the domestic economy, and, as these are the exports of the rest of the world, there is a *feed-back* relationship between activity in the domestic and the rest of the world economies. But for countries which form a small fraction of the total world economy the feed-back relationship is likely to be of minor importance. Australia's demand for the products of the rest of the world is such a small part of total world demand that for practical purposes the level of economic activity in the rest of the world can be regarded as being independent of the level of Australian economic activity.[2] It would not, of course,

---

[1] In section 1 above, the quantities referred to were *ex post*. In the remainder of this chapter, the symbols N, C, I, G, X and M refer to *ex ante* quantities (which may also be equal to their *ex post* values).

[2] Strictly, the feed-back effect for any particular country does not depend simply upon its share of world trade. Rather it depends upon the importance of its purchases in the determination of the level of economic activity of its major customers, and vice versa. Thus, if two small countries were highly dependent upon foreign trade, and each was the major export market for the other, the

be possible to make such an assumption for, say, the United States of America, or the Western European economies. For the purpose of the determination of the short-run level of Australian economic activity, the rest of the world's expenditure upon Australian exports may be treated as an autonomous component of market expenditure and will be written as $X = \bar{X}$.

(b) Expenditure upon imports

In the short run, the level of imports is closely related to the level of market expenditure. An increase in planned market expenditures will stimulate an increase in market supplies, some part of which will be produced domestically and some part imported. The ratio between a small increment in planned expenditure on imports, ΔM, and the increment of planned market expenditure, ΔN (where $N = C + I + G + X$), which induced it will be written as a constant, m. This fraction m is the *marginal import–market expenditure ratio*; its value will be between zero and one.

The specific value of m in any particular economy will be determined by five factors. The first of these is the nature of the increment of market expenditure. The import component of the expenditure by the various sectors, households, firms, government and oversea, is unlikely to be the same. For example, if government expenditure in the form of a programme to clean up public parks is increased, the consequent increment of imports would be much less than for an equal increase in planned investment expenditure in the form of an increase in the desired stocks of raw materials for manufacturing industries, since the latter include a high proportion of imported materials.

Secondly, given the composition of aggregate market expenditure as between the expenditures of the four sectors, the imports consequent upon an increment in any one of the components of market expenditure depend upon the preferences of the domestic buyers of final goods as between goods with different import contents. For example, given that there is an increment of consumption expenditure and that a portion of this is devoted to the purchases of wine, the consequent increment of imports will depend upon consumer

feed-back effect between the two would be substantial. From the viewpoint of any particular country, it is what is happening in the economies of its major trading partners, not the rest of the world in general, which is of primary importance.

preferences as between domestic and imported wines. A switch of tastes towards domestic wines, other factors remaining constant, would reduce the value of m.

A third factor is the relative prices in the domestic economy of imported and domestically produced supplies; for example, given the preferences of Australians as between imported and domestically produced wines, an increase in the price of Australian wine, other factors remaining constant, will cause an increase in the value of m.

The techniques of production in the domestic economy is another determinant of the value of m. Given that there is an increase in the rate of output of domestic industries, the higher the proportion of imported supplies used in the production process, the greater is the value of m. A change in the technique of production could cause a change in the value of m. For example, the development of a successful method of maturing wine in domestically made plastic containers could lead to the replacement of imported wooden barrels. An improvement in managerial efficiency could also have a similar result; for example, the offer by the winemakers to repurchase empty imported wine bottles could both reduce their production costs, and also reduce the level of imports associated with any given rate of output in the industry.

Finally, the availability of supplies will influence the value of m. As domestic economic activity approaches the upper end of the full employment zone the capacity of domestic enterprises to supply extra orders immediately will be strained, and buyers' purchases will 'spill over' more and more on to imported supplies; in the extreme case at the upper limit of the full employment zone, any increment of market supplies must be supplied by the oversea economy and in this case $m = 1$. If the domestic economy's imports are basic raw materials sold on competitive world markets it will always be able to obtain imported supplies at the world price. However, in the case of specialized manufactured goods, it is possible that at times the oversea industries will be working to full capacity; in this case, a domestic purchaser may prefer to buy a less satisfactory and/or more expensive domestically made substitute rather than wait until the foreign sellers can fulfil the order. In practice, it is much more likely that limited availability of imported supplies on the domestic market arises from the operation of quantitative import restrictions. For example, in Australia during most of the decade of the 1950s, the permissible volume of a wide range of imported supplies was limited by a system of licences administered by the Department of Trade. As a result, the demand for Australian-made substitute goods was stimulated.

The exposition is greatly simplified if it is assumed that, given the preferences of buyers, the techniques of production and the relative prices and availability of domestic and imported supplies, imports are a constant, uniform, proportion of all four components of domestic expenditure.[1] The conceptual framework developed below is easily modified to take account of differences in the ratio of imports to market expenditure for different forms of expenditure, and at different levels of domestic activity. For the special case considered here the *marginal* and the *average* import-market expenditure ratios are constant and equal. Planned expenditure upon imports may then be written as

$$M = mN = m(C+I+G+X).[2]$$

[1] A more general case would be to write

$$M = M_1(C)+M_2(I)+M_3(G)+M_4(X).$$

It is unlikely that these import–expenditure ratios M_1, M_2, M_3, M_4 are constants. For example, as personal disposable income increases, an increasing proportion of it may be diverted to imported luxury goods. The analysis developed in this chapter can be adapted to the more general case where separate (linear or non-linear) relationships between imports and each of the four components of market expenditure are specified.

[2] A common alternative treatment of the determination of the level of imports is to regard it as a function of real income. However, there are substantial reasons for treating it as a function of market expenditure. Expenditure upon imports *is* a component of market expenditure, and when market expenditure increases, imports increase, whether or not output and income increase. It is possible to visualize cases where market expenditure and the level of imports increase without any change in output. For example, at the upper limit of the full employment zone, by definition no further increase in domestic output is possible. All further increments of market expenditure spill over entirely upon imports. Alternatively, if the domestic economy is operating with some excess productive capacity, but there is a lag between the response of domestic production to an increase in market expenditure, temporarily the level of imports will increase independently of the level of output. Finally, as was pointed out in the previous footnote, by relating imports to market expenditure it is possible to take account of the differences between the import–expenditure ratios for the different components of aggregate market expenditure.

(c) The equilibrium income

The short-run planned market expenditure function may now be written as

$$N = A + cY_p + \bar{I} + \bar{G} + \bar{X}.$$

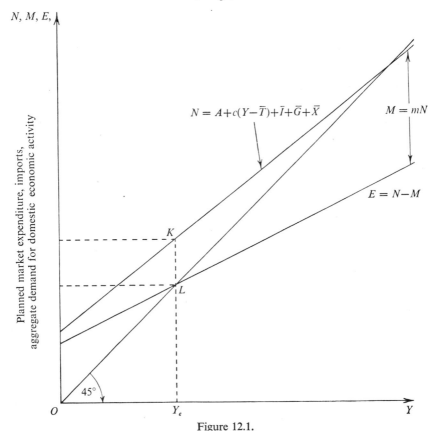

Figure 12.1.

Planned expenditure upon imports was described above as

$$M = mN.$$

In the open economy planned expenditure upon domestic production, that is, $N - M$, gives rise to domestic economic activity. Thus, the aggregate demand function for the domestic economy is

$$E = N - mN$$
$$= (1 - m)N.$$

241

The condition for equilibrium is that aggregate supply (domestic GNP at constant prices) equals aggregate demand. This may be written as

$$E = Y,$$

that is

$$Y = (1-m)N.$$

Planned market expenditure comprises planned investment and government expenditures and exports, which, in the short run, are given, together with planned consumption expenditure, which may be written as a function of real income. The equilibrium level of real income is given by the solution for Y of the equation

$$Y = (1-m)(A+c(Y-\overline{T})+\overline{I}+\overline{G}+\overline{X}).$$

These relationships are illustrated by figure 12.1; there the equilibrium level of income is indicated by OY_e. At this level of income the level of planned market expenditure, Y_eK, is matched by market supplies comprising the GNP together with imports of LK. It should be noted that there is no necessary reason why the level of imports at this equilibrium level of real income should equal the level of exports. The level of imports associated with the equilibrium level of income is equal to a constant proportion, m, of the market expenditure at the equilibrium level of income. An alternative expression for the level of imports at the equilibrium level of income, Y, can be derived as follows:

Since $\qquad\qquad Y = (1-m)N,$

then $\qquad\qquad N = Y/(1-m).$

and as $\qquad\qquad M = mN,$

then $\qquad\qquad M = [m/(1-m)]Y.$

3. The consequences of changes in planned expenditures

(a) The income multiplier

In order to focus attention upon the influence of m in the determination of the multiplier, the government sector is initially omitted. The equilibrium condition is

$$Y = (1-m)(A+cY+\overline{I}+\overline{X}),$$

which solved for Y, is

$$Y = \frac{1}{1-c(1-m)}(1-m)(A+\overline{I}+\overline{X}).$$

It follows that the change in domestic income consequent upon any autonomous change in market expenditure, ΔN, where ΔN may constitute ΔA, ΔI or ΔX, will be:

$$\Delta Y = \frac{1}{1-c(1-m)}(1-m)\Delta N.$$

The multiplier, k, was defined in chapter 10 as the ratio between the total change in income, and the bodily change in the planned expenditure function which occasioned it. The argument of chapter 10 related to a closed economy; in that case planned market expenditure, N, equals aggregate demand, E, and k was defined as being equal to $\Delta Y/\Delta E$.

It would be possible to continue with this definition, and to define the multiplier in the open economy as

$$k = \frac{\Delta Y}{\Delta E} = \frac{\Delta Y}{(1-m)\Delta N}.$$

However, it is more convenient to treat ΔN as the multiplicand and to define the multiplier as

$$k = \Delta Y/\Delta N.$$

If this second form is used, the multiplicand, ΔN, corresponds to the primary increase in demand for *world* production, whereas if the first form is used, the multiplicand, $(1-m)\Delta N$, corresponds to the primary increase in demand for *domestic* production.

Consider the case of an increase in gross investment expenditure of an amount, ΔI. Viewed as a series of rounds, the multiplier process is as follows. The initial, or primary, increase in income is $(1-m)\Delta I$; for $m\Delta I$ represents an initial, or primary, increase in imports. The initial increase in personal disposable income is $(1-m)\Delta I$, and this gives rise to an initial induced increment of consumption expenditure of $c(1-m)\Delta I$. Of this amount, $mc(1-m)\Delta I$ will be met from the output of the rest of the world economy, and the initial increase in the value added generated in the domestic consumption goods sector will be $(1-m)c(1-m)\Delta I$; this will give rise to further rounds of induced consumption expenditure. Table 12.2 sets out the process for a unit increase in investment expenditure.

The total increase in market expenditure is

$$\Delta N = \Delta I + \Delta C = \Delta I + \frac{c(1-m)}{1-c(1-m)}\Delta I = \frac{1}{1-c(1-m)}\Delta I.$$

TABLE 12.2. *The multiplier for a unit increment in investment expenditure**

Round	ΔI	ΔM	ΔY	ΔC
1	1	m	$1-m$	
2	—	$mc(1-m)$	$c(1-m)^2$	$c(1-m)$
3	—	$mc^2(1-m)^2$	$c^2(1-m)^3$	$c^2(1-m)^2$
⋮	⋮	⋮	⋮	⋮
Total	1	$\dfrac{m}{1-c(1-m)}$	$\dfrac{1-m}{1-c(1-m)}$	$\dfrac{c(1-m)}{1-c(1-m)}$

* The leakage of income to saving is not shown.

This increase is divided between the expenditure which generates domestic income, ΔY, and that which induces further imports, ΔM, as follows:

$$\Delta Y = (1-m)\Delta N = \frac{1-m}{1-c(1-m)}\,\Delta I;$$

$$\Delta M = m\Delta N = \frac{m}{1-c(1-m)}\,\Delta I.$$

The value of the income multiplier, and the amount of induced consumption expenditure (but not, of course, the total composition of output), is the same for autonomous increases in gross private investment expenditure, export production, and consumption expenditure.

If there is a government sector, and government expenditure is $G = \bar{G}$ and taxation revenue is $T = tY$, the equilibrium level of income is that where

$$Y = (1-m)\,[A + c(1-t)Y + \bar{I} + \bar{G} + \bar{X}],$$

and for an autonomous increment in market expenditure,

$$\Delta Y = \frac{1-m}{1-c(1-m)(1-t)}\,(\Delta A, \Delta I, \Delta G, \Delta X).$$

Expenditure upon imports operates as a leakage from the domestic income–expenditure–production circuit in a manner similar to taxation and saving. However, the leakages occur at different points of the production–income–expenditure circuit. Taxation is a leakage

244

between the generation of income, and the disposal of income. Personal saving is a leakage between disposable income and consumption expenditure.[1] By contrast, expenditure upon imports represents a leakage between market expenditure and the demand for domestic production; and, as can be seen from the above multiplier for an autonomous increase in market expenditure, the import leakage reduces both the primary increase in the demand for domestic production, and also the amount of the consequent induced increment of production in the domestic consumer goods industries.

(b) Changes in income and the balance of trade

The general principle stated in chapter 4, that the equilibrium level of real income occurs when the total of the *ex ante* leakages is equal to the autonomous, non-consumption expenditures, can be demonstrated to hold in the open economy as follows:

The condition for equilibrium in the domestic level of production is that

$$Y = C + I + G + X - M,$$

where the quantities referred to are *planned* output and *planned* expenditures respectively. Corresponding to Y is the level of personal disposable income $Y_p (= Y - T)$, which is allocated between *planned* consumption expenditure and saving, so that in equilibrium:

$$Y = C + S + T.$$

It follows that

$$S + T = I + G + X - M,$$

and so in equilibrium,

$$S + T + M = I + G + X,$$

that is

$$S = I + B + R.$$

This latter statement describes the equilibrium between planned saving and the sum of planned investment expenditure, net lending to the government and net lending to the rest of the world.

If there is an autonomous increase in any of the items, I, G, or X, initially there will be an increment of demand for domestic production of an amount $(1 - m)$ times the autonomous increment. The new equilibrium level of production will be attained only when out-

---

[1] The role of business saving was discussed in chapter 10. As in the case of taxation, it operates as a leakage between the generation of income and its distribution to households.

put increases by an amount such that the corresponding increases in the leakages from income to saving and taxation, together with the associated leakage from market expenditure to imports, are equal to the autonomous increment in expenditure. Consider, for example, the case of an increase in planned investment expenditure of amount ΔI. The resultant increase in real income is

$$\Delta Y = \frac{1-m}{1-c(1-m)(1-t)}\Delta I.$$

This is divided between C, S and T as follows:

$$\Delta C = \frac{c(1-t)(1-m)}{1-c(1-m)(1-t)}\Delta I,$$

$$\Delta S = \frac{(1-c)(1-t)(1-m)}{1-c(1-m)(1-t)}\Delta I$$

and

$$\Delta T = \frac{t(1-m)}{1-c(1-m)(1-t)}\Delta I.$$

$$\Delta M = \frac{m}{1-m}\Delta Y = \frac{m}{1-c(1-m)(1-t)}\Delta I,$$

and the sum of $\Delta S + \Delta T + \Delta M$ is equal to ΔI.

As a result, the balance of trade, $R\ (=X-M)$ will decline by an amount equal to the change in investment expenditure less the leakages to taxation and saving. That is

$$\Delta R\ (=\Delta M) = \Delta I - (\Delta S + \Delta T).[1]$$

There will be similar changes in the balance of trade for autonomous increases in consumption or government expenditures. In the case of

---

[1] An arithmetical example illustrates the argument. Let $C = 50 + \frac{4}{5}Y_p$, $t = \frac{1}{4}$, $m = \frac{1}{6}$, $I = 100$, $G = 250$ and $X = 200$. Then

$$Y = E = (1-m)[A + c(1-t)Y + I + G + X],$$

that is, $Y = 1,000$.

$$M = m[A + c(1-t)Y + I + G + X], \quad \text{or} \quad [m/(1-m)]Y.$$

That is, $M = 200$. At $Y = 1,000$, $Y_p = 750$, $C = 650$ and $N(=C+I+G+X) = 1,200$, which matches market supplies, $Y+M$. If the value of I is increased by $\Delta I = 12$, then

$$\Delta Y = \frac{1-m}{1-c(1-m)(1-t)}\Delta I = 20$$

$$\Delta R = -\Delta M = \frac{m}{1-m}\Delta Y = 4; \quad \Delta S = s(1-t)\Delta Y = 3;$$

$$\Delta T = t\Delta Y = 5; \quad \Delta S + \Delta T + \Delta M = 12 = \Delta I.$$

an increase in the volume of export expenditure the balance of trade does not increase by the increased export earnings but by a lesser amount depending upon ΔM, the induced increment of imports. That is

$$\Delta R = \Delta X - \Delta M,$$

$$= \Delta X - \frac{m}{1 - c(1-m)(1-t)} \Delta X.$$

For a given value of m, the improvement in the balance of trade consequent upon an increment of export expenditure is greater, the less is ΔY. The greater are the values of s and t, the less is ΔY, and thus the less is ΔM; that is, ΔR ($= \Delta X - \Delta M$) is greater.

Given the values of t and m, the greater is s, the less is ΔY, and the greater is the improvement in the trade balance consequent upon an increase in export expenditure. That is, a high value of the marginal propensity to save, other factors being constant, operates to limit the expansion of income, and gives rise to greater lending to the rest of the world. Similarly, given the values of s and m, the greater is the value of t the less is the expansion of income, and the greater the improvement in the balance of trade.

Given the values of s and t, the greater is the value of m the less is ΔY consequent upon an increase in export production. Consequently, the induced increments of saving, ΔS, and of taxation, ΔT, will be less. It follows from the equilibrium condition

$$\Delta S + \Delta T + \Delta M = \Delta X$$

that ΔM will be greater, and the improvement in the balance of trade will be less.[1]

Because of the relatively large proportion of Australian market supplies which are imported, the import leakage operates to dampen substantially the income multiplier. This has two implications of great practical significance. On the one hand, it operates to modify the impact upon domestic activity of the frequent substantial changes in export proceeds.[2] These fluctuations are unavoidable as long as

[1] Equivalent propositions setting out the effects of changes in the values of s, t and m upon the change in the balance of trade consequent upon autonomous changes in government, investment and consumption expenditures can be derived by similar reasoning.

[2] The estimation of the value of the income multiplier for the Australian economy (for a specified change in market expenditure at a particular time) is a formidable task; such estimates lie in the field of econometrics. In the earlier chapters where the two-sector model was considered the only leakage was personal saving;

Australian exports are dominated by primary products sold on competitive world markets. But on the other hand it means that, when foreign exchange reserves are low, and there is substantial unemployment, the government's use of monetary and fiscal policy to expand internal activity will be tempered by consideration of the effect of the induced imports associated with the increased income.

In the discussion of the techniques of economic policy-making in the closed economy (see chapter 11), it was shown that, because the government can influence all the components of aggregate expenditure it can, in principle, set a monetary–fiscal policy to achieve any desired attainable level of real income, Y^*, with any desired composition of aggregate expenditure, C^*, I^* and G^*. In the open economy, if the government were not constrained by the need to maintain international solvency, it could, in the light of the expected value of export proceeds, $\bar{X}$, set its monetary–fiscal policy to achieve a target level of real income

$$Y^* = (1-m)(C^*+I^*+G^*+\bar{X}).$$

Moreover, if the value of $\bar{X}$ or of m were to change, Y^* could be sustained by appropriate changes in monetary–fiscal policy.

However, changes in income cause changes in the balance of trade. If the value of export sales is $\bar{X}$, and if the current relationship between market expenditure and imports is such that, at Y^*, imports of M' will be purchased, the attainment of Y^* will be associated with a particular balance of trade, R' ($= \bar{X}-M'$).

If, initially, the actual level of income were Y^*, and R' is acceptable to the policy-makers, the government can use its monetary–fiscal weapons to offset any autonomous shifts in consumption and investment expenditures without causing a deterioration in the balance of trade. For example, if gross investment expenditure falls by \$$x$, the government could increase its own expenditure by \$$x$, or reduce net taxation in such a way as to cause consumption expenditure at Y^*

---

in that case a value of c of 0·9 meant that the multiplier was 10. In the full economy there are additional leakages and the value of the multiplier is certainly closer to unity than to ten. The marginal import-market expenditure ratio is a most important factor in the determination of the value of the multiplier. It was pointed out above (see p. 239) that as domestic industries approach full capacity the ratio $\Delta M/\Delta N$ increases. In the extreme limiting case where no further domestic production is forthcoming this ratio has a value of unity, and the value of the multiplier is zero.

to increase by x. Market expenditure at Y^*, and hence M' and R' would be unchanged.[1]

In the case where the export component of market expenditure falls by, say, ΔX, there will be both a fall in income and an adverse change in the balance of trade. If monetary–fiscal techniques are used to restore Y^*, the balance of trade will be $R' - \Delta X (= \bar{X} - \Delta X - M')$. If this balance of trade is considered by the government to be unacceptable, it may revise downward the target for economic activity. Alternatively, if the government is not prepared to allow an increase in unemployment in order to improve the balance of trade, it can change its trade policy—for example, it can increase the tariff rates in order to discourage imports. Such changes are discussed in some detail below. For the present the argument proceeds upon the assumption that trade policies are unchanged; this focuses attention upon reductions in Y^* as a method of improving the balance of trade.

During the severe depression of the 1930s, the monetary authorities, for a variety of reasons, did not take strong measures to stimulate the level of expenditures. One major Australian economist has argued that, had Australian Governments implemented expansionary policies, this would have given rise to insurmountable problems of international solvency.[2] Post-war Australian Governments are much better equipped to implement their economic objectives; there has been great progress in the understanding of the working of the economic system, and there is available now a much greater range of techniques of economic control. Nevertheless, in situations where international reserves are low, a fall in export proceeds is likely to lead the government to set Y^* at a lower level. In these circumstances an increase in exports, ΔX, will cause an increase in economic activity of

$$\Delta Y = \frac{1-m}{1-c(1-m)(1-t)} \Delta X,$$

and lead to an improvement in the balance of trade ΔR, which will permit the government to initiate a further expansion of income of $\Delta Y_2 = [(1-m)/m] \Delta R$. This further increase in income will give

---

[1] The argument would have to be modified if the marginal import–expenditure ratio was not the same for the various components of market expenditure.

[2] See L. F. Giblin, *Growth of a Central Bank* (Melbourne: Melbourne University Press, 1951), pp. 79–81. The onset of the depression was marked by the fall in export proceeds and it was made worse by the subsequent drastic curtailment of the capital inflow.

rise to additional imports ΔM_2 ($= [m/(1-m)]\Delta Y_2$), so that over-all the balance of trade will be as it was before the increase in exports.[1]

An alternative case involving similar considerations is that where an initial increment to the international reserves is obtained from an increased capital inflow. For example, assume that the government raises $\$x$ in foreign currency from an oversea loan. It was explained in chapter 7 that the Commonwealth Government has unlimited access to Reserve Bank finance, and it does not need to borrow oversea to pay for its own domestic expenditures. But if the balance of payments position is adverse, the proceeds of oversea borrowing permit a higher level of imports (and hence a higher level of income) without a net loss of international reserves. The government could permit an increase in income of $[(1-m)/m]x$, and this would result in increased imports of $\$x$. The increase in income need not neces-sarily be stimulated by increased government expenditure. It would be a question of social priorities as to how far the possible expansion of income should be absorbed by the public sector.

Only in the special case where $\Delta M/\Delta N = 1$ would the increment of market expenditure, consistent with induced expenditure upon imports of an amount equal to the proceeds of a foreign loan, be limited to the amount of the loan. Two examples illustrate this case. First, it would arise if the loan was floated specifically to finance the purchase of imported goods, such as foreign-made aircraft. Secondly, where the economy is operating at the upper end of the full employ-ment zone, by definition, any increase in market expenditure will lead to an increment of imported supplies equal to the increased expendi-ture.

At the other extreme is the case where the increased expenditure made by the entity which raises the foreign loan does not cause a direct increase in imports. For example, suppose that General Motors

---

[1] An arithmetical example illustrates the argument. Assume the economy postu-lated in the footnote on p. 246. Suppose that $\Delta X = 12$; this will cause $\Delta Y = 20$, $\Delta M = 4$, and $\Delta R = 8$. The government could permit a further increase in income of 40; for example, it could change the cost and availability of credit to stimulate an increment of investment expenditure of 24. The consequent further increase in income $\Delta Y_2 = 40$ would lead to further imports $\Delta M_2 = 8$. The total expansion of income of 60 causes a total increment of imports of 12, which equals ΔX. It should be noted that the expenditure plans of Australian businessmen are sensitive to changes in export prospects, and in practice it may be unnecessary for the government to take positive action to stimulate expenditure.

Acceptance Corporation, Australia (the company which arranges much of the consumer credit for the purchase of General Motors–Holden's motor vehicles) requires additional finance, and that it obtains this by floating a loan in the United States. If it uses the proceeds (converted to Australian dollars through the banking system) to make increased finance available to Australian car-buyers, and if the import content of the cars is nil, the transactions involving the General Motors group will not give rise to any additional imports, so that initially the international reserves will increase by the amount of the loan raised.

(c) Changes in export prices

The discussion in the previous sections is based on the assumptions that the prices of exports are constant, and that, in the short run, increased planned expenditure by the rest of the world on the products of the domestic economy results in a commensurate increase in production and employment in the domestic country's export industries. These assumptions are satisfactory for a country, such as England, whose exports are mainly manufactured goods.[1]

In the Australian case, exports are predominantly primary products; in the period between planning decisions (for example, between seeding operations) output is not greatly responsive to increased demand. Consider the extreme case, where exports are produced by a farm sector, and where domestic entities do not purchase export-type goods, so that, in the short run, the *quantity* of export produce is given. In this case, if oversea demand increases, exports prices will increase, but employment and production in the farm sector will remain unaltered. Suppose that the increase in export proceeds is ΔX_p. The consumption expenditure of farmers will increase by $c(1-t)\Delta X_p$. To the extent that this is not met from imports, there will be increased production by the non-farm sector.

---

[1] One complication, not considered in the text, is that potential exports are frequently potential domestic consumer goods; a rise in personal disposable income in the domestic economy, because of, say, an increased oversea demand for one type of exports, could lead to greater domestic absorption of other potential exports. For example, in the case of England, increased economic activity because of increased foreign demand for one category of British exports, say, investment goods, could lead to reduced exports of cars and household durable goods, if those industries were operating close to full capacity. In the Australian case the low domestic income–elasticity for export-type goods means that the diversion of potential exports to domestic consumption as disposable income rises is unlikely to be great.

The total increase in production in the non-farm sector will be equal to the sum of the series of induced consumption expenditures net of their import contents:

$$(1-m)c(1-t)\Delta X_p + c^2(1-m)^2(1-t)^2\Delta X_p + \ldots$$
$$= \frac{c(1-m)(1-t)}{1-c(1-m)(1-t)} \Delta X_p.^1$$

This represents the increase in domestic production when all quantities are valued in constant prices, and it is the appropriate indicator of the change in the level of domestic activity.

The increase in production is confined to the consumer goods sector. It is associated with an increment of imports, ΔM, of $[m/(1-m)]$ times the increment of production (see p. 242). That is,

$$\Delta M = \frac{mc(1-t)}{1-c(1-m)(1-t)} \Delta X_p.$$

In the case considered in the previous section (see pp. 246–9) of an increase in export expenditure, ΔX, which gives rise to increased output of the export sector at unchanged market prices, the increments in domestic economic activity and imports were:

$$\Delta Y = \frac{1-m}{1-c(1-m)(1-t)} \Delta X,$$

and
$$\Delta M = \frac{m}{1-c(1-m)(1-t)} \Delta X, \text{ respectively.}$$

The case where a given increment in export proceeds is due to an increase in export prices may now be compared with that where an equal increment in export proceeds is earned by increased output sold at unchanged prices. It can be seen that the increment of economic activity is greater in the latter case, but that, because the increment of imports is greater, the improvement in the balance of trade is less.

4. Changes in the import–market expenditure ratio

So far, the argument has proceeded upon the assumption that the functional relationship between expenditure upon imports and market expenditure is constant. In practice, this relationship may change. Given the availability of supplies, the most likely cause of a change in the proportions of market expenditure devoted to imports is a

---

[1] The same change in the output of the non-farm sector would result if the increased demand were for, say, wheat, and the Australian Wheat Board drew upon accumulated stocks of wheat.

change in the *internal–external price relation*, that is, the relation between the general level of prices in the domestic economy–*internal prices*, and the general level of prices paid by domestic entities for those goods and services traded internationally which are relevant to the domestic economy–external prices.[1] If other factors are unchanged, an increase in internal prices relative to external prices will cause domestic purchasers to substitute the relatively cheaper imported supplies; consequently the aggregate demand for domestic economic activity will be reduced.

The most important likely causes of changes in the internal–external price relation are differences in the rates of increase in money wages (which may reflect differences in inflationary pressures), differences in the rates of increase of productivity, changes in tariffs, changes in the prices of internationally traded commodities resulting from changed conditions of supply and demand, and changes in exchange rates. These changes may influence the magnitude of planned market expenditure, as well as the proportion of market expenditure devoted to imports. It is also possible that a change in the proportion of given planned market expenditures devoted to imports may occur independently of the above factors and two such cases are now considered.

First consider the case where there is a change in the preferences of domestic buyers as between imports and domestic supply. Such a change would result, for example, from a successful campaign to induce domestic entities to buy Australian-made goods. This case is illustrated by figure 12.2. Planned market expenditure is represented by NN. Initially the aggregate demand for domestic production is given by E_0E_0, the equilibrium level of income is OY_0, and imports are equal to AC. Following the change in buyers' preferences in favour of domestic products the aggregate demand for domestic production shifts autonomously upwards to E_1E_1, and the equilibrium level of income increases by Y_0Y_1. The increase in income exceeds AB, the

[1] Broadly speaking, the 'relevant' goods and services in this context comprise those goods and services actually imported by the domestic economy and also those which are potential imports. The concept of the internal–external price relation involves complicated index number problems; for the purposes of this book it is not necessary to discuss these. In the examples used in the text the *direction* of the change in the internal–external price relation is quite clear, and this is sufficient for the purpose of the argument. It should be noted that the relation is defined so that the imposition of a tariff upon imports (which will raise the prices paid by domestic buyers) raises external prices relative to internal prices, even if the price of the goods on the world markets is unchanged.

increase in aggregate demand for domestic production at the initial level of income by FG, the induced increment of production in the domestic consumption goods industries. Where planned market expenditure as a function of real income is given and described by

$$N = A + c(1-t)Y + \bar{I} + \bar{G} + \bar{X},$$

the effect of a change in the import–market expenditure relationship can be determined from the income multiplier

$$\Delta Y = \frac{1}{1 - c(1-m')(1-t)} (m-m') N_0,$$

where m is the initial, and m' the new fraction of market expenditure devoted to imports, and N_0 is the market expenditure corresponding to the initial equilibrium income, $O Y_0$.

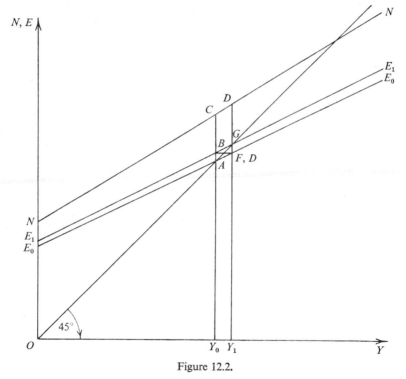

Figure 12.2.

The increment of income, ΔY, comprises the response of production to the increment in aggregate demand at the initial level of income, $(m-m')N_0$, together with the induced increment of production in the domestic consumer goods industries,

$$\frac{c(1-m')(1-t)}{1-c(1-m')(1-t)}(m-m')N_0.^1$$

If buyers' preferences remain unaltered, but quantitative import restrictions are imposed there will be a similar diversion of market expenditure towards domestic production. The case where planned market expenditures are unaltered by the imposition of import restrictions is illustrated by figure 12.3. It is assumed that the landed price of imports is unchanged, that domestic buyers are able to substitute domestic goods where imported supplies are unavailable, and that planned market expenditures are unchanged.

In figure 12.3 planned market expenditure is represented by NN. Initially imports are freely available; the aggregate demand for domestic production is indicated by $E_0 E_0$, the equilibrium level of income is OY_0, and initially imports are equal to AC. Assume now that imports are restricted to the quantity $LK = BC = FG$. The increased expenditure upon domestic production at OY_0 is equal to the reduction in the flow of imports consequent upon the introduction of the import quotas. As no further import supplies are permitted the import leakage is zero, and the total increase in income is $1/[1-c(1-t)]$ times $AB.^2$

---

[1] An arithmetical example illustrates the argument. Let $C = 25+\frac{4}{5}Y_p$, $t = \frac{1}{4}$, $\bar{I} = 30$, $\bar{G} = 180$, $\bar{X} = 155$, $m = \frac{1}{5}$ and $m' = \frac{1}{6}$. Then

$$Y = (1-m)(A+c(1-t)Y+\bar{I}+\bar{G}+\bar{X}),$$

which, solved for Y, gives $Y_0 = 600$. The market expenditure corresponding to this level of Y is $N_0 = 750$, which is matched by market supplies of imports, $M_0 = 150$, and $Y_0 = 600$.

As a result of the increased preference for domestic goods the increment of income, ΔY, is

$$(m-m')N_0+\frac{c(1-m')(1-t)}{1-c(1-m')(1-t)}(m-m')N_0 = 25+25 = 50.$$

The new equilibrium level of income, $Y_1 = Y_0+\Delta Y = 650$; the corresponding level of market expenditure is $N_1 = 780$, which is matched by market supplies of imports, $M_1 = 130$, and $Y_1 = 650$. The change in the level of imports, $\Delta M = M_0 - M_1 = -20$ can be regarded as the algebraic sum of the reduction in the imports at the initial level of income, 25, together with the additional imports of 5, associated with the expansion in economic activity.

[2] In practice it is likely that import restrictions will lead to an increase in the domestic prices of imports, for example, as importers take advantage of the reduced supply of imports to increase their profit margins. As a result, the internal–external price relation will fall, and so the profitability of producing goods competitive with imports will improve.

These two examples demonstrate that, where the level of planned market expenditures is constant, a decrease in the proportion of market expenditures devoted to imports will cause an increase in the level of income. In these two cases the change in the import–market expenditure function was not due to a change in the internal–external price relation. When there is a change in this relation, it will

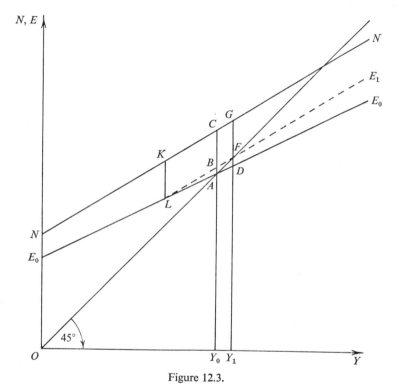

Figure 12.3.

not only affect the proportion of a given level of real market expenditure devoted to imports, but it may also affect the relationship between real market expenditure and the level of domestic output.

The reason why a change in the internal–external price relation may affect this latter relationship is that consumption expenditure is a function of the level and distribution of real income; in an open economy the real income[1] corresponding to any level of domestic

---

[1] Real income in this context is the command over goods and services accruing to the domestic recipients of the incomes earned in the production process.

output depends upon the *terms of trade*, that is, the ratio of the world prices of exports to those of imports. These may change with changes in the internal–external price relation. For example, suppose that the world price of imports rises so that the terms of trade deteriorate. Real income, at any given level of domestic output, will fall and with it consumption expenditure. In itself this will cause a fall in domestic activity, which may or may not be offset by the diversion of real market expenditure from imports to domestic production consequent upon the change in relative prices.

A second example relates to the effect of a change in the internal–external price relation upon the distribution of real income. Suppose that domestic money wages are increased. The domestic price level will rise, but less than proportionately, because the price to domestic buyers of imports will not change. It follows that the real incomes of wage-earners will rise while those of farmers, whose gross incomes are determined by export prices, will fall. If wage-earners have a different marginal propensity to consume from farmers, consumption expenditure at given levels of real income will change.

If attention is focused upon those movements in the internal–external price relation which are not associated with significant changes in the terms of trade, and if consumption expenditure is not sensitive to the distribution of real income, an increase in the level of internal prices relative to external prices will divert expenditure from domestic products to imports; and a decrease in the level of internal relative to external prices will divert expenditure from imports to domestic products. It follows that, in the former case, domestic economic activity will be reduced and the balance of trade will deteriorate, while, in the latter case, domestic activity will be stimulated and the balance of trade will improve.

An example of this latter case is where a devaluation of the foreign exchange does not lead to a change in the terms of trade, and the changes in the distribution of income do not affect the consumption function. Suppose that the rate of exchange between the domestic currency and other currencies is depreciated by 20 per cent. In the Australian case this would mean that the banking system would buy and sell £100 sterling for $300, instead of the present $250. If the domestic economy is a small part of the world economy, its purchases of imports will not influence the world price. However, domestic purchasers of imports will have to pay 20 per cent more for them; consequently, domestic industries will enjoy an improvement in their competitive position. If the volume of the exports of the domestic economy does not influence world prices, the terms of trade will be unchanged. However, the price of exports in terms of domestic currency will increase by 20 per cent; consequently the distribution of domestic real income will change in favour of exporters, and against other income recipients (who will face higher domestic prices for both imports and exportable goods). If there is no significant difference between the relevant marginal propensities to consume, domestic economic activity will increase because of the diversion of expenditure towards import-competing industries. Moreover, if the improved domestic prices of exports induce a greater output this represents a further increase in production.

A second method whereby the government can change the internal–external relation is by a change in tariff policy. For example, suppose that a government wished to reduce the magnitude of an export surplus. It could do so by reducing the level of tariff duties. If the country was not an important buyer of imports, their price on world markets would be unaffected; however, the price paid by domestic purchasers would fall. Consequently, market expenditure would be diverted away from domestic industries, and, in itself, this would cause domestic economic activity to fall. However, the reduction in tariff rates is an example of a reduction in the rate of sales taxation; the process whereby such a change would, in itself, increase economic activity was explained in chapter 11, section 3(b) (iii). If the government made compensating changes in the tax structure (for example, by increasing the rates of income tax) to keep real consumption expenditure at the initial level of real income constant, there would be a net decrease in real aggregate demand because of the change in the import–market expenditure relationship following upon the increase in internal prices relative to external prices.

In the final chapter it is explained how by simultaneously changing the internal–external price relation and using monetary–fiscal policy to change the level of aggregate demand, the government can manipulate the economy towards a target defined in terms both of the level of employment and the balance of trade.

13

THE INTERACTION
BETWEEN PLANNED EXPENDITURES AND
FINANCIAL FACTORS

The analysis developed in the previous chapters can be used to explain how, in a simplified model of a full economy, the level of economic activity is determined, and how this level will respond to given changes in the expenditure plans of the various sectors. One important limitation of the argument developed so far is that, in general, it has proceeded on the assumption that the cost and availability of finance are determined independently of the level of economic activity.

In chapter 6, it was explained that the cost and availability of finance influence economic activity because they have a significant effect upon the level of investment expenditure, and, to a lesser extent, upon consumption expenditure, and this influence was considered in some detail in chapters 8 and 9 respectively. The possible methods whereby the monetary authorities can exercise an influence upon financial conditions were discussed in chapter 7. The analysis of subsequent chapters has been concerned with situations where the cost and availability of finance were assumed to remain constant. This assumption greatly simplified the exposition of the effects of changes in expenditure plans, but it is not in accord with reality, and will now be discarded.

1. Interaction between the production and financial sectors in a simplified two-sector economy

It was explained in chapter 6 that the cost and availability of finance reflect the willingness of those holding money balances to part with them. Changes in the cost of finance may result from a change in the demand to hold money *vis-à-vis* other assets, or from a change in the supply of money. The demand for money was shown to depend upon the desired rate of spending, and also upon the proportion of their assets which wealth-holders wish to hold in the form of money. Clearly, there is a link from an increase in the propensity to spend by any of the sectors, through an increased demand for transaction balances, to the cost and availability of finance. This link may be illustrated by consideration of the simplified two-sector economy, in which it is assumed that the quantity of money is given. It will further be assumed that the only non-money financial assets are fixed-interest bearing securities issued by the trading enterprises. It is also assumed that the capital market is perfectly competitive, so that any credit-worthy borrower can obtain funds at the going rate of interest. The economy is in an initial equilibrium position where

$$Y = A + cY + I.$$

The capital market is also assumed to be in equilibrium.

Suppose that there is an increase in the propensity to consume, so that for each period households wish to spend from their current incomes an additional amount, ΔA. Then (as was shown in chapter 10) given that the level of planned investment expenditure remains unchanged, there will be an increment of income

$$\Delta Y = \frac{1}{1-c} \Delta A.$$

However, an increased rate of production means that trading enterprises will require greater money balances to finance the higher level of wage payments, stocks, and trade debtors.[1] Given that the existing preferences of wealth-holders are unchanged, it will be necessary to offer an increased rate of interest in order to induce them to provide funds to the trading enterprises. Such an increase will be referred to as an *induced* change in the rate of interest; that is, a rise induced by a change in aggregate demand.

It was demonstrated in chapter 9 that an increase in the cost of finance will have a dampening effect upon planned investment expenditure; consequently, the conclusion reached in chapter 10 that an autonomous increase in consumption expenditure will cause a total change in income of $[1/(1-c)]\Delta A$ must be modified. It remains true that *other factors being unchanged,*

$$\Delta Y = \frac{1}{1-c} \Delta A,$$

[1] If the increase in planned consumption expenditure is associated with an increase in the general level of prices and money wages, this will further increase the demand for money; the transactions demand is a function of transactions in terms of current prices. Situations where the price level changes are considered in the next chapter.

but the new equilibrium position will be such that the level of income exceeds the initial level by

$$\Delta Y' = \frac{1}{1-c}\Delta A - \frac{1}{1-c}\Delta I',^1$$

where $\Delta I'$ is the change in investment expenditure consequent upon the induced rise in the rate of interest. Corresponding to this higher equilibrium level of output will be a higher equilibrium rate of interest. At this higher rate, wealth-holders will be prepared to part with the money required by trading enterprises for their increased transactions balances.

It can be seen that the change in income, $\Delta Y'$, can be obtained by applying the income multiplier, both to the autonomous change in consumption expenditure, ΔA, and to the change in investment expenditure induced by the higher rate of interest, $\Delta I'$.

Given the value of the multiplier, $1/(1-c)$, the magnitude of the difference in the change in income where financial conditions are assumed to be unchanged, ΔY, and the change where account is taken of the induced change in financial conditions, $\Delta Y'$, is determined by the extent of the induced fall in investment expenditure, $\Delta I'$. This in turn depends upon two factors. First, it is related to the sensitivity of investment expenditure to an increase in the rate of interest; this was discussed in chapter 9. In the extreme case where investment expenditure is independent of the cost of finance, the interaction of expenditure upon financial conditions causes only a change in the rate of interest, and

$$\Delta Y' = \Delta Y = \frac{1}{1-c}\Delta A.$$

Secondly (given that investment expenditure has some sensitivity to the rate of interest) $\Delta I'$ depends upon the effect upon the rate of interest of changes in the level of expenditure. This in turn depends upon two relationships. The first of these is the ratio between the increment in the demand for transactions balances,[2] and the increment of expenditure which gave rise to it. In the short run this is a stable relationship reflecting such factors as the proportion of intermediate transactions to final expenditures. Other factors being constant, the lower is this ratio, the less will be the induced rise in the rate of interest. The second influence upon the rate of interest is the terms upon which entities which are holding idle balances are

---

[1] It is assumed that the consumption function is not affected by changes in the rate of interest.

[2] The argument assumes this demand to be independent of the rate of interest.

prepared to exchange them for securities. This was discussed in chapter 6. Given the additional transactions balances required to finance a given increment of expenditure, the nearer are securities regarded as a substitute for money by wealth-holders, the less the rise in the rate of interest which will be necessary to induce them to part with money. In the extreme case where only a fractional change in the rate of interest is needed to induce holders of idle balances to substitute non-money financial assets in their portfolios, $\Delta Y'$ will approximate ΔY.

One conclusion of general applicability which emerges from the consideration of this simplified economy is that equilibrium of the economic system requires both that the level of output should be in equilibrium, and also that the financial sector should be in equilibrium. The respective equilibrium conditions are that aggregate demand equals aggregate supply, and that, at the current rate of interest, entities are not trying to change the composition of their financial assets. The analysis above shows that other than in the extreme theoretical cases referred to in the preceding paragraphs, it is not possible to have a stable equilibrium in one sector, unless the other is also in equilibrium. For example, if the financial sector is currently in equilibrium, but the level of economic activity is below the equilibrium level, the increase in output will cause a change in the financial sector. For expositional purposes it is convenient to focus in turn upon each sector by assuming that conditions in the other sector are unchanged. In fact, a change in the production sector will cause changes in the financial sector, and vice versa.

2. Changes in expenditure and financial conditions in the full economy

The argument of the previous section suggested that the movement of the level of output to a higher level consequent upon an autonomous increase in aggregate demand would be somewhat restrained by the consequent induced changes in the financial sector. In the full economy, however, changes in aggregate demand will affect the supply of money, as well as the demand for money.

Consider the case of a full economy with a central bank, where the money supply is in the form of trading bank deposits. As in the previous section a competitive capital market dealing in fixed interest securities is assumed. The full economy has two additional components of aggregate demand, government expenditure and export demand, and two additional leakages, taxation and imports. The latter two factors operate both as leakages from the income–expenditure circuit, and also as leakages from the banking system. As was explained in chapter 7, section 3(c), payments made by the domestic payments sector to the government and oversea sectors cause matching reductions in the public's deposits with the trading banks.[1] They also have an adverse effect upon the liquidity position of the trading banks, and if the latter do not have excess liquid assets they will be forced to reduce the level of advances, which will cause a further fall in the money supply. Consequently, in the full economy, an increase in the level of planned expenditure which occurs without an increase in the money supply will result in both an increased demand for transaction balances and a reduction in the money supply; both factors operate to increase the cost of finance.

However, in the cases where the increased domestic production is in response to increased government expenditure, ΔG, or improved export earnings, ΔX, there will be an initial increase in the public's money supply matching the initial increase in personal disposable income consequent upon the increase in the level of planned market expenditure, and this will be associated with an improvement in the liquidity position of the trading banks. That is, the increase in aggregate demand will be associated with an increase in the money supply, which, in itself, would tend to reduce the cost of finance, and so stimulate investment expenditure. As production increases in response to the higher level of aggregate demand, the increased transactions demand and the leakage of deposits to imports and taxation receipts will operate to offset the effects of the initial increase in the money supply. Overall, the change in the level of income is likely to exceed that deduced by the simple income multiplier.

It was shown in chapter 12, section 3(b), that, given an increase in government expenditure of amount ΔG and assuming that the other components of aggregate demand are unchanged, the new equilibrium level of income will be such that

$$\Delta G = \Delta S + \Delta T + \Delta M.$$

That is, at the higher level of activity predicted by the simple income multiplier, the net change in the quantity of money consequent upon

---

[1] It was explained in chapter 7 that the public's demand for notes and coins is closely related to the level of economic activity. The conversion of deposits to currency represents another source of pressure on trading bank liquidity. In practice, this is a relatively minor factor and is not discussed in the text.

the increased expenditure and the induced leakages to taxation and imports is positive, and the liquidity position of the trading banks will also be improved. On the other hand, there will be a greater demand for transactions balances.[1]

Similarly, if the rates of taxation are reduced the primary increase in aggregate demand will be associated with an increase in the quantity of money, which will be partially offset by the induced increments of taxation and imports consequent upon the increased production. The initial impact of a budgetary change involving either an increased level of government expenditure and/or reduced rates of taxation is to cause an expansionary change in both the production and financial sectors. A similar effect occurs where there is an improvement in the balance of trade because of an autonomous increase in export proceeds at an initial level of income.

3. Elasticity in the financial sector

The argument above has focused upon the direct effects of changes in market expenditure upon the demand for and supply of money in an economy where the only financial institutions are the trading banks. Changes in economic activity may have important indirect effects upon the financial sector. In particular, the willingness of domestic and oversea investors to lend to, and invest in, Australian enterprises is influenced by the level of economic activity. There may be a substantial private oversea capital inflow and an increased mood of confidence among the public consequent upon an increase in economic activity, and these will operate to promote easier financial conditions.

Furthermore, the analysis above was in terms of a perfectly competitive capital market, where the only financial assets were current deposits with the trading banks, and fixed interest securities; and the only financial institutions were trading banks. In fact, there are many financial assets which the Australian public regard as close substitutes for money. In particular, fixed (interest-bearing) deposits with trading banks, and savings bank deposits, comprise a stock of near-money which in mid-1965 was approximately three times the level of current deposits.

If the rates of return on other financial assets increase relative to

---

[1] Those entities which are saving will enjoy an increment to their wealth holding which, initially, is likely to be in the form of an increment of money. Their preferences as between holding their additional wealth as money or as securities will influence the total demand for money.

the rates of interest paid on savings bank and fixed deposits, and/or if the public's mood of confidence improves, people will tend to move out of these assets, and in doing so will make funds available to the capital market. The Australian public's holding of fixed interest deposits comprised approximately 40 per cent of their total trading bank deposits in mid-1965. While depositors can not write cheques against fixed deposits, they can transfer them to current account deposits with little difficulty. As the S.R.D. and L.G.S. ratios are based upon total deposits, such a switch does not affect the liquidity position of the banks. It is an even simpler matter to convert a savings bank deposit to a current account, and, so long as the savings banks do not respond to such a loss of deposits by selling securities on the open market and/or by reducing their rate of lending, the liquidity position of the trading banks will be improved.

The argument above follows the somewhat mechanistic approach to the banking system developed in chapter 7. There, the trading banks were regarded as being likely to respond to an increase in their excess reserves by increasing their advances by some multiple of their excess reserves. It was also assumed that the level of advances was determined by the bankers, not by their clients.

In fact, the trading banks frequently have substantial excess reserves; that is, the actual ratio of their L.G.S. assets to their deposits exceeds the agreed minimum ratio.[1] Consequently, in the short run an increase in advances up to the limit consistent with maintenance of the agreed L.G.S. ratio is possible. Furthermore, an increase in advances may occur without any action by the trading banks. The Australian trading banks set upper limits to the overdraft which a client may draw upon. At times the percentage of actual overdrafts to the limits extended has been as low as one-half; that is, should all clients decide to write cheques to the limit possible under their agreements with their banks, the volume of actual overdrafts would double.[2]

Entities, other than the banking system, may also have excess cash holdings. For example, trading enterprises may, through past company saving, have accumulated liquid assets. Also, other financial

[1] The excess reserves are held for a variety of reasons. There may not be suitable investment outlets available; they may represent a buffer against possible increases in the S.R.D. ratio; they may represent a buffer against a greater use by the public of existing overdraft limits; and so on.

[2] In practice an increase of such magnitude would not occur, but an increase in the percentage of limits used of 10 per cent or more within twelve months is quite feasible.

intermediaries, such as the finance companies, may have excess cash balances. This may occur because the finance companies wish to be in the position to take immediate advantage of any increased demand for loans, or because in the immediate past the demand for loans has been insufficient to utilize all the funds borrowed from the public by the finance companies.

It was explained in chapter 7 that the Australian monetary authorities determine directly certain key interest rates. One effect of this is to offset the extent to which the cost of finance increases when economic activity increases. This effect may operate directly, as, for example, where the bank overdraft interest rate is fixed and persons wishing to increase their rate of expenditure obtain increased bank accommodation. It may also operate in a less direct manner, as in the case noted above, where holders of interest-bearing bank deposits switch out of these deposits into other securities bearing interest rates not determined by the authorities. Another example of this effect arises where the monetary authorities peg the rate of interest on government securities. If the Reserve Bank is to prevent a rise in the rate of interest as the public attempt to switch out of government securities, it must intervene in the market and act as a residual buyer, prepared to purchase all bonds offered for sale at certain prices. This not only enables the bond holders to switch from securities to cash at these minimum bond prices, it also increases the liquidity position of the trading banks (see chapter 7, pp. 103–4).

Through these, and other ways, the tendency for an increase in planned expenditures to cause an increase in the cost of finance, is offset. The interrelationship involved is complex, and the magnitudes of the relevant variables cannot be predicted with any great precision. It may be, that by their very nature, some of the key factors, such as the degree of confidence of the public, will never be predicted accurately. However, a study of post-war Australian experience suggests certain important conclusions. First, that except where the monetary authorities were following an aggressive policy of credit restraint, an increase in the desired rate of spending did not give rise to such an increase in the cost of finance as greatly to dampen expenditure plans. And secondly, that, other factors being constant, a marked swing in the balance of payments has a significant effect upon financial conditions; for example, an improvement in export prices will increase the availability of finance and tend to reduce interest rates.

14

INFLATION

1. Introduction

The general levels of prices in most advanced countries have risen substantially over the post-war period, but not at a steady rate. For example, in Australia between 1947 and 1952 the consumer price index rose at an annual rate of 9·9 per cent; between 1953 and 1960 at an annual rate of 2·7 per cent; from 1961 to 1963 the rate of increase was only 0·5 per cent. But over the years 1964 and 1965 the annual rate of increase was 4·0 per cent. One of the declared aims of the governments of the advanced countries has been to attain full employment with price stability. The problem of rising prices has been at the forefront of discussion of economic policy by economists, newspaper editors and other commentators. Various groups in the community have been singled out as responsible for rising prices —trade unions, the Arbitration Commission, businessmen with monopoly power.

In this chapter an analysis is made of the forces which cause prices to rise. It is recognized that prices may increase for a variety of reasons, but the term, *inflation*, is used to describe any situation marked by a *rise in the general level of prices*. A warning is necessary at the outset. So far discussion has been confined to the forces which determine the positions of *equilibrium* and, apart from chapter 10, little attention has been given to an analysis of the *process* by which an economy moves from one equilibrium position to another. Thus, in chapter 4 it was shown that, in the short run, real income will tend to settle at the value indicated by the intersection of the aggregate demand and supply schedules. And the multiplier analysis of chapter 10 was mainly concerned with the ultimate change in income that results when the economy moves from one short-run equilibrium position to another. The essence of inflation, however, is that it is a process associated with situations of *disequilibrium*, which may endure for substantial periods of time.

The tools that were developed in earlier chapters can be adapted for an elementary analysis of the inflationary process. The treatment must necessarily be oversimplified because it is not possible to discuss the significance of all the various institutional and behavioural factors which are relevant to a full account of the inflationary process. It is necessary to restrict the discussion to simple models of the determination of the price and investment policies of individual firms; and, for the most part, the simplifying assumptions that the real consumption demands of households are determined by their real personal disposable incomes is retained.[1] Initially, the assumption is made that the inflationary process occurs in a situation where there is no change in the terms on which economic entities can obtain finance.

In the post-war years economists have debated at length the issue of whether 'the' cause of rising prices has been *cost-pushes*— particularly those attributable to higher money-wage rates achieved by trade union pressure—or *demand-pulls*, that is, pressures arising from the existence of excess aggregate demand as defined in chapter 5. The first step is to examine the relationship between short-run changes in the level of aggregate demand and the general price level. This enables an analysis in section 3 of the nature of the 'cost-push', 'demand-pull' controversy. In the final section the question of whether or not inflationary processes will continue indefinitely in the absence of government intervention is discussed.

2. Price formation and aggregate economic activity

In the earlier chapters the analysis was in real terms. For the two-sector economy it was demonstrated that the equilibrium level of output was the outcome of producers' responses to the real levels of spending of households and firms on consumer and investment goods respectively; and the impact of autonomous changes of the consumption and investment functions was also discussed in real terms. It is now necessary to consider the short-period relationship between autonomous changes in the determinants of real aggregate demand and the general price level. This analysis will reveal the way in which

[1] Readers familiar with microeconomic analysis will be aware that heroic assumptions about the behaviour of firms are made in this chapter. The great variety of patterns in business behaviour are ignored, but the general approach can be adapted to cases other than the simple cases specifically discussed. Similarly, the general approach could be modified to take account of the influence of factors such as the effect of inflation on the real value of the financial assets held by the public, and hence upon their real consumption expenditures.

GNP in current market prices, or money GNP, changes with economic activity. And it leads to a consideration of the impact of price changes upon real expenditures and the likelihood that the price changes will be associated with a movement towards (or away from) a new equilibrium level of activity with stable prices. For simplicity of exposition the analysis is developed initially for the simplified two-sector economy.

The general price level is determined by the multitude of individual product prices. The four most important factors determining the price prevailing in an individual industry are, first, the nature of the

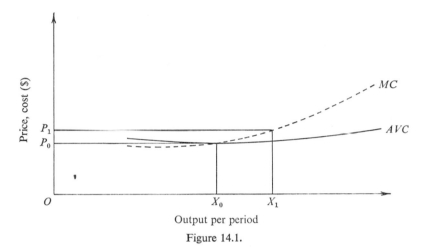

Figure 14.1.

cost–output function, given the prices that the firm pays for its inputs; secondly, the level of prices of its inputs; thirdly, the level of demand for the product; and, fourthly, the degree of competition prevailing in the industry, which determines the degree of discretionary power of the individual firms in setting their prices.

In situations where the capital equipment of a firm is given, and where the prices of the inputs (that is, money-wage rates and raw material prices) are constant, the relationship between the output and average variable costs of individual firms is typically as in figure 14.1.

Firms in highly competitive industries must accept the price prevailing in the industry, that is, they are *price-takers*. They can vary the rate of their output, but cannot influence the market price. Each faces competition from the other competitors, and in order to make

269

sales, each must match the prevailing market price. By contrast, where a firm has some discretion as to the price it will charge for its product, it is referred to as a *price-maker*.

As long as the market price exceeds the minimum short-run average variable costs, AVC, the firm will have an incentive to produce; and its most profitable output at any given market price is that at which its marginal cost, MC, equals the market price. For example, the price-taking firm depicted in figure 14.1 would produce so long as the price exceeds OP_0, and would produce OX_1 when faced with the market price, OP_1.

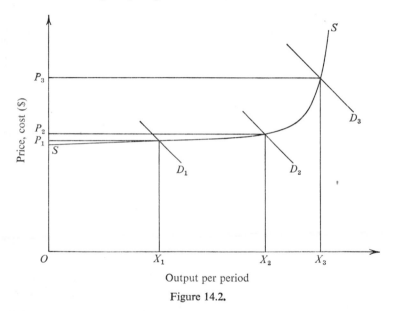

Figure 14.2.

In the case of the competitive industry, the total supply at any given market price is the horizontal summation of the individual firms' outputs. Given the cost functions of the potential producers, an increase in demand causes an increase in market price and induces an increase in output. Such a change is illustrated in figure 14.2 by the outward movement of the demand curve from D_1 to D_2 and the consequent increases in market price (from OP_1 to OP_2) and output (from OX_1 to OX_2).

If, as is most common, the differences in minimum short-run average costs between firms are not great, then the increasing slope of the industry supply curve is attributable primarily to the increased costs associated with operating at output levels in excess of those considered 'normal'. The capital equipment of a firm is designed to minimize average costs when operated at a certain level. If demand exceeds this level, increases in output are possible by more intensive use of the capital equipment, but this involves a more than proportionate increase in the inputs, particularly of labour, and this results in rising marginal costs.

When the demand for the industry's output is depressed, as represented by D_1 in figure 14.2, an increase in demand to levels nearer to planned capacity can be accommodated by utilizing capital equipment previously under-utilized, or idle. Thus an increase in demand, such as a shift from D_1 to D_2 in figure 14.2 is associated with little increase in the equilibrium market price. But an increase to D_3 means that the firms will be operating at levels beyond their designed normal capacity;[1] that is, they will be facing steeply rising MC curves and the market price will rise significantly.

The supply curve of figure 14.2 is drawn on the assumption that the prices of inputs are constant. The rising costs of the firms are explained by the declining productivity of the purchased inputs, associated with the more intensive use of the limited stock of capital equipment.

If it is assumed that the increase in demand is restricted to the product of the particular industry under consideration then, as long as this industry does not use special types of labour or raw materials, it is reasonable to assume that being a small segment of the whole economy, its increased purchases of inputs will not lead to significant increases in their prices.

However, this analysis is not primarily concerned with changes in the demand for an individual product, but with the consequences of changes in *aggregate demand*. Where an autonomous increase in aggregate demand carries the demand for most industries to levels where plant capacity is close to full utilization, product prices increase not only for the reasons discussed above but also for another

[1] In chapter 9 it was pointed out that businessmen can be thought of as having in mind expected levels of sales when making current investment decisions. The potential short-run output of the firm exceeds the planned normal rate since the firm can use more labour, including overtime work, and can draw on obsolete machines retired but not discarded. However, if it is believed that rates of output higher than normal can be sustained, the firm would plan to install additional capital equipment.

substantial reason: there will be a *general increase in the prices of inputs*. All firms, in an attempt to take advantage of the profitable opportunity to expand production, will be competing to win, or to retain, workers. Even if trade unions are passive, firms have an incentive to offer higher wages to overcome their (individual) difficulties in recruiting more labour, or to hold their existing labour force.

When an individual competitive industry is considered in the context of an increase in aggregate demand, account must be taken not only of the effect of the outward shift in the industry's demand curve upon the product price; but also of the impact of the shift in the firm's cost–output function, and hence the shift of the industry supply curve. A rise in input prices causes a bodily upward shift in the firm's cost function, as illustrated in figure 14.3 a. The corresponding shift in the supply schedule for the industry is illustrated in figure 14.3 b.

Figure 14.3 b illustrates the case of a typical individual competitive industry which experiences an increase in the demand for its product, shown by the shift of its demand curve from D_1 to D_2, in a situation of a general increase in aggregate demand. This latter causes an increase in money–wage and material costs, and so shifts the supply curve bodily from S_1 to S_2. The total increase in price, P_1P_2, is the result of the change both in demand and in cost, or supply, conditions.

Because microeconomic theory has not produced a generally accepted theory of pricing under conditions of imperfect competition (that is, where firms have some discretion as to the prices they can charge), it is not possible to analyse the impact of changes in aggregate demand upon prices in the imperfectly competitive industries with the same rigour as for the highly competitive sector. Nevertheless, some general propositions can be stated.

Typically, the imperfect competitor also operates under conditions of approximately constant short-run variable costs. If the firm is in the relatively rare position that it can set its prices independently of the prices set by other firms, then an increase in demand for its product normally raises the profit-maximizing price,[1] as illustrated in figure 14.4.

If the increase in demand is not confined to the product of the

---

[1] Under these conditions the profit-maximizing price is that corresponding to the output at which marginal revenue equals marginal cost. The proof of this is given in any textbook on price theory.

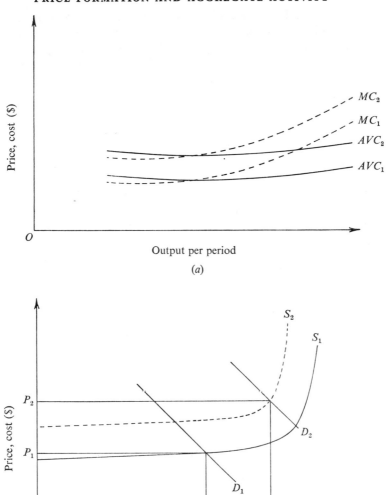

(a)

(b)
Figure 14.3.

particular firm, but is associated with an increase in aggregate demand which brings most firms close to their full capacities, the particular firm will experience the same increase in its input prices as will the highly competitive firms, and the consequent upward movement of its cost functions will cause a further increase in the profit-maximizing price.

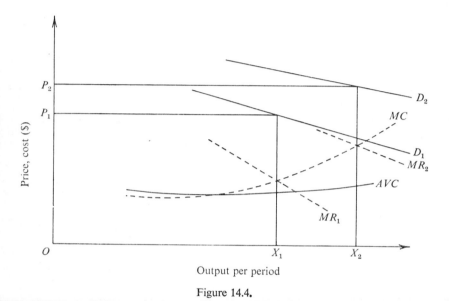

Figure 14.4.

In practice few imperfectly competitive firms are able to adopt the rather mechanical pricing technique of setting output at that level where marginal revenue equates marginal cost, and charging the corresponding price. Over a large part of industry, individual firms are conscious that any significant changes in their product prices will bring a change in the sales policies of their competitors. Commonly, a firm is acutely aware that its own sales depend upon the pricing, advertizing and selling policies of a relatively few rival firms. Such competitive relationships are described as oligopolistic.

In a situation where the members of the oligopolistic group are producing a homogeneous product, for example, a group of say five firms producing cement, it is likely that the firms will reach a specific agreement on prices. Where the products of the group are not identical, for example, in the cigarette industry, some differences in

274

prices in line with product differences is possible. But the essence of the oligopolistic relationship is the close link between the sales of one firm and the policies adopted by the other members of the group; in these circumstances it is likely that, either by tacit or specific agreement, the members of the group will strive for a pattern of prices which is mutually acceptable. This set of prices may be such that an individual firm may consider that, so long as the others would not change their policies, a change in its own price would be to its advantage. However, such a unilateral change is not possible. The set of prices is an acceptable compromise which offers all of the firms the possibility of making some profits, and it has the great advantage to the firms of preventing a continuous competitive price struggle.

Once a consensus on pricing policies is reached the firms face the problem of finding a method for preserving the arrangement in the face of changing cost and demand conditions. A common arrangement is for the individual firms to set their prices on the basis of the average variable costs,[1] plus a given percentage *mark-up*. This percentage mark-up may differ as between firms, for example, because they have different cost–output relationships. When all the members of the group experience an increase in their operating costs, for example, because of a wage increase or an increase in raw material prices, the relative price structure within the group is maintained by applying these mark-ups to the higher average variable cost levels.

If the cost–output relationship for a particular firm is constant, then, over that range of output where average variable costs are approximately constant, an increase in demand for the firm's product permits greater sales at approximately the same *absolute* gross profit per unit of output. Such a situation is illustrated by figure 14.5.

Assume that originally this firm, in explicit or tacit agreement with its competitors, sets a price of OP, and that the initial sales level is OX_1 so that the gross profit margin is CP. For increases in sales up to the level OX_2, the firm will earn the same gross profit margin.[2]

[1] As pointed out above, the average variable cost is likely to be approximately constant over a large range of output. One technique of price making is to use the average variable cost at some specific level of output as the appropriate cost.

[2] Figure 14.5 does not show the fixed costs, that is, those costs incurred independently of the level of output, so that the net profit is not shown. Since, by definition, fixed costs do not increase with output the increment of gross profit, CP times $X_1 X_2$, associated with an increase in sales from OX_1 to OX_2 is also an *increment* of net profit, and the increase in sales will involve a more than proportionate increase in the firm's total net profit.

If demand at price OP increases beyond OX_2, the firm can increase its *total net profit* by expanding sales up to OX_3, but beyond that level of production the marginal production cost exceeds the price.

The firms in oligopolistic industries are usually reluctant to change their prices, but if high levels of demand are expected to endure, an increase in prices is likely. If demand for the products of the industry is such that, at the price OP, the sales of the firm illustrated in figure 14.5 increase beyond OX_2, the absolute profit margin will be

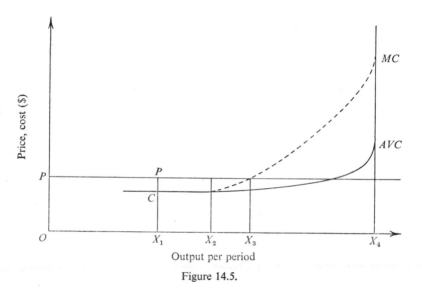

Figure 14.5.

reduced. And, if at price OP, demand exceeds the absolute capacity of the firm, OX_4, the firm will be faced with lengthening of its order books and other symptoms of excess demand. If the high level of demand is expected to endure, there is likely to be a general increase in prices set by the group; and, of course, for sales levels beyond OX_2, firms can argue that higher operating costs 'justify' the price change.

When there is an increase in aggregate demand such that many industries are operating close to capacity and labour is scarce, the average variable cost curves of the individual firms will be raised bodily because of the increase in the cost of labour and raw materials. Where the oligopoly group is adhering to a rigid price formula with constant percentage mark-ups there will be an 'automatic' increase in product prices. If the pricing procedure is not as mechanical as this,

276

the squeeze in the firms' gross profit margins, together with the fact that prices in other industries are rising,[1] will provide both the incentive and justification for price increases. Furthermore, as was argued above, at high levels of sales the oligopoly group may take the opportunity to widen the percentage mark-ups.

Thus in both the competitive and imperfectly competitive sectors of the economy, an increase in demand will tend to cause an increase in prices. However, prices in the competitive sector tend to be more sensitive to changes in demand. The competitive industries are mainly those producing primary products, and it is often not possible to increase their rate of output in the short run. On the other hand, the imperfectly competitive sector comprises much of the manufacturing industry, where frequently excess capacity can be drawn upon to meet increased demand. Furthermore, in a competitive industry the market price at any time is that which just clears the quantity supplied and hence the price changes continually with market conditions. By contrast, imperfectly competitive firms usually prefer to change their prices only after considerable time intervals; for example, to coincide with the introduction of new models. In the short run many price-makers prefer to meet increased demand by increasing output and/or drawing upon stocks, and when these possibilities are exhausted they will frequently quote longer delivery dates rather than immediately increase their prices. This latter consideration means that if an increase in aggregate demand has been sustained for only a few months, and if money-wage rates have not risen greatly, there may be little change in the prices charged by imperfectly competitive firms.

3. Price increases—cost-push or demand-pull?

(a) Pure demand and pure cost inflation

In the previous section it was shown how the prices of particular products are likely to respond to changes in the general level of economic activity. It was shown that as the level of aggregate output is increased towards full capacity, some types of labour will become relatively scarce, and so the money-wage rates offered by employers and/or asked by the scarce workers are likely to rise. And it was also

---

[1] It was argued above, that in the competitive sectors, where price is not consciously determined by individuals, product prices would rise. There is frequently a certain amount of moral pressure, both from outside and within an industry, to avoid price increases. This is weakened by a *series* of price increases. In a sense price rises are contagious.

shown that some product prices, in both the competitive and imperfectly competitive sectors, are also likely to rise, even if money-
wage rates in the particular industry do not rise. For other products
the increase in demand may not lead to a shortage of labour nor to
a demand-induced increase in prices—but their prices may rise if the
inputs used in their production have risen in price. For example, a
demand-induced increase in the price of, say, raw wool may cause
a cost increase in the production of another good, say, woollen
textiles. Price rises are the outcome of both demand and cost (or
supply) factors, and the factors are interrelated.

Only in a very special, and unrealistic, case is it possible to isolate
'pure demand inflation' from 'pure cost inflation'. Consider the case
of the simplified two-sector economy where the following conditions
are fulfilled: the labour force is homogeneous; the number of workers
and the length of the working week are given; there is a minimum
money-wage rate, but the labour market is competitive in all other
respects (so that businessmen offer higher money wages when they,
individually, find labour scarce); the average productivity of labour
is constant (this implies that the ratio between employed labour and
utilized capital is constant up to full employment); the prices of
products are determined by firms adding a given percentage mark-up
to their average variable costs.

Under these conditions a unique, full employment level of output,
in the sense of an absolute upper limit to aggregate output, can be
identified. Up to this level of output, prices are constant, and only if
planned money expenditure should rise so as to exceed the full
employment output valued at the former price level would there be
an increase in prices. In this case the relationship between output and
the price level would be as illustrated by figure 14.6. The full employment output is indicated as Y_f. When aggregate demand exceeds the
full employment level of output it would also be possible to identify
an 'inflationary gap', in the sense of the unique reduction in real
aggregate demand necessary to restore price stability with full
employment. This is illustrated by figure 14.7 where, if aggregate
demand is at E_2, GF is the required reduction in real aggregate
demand.

This special case is one in which 'pure cost inflation' can be
isolated. Assume that this particular economy is operating below full
employment and that the minimum money-wage rate is increased;
then the general price level will rise, despite the existence of un-

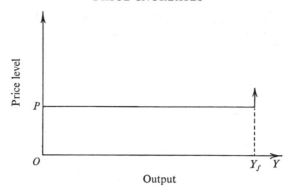

Output

Figure 14.6.

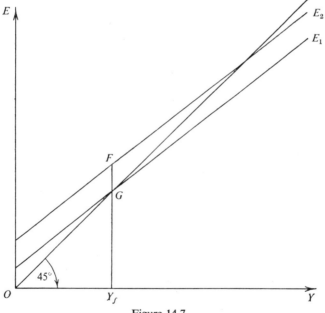

Figure 14.7.

employed resources. If finance is available to permit real expenditure to be maintained, the level of real activity may remain unchanged.[1]

In this case the increase in the minimum wage rate could be singled

---

[1] It was explained in the previous chapter that, other factors being constant, an increase in the quantity of money will be required if the cost of finance is to be held constant.

out as the cause of the inflation. The wage increase could be the result of the decision of a wage-fixing authority, or it could be the result of collective bargaining between unions and businessmen. A second form of pure cost inflation, that due to increases in the profit mark-ups set by the imperfectly competitive industries, can also be distinguished.

The pure demand inflation case occurred because of the excess of real planned expenditure; in that case, the price level could be stabilized by reducing real planned expenditure while maintaining the full employment level of output. However, in the case of the pure cost inflation, while a reduction in real aggregate demand would reduce output, it would not prevent rises in the price level resulting from cost increases made independently of aggregate demand. The same phrase, 'inflation', describes the change of the price level, but, clearly, the rise in prices in the two cases is the outcome of quite different economic forces.

A clear distinction between pure demand inflation and pure cost inflation cannot be made in the real world. Increases in aggregate demand may produce shortages of particular types of labour before the whole labour force is employed. Particular industries may reach full capacity and increase their prices before others. This effect will be greater the more the increase in aggregate demand is focused on a few sectors; for example, the rise in aggregate demand may be largely concentrated on the output of the construction industries, where both money wages and profit mark-ups are particularly sensitive to demand conditions.

Another factor influencing the response of prices to an increase in aggregate demand is the general adequacy of the capital stock. If in the past entrepreneurs have been optimistic about future sales and made investment expenditures to increase their capacity at a rate which has resulted in a significant increase in the productive capacity of the current capital stock, firms may continue to have excess capacity even when unemployment has been reduced to low levels.

The fact that, in the real world, increases in aggregate demand within the full employment zone result in increases in money wages for particular types of labour and particular product prices, which in turn raise the costs of production in other industries, does not, in itself, mean that the inflation is a mixture of excess demand and cost inflation. If the cost increases can be regarded as being *induced* by the increased aggregate demand, it would still be a reasonable use of words to say that there is an 'excess demand inflation', and to say that 'pure cost inflation' is the result of increases in money costs—higher wages or profit margins—which occur independently of the level of aggregate demand. But, in practice, it is extremely difficult to sustain this dichotomy in situations where the level of unemployment is low; for here the circumstances are favourable for unions to press for higher wages and for businessmen to increase their profit margins.

(b) Increases in productivity

The model postulated in the special case considered in the previous section is a useful device for tracing out the effect of increases in productivity. In the short run, increases in output from a fully employed labour force involve either an increase in the working week, or in the productivity of labour (defined as GNP at constant prices per worker).

Labour productivity could be increased if workers chose to work harder, but under normal peace-time conditions, it would be unrealistic to expect this to be a significant source of increased output. The productivity of labour can be increased by increasing the quantity of capital equipment used by the labour force, but in the short run the possibility of doing this is limited. Even if the current rate of production of investment goods is increased, there is a time lag—the gestation period—until the increased investment goods are ready to be used in the production process. Notwithstanding this, the most likely source of increased productivity in the short period arises from the use of the net increment of capital equipment which occurs during the period. This comprises the new equipment installed in the period (which reflects investment expenditure decisions made in the past) less that existing equipment which is scrapped. There may also be some increase in productivity consequent upon the improvement of technological and managerial techniques. In practice, the annual rate of increase in productivity is not large; in the case of post-war Australia, it has probably been at a rate of about 2 per cent per annum.

Suppose that, in a given short period, the full employment level of output in the economy postulated in the previous section is x per cent greater than that of the previous period. If the schedule of real aggregate demand was initially that described by E_1 of figure 14.8, so that in the previous period actual output coincided with the past

281

period's full employment level of output, OY_f, the new full employment output, OY_g, would not be achieved unless there were an autonomous increase in real planned expenditure of an amount BA.[1]

It can be seen from figure 14.8 that BA, the required autonomous increase in planned expenditure necessary to ensure that full employment is achieved in the current period, falls short of $Y_f Y_g$ by CD, the

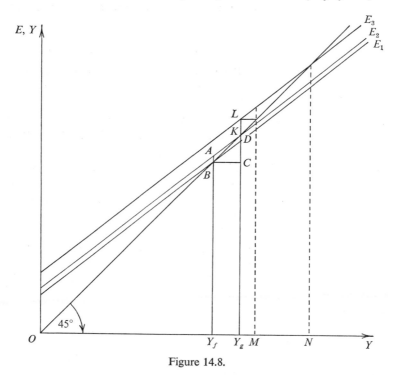

Figure 14.8.

amount of induced consumption expenditure associated with the increase in full employment income (see chapter 5, p. 70). In general terms, it can be stated that the upward movement in the aggregate demand schedule necessary to ensure that the potential growth in output is realized is equal to $s\Delta Y_f$, where ΔY_f is the increase in the full employment output, and s is the marginal propensity to save.

[1] Paradoxically, unless planned aggregate demand were to increase, businessmen would consider thatt heir past investment expenditures were unwise; this would dampen their enthusiasm for current investment expenditure, and aggregate expenditure would fall below E_1.

A similar approach can be used to answer the question: what increase in productivity would be required to eliminate an excess demand gap? If, in the current period, the full employment level of output is represented by OY_g in figure 14.8 and planned real expenditure is represented by E_3, so that the demand for real output exceeds the full employment output OY_g $(= Y_g K)$ by KL, the required increase in real output necessary to eliminate the excess demand exceeds KL. If, for example, it were possible in the present short period to increase the productivity of labour, the required increase in output would not be $Y_g M$ $(= KL)$, but $Y_g N$. The argument can be illustrated by an arithmetical example.

Suppose that OY_g is \$10,000m., that the labour force consists of 10m. workers, that the excess demand gap, KL, is \$100m. (which equals 1 per cent of the full employment output), and that the *mpc* is $\frac{4}{5}$. If productivity per worker were increased by 1 per cent, by, for example, an increase in effort, or in working hours, there would be an increase in output of \$100m. But this would be matched by an increase in incomes, and an increase in planned consumption expenditure of \$80m. The net reduction in excess aggregate demand would be only \$20m., that is, the amount saved from the additional real income. The total increase in output required would be that which gave a net increase, over and above the induced consumption expenditure of \$100m. This would amount to \$500m.; that is, the required increase in production per worker is 5 per cent.[1] In general terms, the required increase in productivity, as a percentage, is $[(1/s)E]/Y_g$, where E measures the inflationary gap at the *initial* full employment level, Y_g.

If the hourly money-wage rate is constant, and labour productivity increases in all industries, this will cause a bodily downward movement in the average variable cost curve of each firm. In competitive industries this will cause outward movements of the supply functions and a fall in prices; and where product prices are determined by the addition of a fixed percentage or an absolute gross mark-up to average variable costs, prices will also move to a lower level. If the

[1] Economists who advocate measures to reduce aggregate demand to combat excess demand inflation are sometimes rebuked as being defeatist. This analysis suggests that, in the short run, it is not feasible to counter excess demand by an increase in output. In the real world the required increase in productivity is less, since the marginal rate of taxation on increases in real income also operates to reduce the induced consumption expenditure consequent upon the increase in real income. On the other hand, wage demands are likely to be influenced by increases in productivity.

hourly money wage is increased in the same proportion as the uniform increase in productivity so that labour cost per unit of output remains unchanged, or if the profit mark-up is increased to absorb the decline in costs, the price level will remain constant. These cases can be thought of as examples of cost-push inflation offset by increases in productivity.

(c) Institutional factors in wage determination

The level of money-wage rates actually set in any short period is the outcome not only of the level of aggregate demand and the accompanying rate of unemployment, but also of important institutional factors. These latter affect both the money-wage demands made by trade unions in different occupations and the levels granted by employers. In addition, in Australia, they also greatly influence the level of the basic wage and margins awards granted by the Arbitration Commission. These institutional factors can be discussed under the following headings: the *wage–wage* link, the *wage–price* link, and the *wage–productivity* link.

The wage–wage link refers to the conventionally established structure of wages between different occupations, which trade unions and employers have come to regard as the 'fair' relative differences in the money-wage rates of the different occupations. The differences are thought to indicate differences in rewards which compensate for the differing degrees of skill, or difficulty, or dirtiness of different occupations. In Australia the Arbitration Commission awards at regular intervals, and in great detail, differing margins over the basic wage for various occupations. The margins are modified from time to time, but the relative wage structure changes little in the short run. In an economy, such as the United Kingdom, where a system of collective bargaining is used to set money-wage rates, the same notions hold in a less formal, but nevertheless rigid manner. If relative wages are linked in this way, an autonomous rise in the wage rate of one occupation can set off a series of rises in the wage rates of related occupations, in order to maintain the conventionally established relativities. For example, in the United Kingdom in recent years, a familiar process has been the annual round of wage demands. In this process, individual unions take the first increase granted to the members of a prominent union to which they traditionally look as the base for the percentage increase they will demand in their own wage rates. This wage–wage link is a lagged process; it takes some time to move from the first wage increase granted to the other increases. In the case where the wage–wage link is absolutely rigid, an increase in the relative wage of an individual group would cause an eventual rise of the same proportionate amount in the wages of all other groups and therefore of the entire wage structure.

The second link is the wage–price link. Either formally or informally, the increases in money wages asked for and granted in any short period may be related to the rate of increase in the prices of consumer goods in the previous period. Underlying this link is the notion that it is 'fair' to maintain the *real* value of the money incomes of wage-earners. Up to 1953, in Australia there was an automatic adjustment every three months of the money basic wage. The adjustment was determined by the rise for the previous quarter in an index of retail prices. Since 1953 there has been an annual review of the basic wage, and the increase in consumer good prices over the previous year has been an important factor in the determination of the award by the Arbitration Commission. The wage–price link is also a lagged process, with the change in money wages of the *current* period reflecting the happenings of a previous period.

Finally, the rate of increase in productivity in the *economy as a whole* has an important influence on increases in the money-wage rates demanded in *particular* occupations. A concept of 'fairness' also underlines this link. In a closed economy, increases in productivity would result in proportionate price reductions, and these would raise the real incomes of all members of the community. In the real world, prices tend to be 'sticky'[1] so that increases in money wages are a mechanism whereby real wages can be increased. In general, provided that changes in money-wage rates keep in step with increases in productivity, the general level of prices will remain approximately stable. Consequently, if all money-wage rates rise at approximately the rate of increase of productivity in general, all workers (and thereby other groups in the community whose money incomes have been improved) will share in the general increase in the available supplies of goods and services. The Arbitration Commission regards the increase in productivity as an important factor in its determination of the money basic wage. It, too, is a lagged process— last year's change tends to influence this year's level of money wages.

[1] A major reason for this 'stickiness' is the reluctance of many sellers—public utilities, professional workers, and firms in imperfectly competitive industries—to change their prices unless there has been a substantial change in cost and/or demand conditions.

If prices do not fall when productivity actually rises, there is a short-run shift to profits, which the wage–productivity link eventually removes.

Because the wage–wage link and the wage–price link are lagged, and because wages are not the only components of the costs of products, an autonomous rise in either a money-wage rate or in prices[1] *need* not set off a process of *continuously* rising prices and wages. Thus, an increase in wages of 10 per cent may raise prices by only 5 per cent in the first three months after the increase; if the consequent rise in wages in the next quarter is less than 5 per cent, there will be a convergence to a new, higher *level* of prices and wages. However, if productivity changes also influence the level of money wages, the combined result of all *three* links may be such that a convergent process does not ensue. Rather, the process may be *continuous* or even an *explosive* one. These points are discussed further in the next section. Here it is sufficient to note that the price level is the *joint product* of all these forces, and it is impossible to disentangle the contribution of any *one* of them.

4. The process of inflation

The discussion above was concerned with an analysis of the factors which influence the change in the level of prices over a short period, consequent upon some specified initial increase in aggregate demand, productivity, money-wage rates, or profit margins. It was *not* a complete account of the process of inflation because it did not consider the 'feed back' of the effect of the changes in the price level upon expenditure plans. Furthermore, as the discussion was concerned only with the price change over a short period, it avoided the issues as to whether, once prices begin to increase, they will continue to do so, and if so, at what rate. The analysis did not purport to trace the effects of the changes through to the new equilibrium positions; nor was the question of whether or not such a position existed discussed. This section deals with these questions.

Consider, first, a simplified, two-sector economy. Assume that the economy is initially at the full employment level of output, $O Y_f$, and that this is \$10,000m. in the prices of the base period. Initially the

---

[1] *An autonomous rise* may be interpreted as a rise inherited from a previous period; or a once-and-for-all change in the relative position of a particular wage rate, or, in the case of an open economy, as a rise in the price of a group of commodities, the prices of which are determined by conditions external to the domestic economy.

aggregate demand schedule is described by E_1, and the current level of prices is stable. Assume further that, initially, planned fixed investment expenditure is \$1,500 m. and planned consumption expenditure is described by $C = 500 + \frac{4}{5} Y_p$, where both are measured in prices of the initial or base period. Figure 14.9 illustrates the position.

If planned real fixed investment expenditure rises to \$2,000 m. this will create an excess demand gap of \$500 m., initially in the invest-

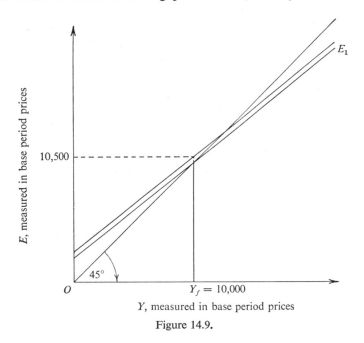

Figure 14.9.

ment goods industries. The consequent increase in prices and the possibility that a new equilibrium will be achieved depends upon the pricing policies of businessmen, the process of money-wage determination, and the lags in the system.

One possibility is that, despite the increased demand, producers of investment goods do not raise their prices. In this case, there will be a *suppressed excess demand* which will take the form of lengthening of order books. The actual allocation of the limited output of investment goods will depend upon how the sellers decide to allocate supplies. Would-be buyers of investment goods to the value of \$500 m. will be unable to obtain supplies. There will be no increase in the money

287

incomes of any sector. This disequilibrium situation could continue indefinitely; but, since sellers of investment goods have an incentive to raise their product prices, such suppressed excess demand always represents a potential source of price inflation. Moreover, even if they do not directly raise their prices, their increased demand for labour is likely to cause an increase in the wage rates that they pay, and in this way, to influence prices.

If the investment expenditures are planned in money terms, that is, if entrepreneurs plan to spend a total of $2,000 m. in terms of market prices on investment goods, then a rise in the prices of these goods of $33\frac{1}{3}$ per cent will result in the elimination of the excess demand for investment goods. But only if the increased money incomes of $500 m. earned by those in the investment goods industry are *all* *saved*, will there be no induced increased real demand for consumer goods. If the businessmen in the investment goods sector do not offer higher money-wage rates but, instead, raise their profit margins, then, as long as the *mpc* from profits is zero, there will be no induced expenditure on consumer goods. In this extreme case, the price rise has served to eliminate all excess demand.[1]

At the other extreme is the case where prices and money wages immediately rise in an explosive manner. If investment plans are made in real terms, and price increases do not influence the desire and ability to invest, the rises in the prices of investment goods will not eliminate excess demand. And if the *mpc*'s of profit-recipients and wage-earners are the same, and positive, there will be an excess demand for consumer goods induced by the increased incomes of those in the investment goods sector, and this will endure regardless of price changes and of shifts in the distribution of income between profits and wages. If there are no income–expenditure, expenditure–production, or production–income distribution lags, and if product prices and money wages are continuously revised, the price level will rise at an infinite rate. This case would also require the supply of money to be infinitely elastic. If it were not, the increase in the price level would reduce the ratio of the quantity of money to national income valued in market prices; as a result the cost of finance would tend to rise and this would discourage expenditure.

---

[1] The increased profits in the investment goods sector may lead to an increase in the *desired* capacity in this sector. Whether or not this results in excess demand in the future depends upon the total level of planned expenditure in the future periods.

The effect of price increases upon planned consumption expenditure will now be considered in detail. Under what circumstances will rising prices lead to a reduction in consumption expenditures in real terms? One possibility is that there are in the community, groups whose *money* incomes are either fixed, or increase in response to price changes only after a considerable lag. Examples are persons whose incomes are derived from fixed-interest securities, pensioners, professional men such as doctors and dentists whose fees are fixed in the short period, and salaried groups such as teachers and public servants, whose scales of payment are revised only after considerable intervals. If these groups react to the cuts in their real incomes by reducing their real expenditures, aggregate planned consumption expenditure in real terms from any given level of personal real disposable income will be reduced. This cut in real consumption will be forced on those persons who have no accumulated liquid assets, and who already consume all of their money income. Many old age pensioners are in this position. Other persons who are not currently spending all of their money income, are likely to react to the fall in their real incomes by reducing both their real consumption expenditure and their saving.

The following example illustrates the argument. A simplified, two-sector economy with a given level of full employment income is assumed. Suppose that there are two income groups in the community—a group who are active in the production process and who earn profits and wages, so that their money incomes automatically reflect any rise in prices (for simplicity, they are assumed to have the same *mpc*), and a retired group of superannuated persons whose money incomes are fixed in the short run and who are assumed to spend all their pensions on consumption goods. The consumption function of the active group is

$$C_a = 600 + \tfrac{3}{5} Y,$$

where C_a and Y are measured in base period prices.

The consumption function of the retired group is

$$C_r = \frac{500}{P},$$

where 500 is the autonomously given amount of superannuation payment. C_r is measured in base period prices, and P is the ratio of current to base period prices.

The aggregate consumption function is therefore

$$C = 600 + \frac{500}{P} + \tfrac{3}{5} Y$$

similarly measured.

Suppose that the full employment level of real income is 5,000 and that gross investment expenditure is 1,000 in real terms and this is independent of the price level. Aggregate planned expenditure in real terms at the full employment level of real income, $C+I$, is then:

$$1,100 + \tfrac{3}{5}(5,000) + 1,000 = 5,100,$$

and there is an excess demand of 100. If prices were to rise by 25 per cent, the money incomes of the active group would also rise by this amount, so that their real expenditure would be unchanged. However, the retired groups' real income and, therefore, their planned expenditure on consumption goods would be reduced to 400. The excess demand would therefore be removed by the rise in prices and, in this case, an equilibrium position at a higher price level would be possible.

Such a process depends upon the existence in the economy of significant groups who cannot *fully* protect themselves in the short run against the fall in real income due to rising prices. It also supposes that an expectation of rising prices does not lead to an upward shift in the consumption functions of these groups, such that even as their *real* incomes fall, nevertheless, their consumption expenditure in real terms remain constant. Thus, in figure 14.10, if a particular group had a fixed money income OA in the short period of (measured in base year prices), the impact of a rise in prices which reduces its real value to OB may at the same time lead to a bodily shift upwards in the consumption function from $C'C'$ to $C''C''$, so that the planned consumption expenditure remains unchanged ($AC_1 = BC_2$). While few pensioners may be able to do this, other fixed income groups, who have saved in the past and are currently saving, can do so for some time. And those persons who have invested their past savings in assets, the values of which appreciate in periods of rising prices, may be able to do so indefinitely.

It has already been suggested that money wages may for a short time lag behind a rise in prices, so that there is a shift to profits in the short run. If the *mpc* of wage-earners is greater than that of profit-earners, the aggregate consumption function will shift downwards. However, this effect may be offset by an upward shift in the consumption function of wage-earners, if they anticipate that rising prices will continue and/or that they will be able to take effective action to raise their money wages in the near future. It is unlikely therefore that the fall in real consumption demands associated with the initial rise in prices will be maintained for any length of time.

As was shown in chapter 8, expenditure on durable goods is influenced by factors other than current income. If the prices of these

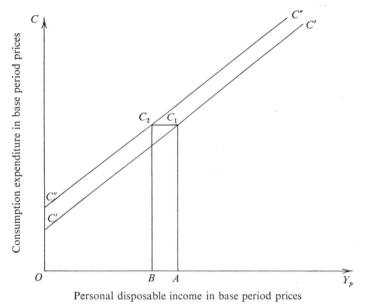

Figure 14.10.

goods are rising but the credit facilities (especially hire-purchase loans) for the finance of their purchase are not expanded proportionately, real demands for durable goods may fall. In the Australian case, except in the event of an aggressive contractionary monetary policy by the government,[1] it is most unlikely that con-

---

[1] See chapter 13, pp. 264–6. In Britain, monetary policy has on occasions been specifically directed towards restraining consumer credit. The British government has set minimum deposit and maximum repayment conditions. In Australia, in 1955, the Prime Minister persuaded the finance companies to exercise voluntary restraint on the rate of their lending, and in 1960, the Commonwealth Government temporarily altered the taxation legislation in such a way as to make it unprofitable for the finance companies to increase their own borrowing from the public. These measures did check the rate of increase of expenditure upon durable goods.

sumer credit facilities would not expand. In fact, in an inflationary situation, demands in real terms for these goods may actually rise.

So far a closed economy in which there was no taxation has been assumed. If, now, the government and oversea sectors are introduced, the analysis of the impact of a price rise on real expenditure must be modified to take account of the influence of net taxation, and of international trade. First, if rates of income taxation are progressive and related to *money* incomes, the rise in the real disposable income of active earners will not match the rise in their real *pre-tax* incomes. Indeed, the same real pre-tax income will now be associated with a lower *real* disposable income.[1] This will have a dampening effect on real demands. There will be a similar effect if the rates of social service benefits in money terms are increased less than proportionately to the price increase.

In an open economy, where domestic prices are rising at a faster rate than those of the rest of the world, if (as in the case of most Australian exports), the prices of exports are determined independently of domestic costs, the real income, and hence real expenditures, of exporters will fall. A second consequence will be a switch of expenditure from domestically produced goods to expenditure on imports. This will take the form both of direct substitution of imported goods for final home-produced goods, and also of an increase in the import *content* of domestically produced goods.

In effect, there will be an increase in the ratio of imports to market expenditure, which will operate to reduce the level of economic activity in the domestic economy. This will be reinforced by the financial effects of the higher level of domestic prices and money incomes. The consequent increased taxation payments will not only operate to reduce real disposable income (as explained above) but

---

[1] Suppose that the marginal tax rates on each additional $500 of income are:

Income range ($)	Marginal tax rate
0–500	0
501–1,000	5
1,001–1,500	7
1,501–2,000	10
2,001–2,500	15

The money disposable income associated with a money income of $2,000 is $1,890. If prices and money incomes both rise by 25 per cent, the real disposable income associated with a real income of $2,000 (money income of $2,500) is $1,852.

also will operate to reduce the supply of money. The increased flow of imports will also have this effect, and the transactions demand for money will increase because of the higher level of prices. These factors will operate to increase the cost and reduce the availability of finance. This will tend to reduce planned expenditures by domestic entities, and this, together with the effect of the rise in the ratio of imports to market expenditure, may lead to the attainment of a new equilibrium level of economic activity, but this level may be associated with a serious balance of payments problem.

If the domestic price level is stable, and the world price of imports increases, this will have the effects upon the aggregate demand for domestic production discussed in section 4 of chapter 12, and in the footnote on p. 301 of chapter 15. The increased price of imports will also be a source of a cost–push pressure upon the domestic price level, and this in turn is likely to cause further cost pressures through the wage–price link. The practical importance of such an 'imported cost inflation' depends upon the ratio of imports to market supplies. If, as in the Australian case, this ratio is high, a rise in import prices will have significant effects on aggregate demand (because of the decrease in internal prices relative to external prices and also because of the change in the terms of trade), as well as upon the level of domestic costs.

The analysis to date has been confined to one short period. In effect, the following question has been asked: suppose that initially the price level is stable and the economy is in equilibrium, and that aggregate market expenditure or the level of costs autonomously increase; what will be the level of prices by the end of the short period concerned? It has been shown that the answer to this depends upon a host of factors—the existing capital stocks of the various industries and especially of the investment goods sector, the number of un-employed workers and the extent of idle productive capacity, the mobility and flexibility of the available labour supply, the pricing policies of the various industries in the economy, the nature and extent of the various lags in the system including those which influence the rate of change in money wages, and, of course, the size of the rise in market expenditure.

Throughout the chapter attention has been concentrated upon the consequences for the price level of an increase in aggregate demand, or of a sustained high level of demand. In fact aggregate demand fluctuates from time to time, and there are periods when economic activity declines. Much of the argument of this chapter can be applied in reverse to situations where aggregate demand falls. However, both wages and prices are much less flexible downwards than they are upwards. While there are some industries where prices are highly sensitive to the state of demand, for example, the building industry and many primary industries, in general, a decline in demand has its major impacts upon the levels of output and employment, and the size of order books and the promptness with which orders are fulfilled.

It is not correct to regard prices as being subject to a 100 per cent ratchet effect, that is, capable of rising but never falling. While it is true that award wages are highly inflexible downwards most employees receive over-award payments, and these are influenced by the demand for labour. And in times of reduced demand some product prices do fall somewhat. The measurement of these is difficult since nominal prices may be unaltered, but discounts and trade-in allowances may be increased, or credit terms liberalized, or model improvements made, or sales at reduced prices may be more frequent. Furthermore, the continuous increase in labour productivity arising from the growth in the capital stock, improvement in labour skills and improved business administration operates to reduce average costs, so that, if the overall demand pressure were sufficiently reduced, this would show itself as a fall in the level of prices.

Now a further question is asked: given that the level of prices has begun to rise, will a new price level be reached, or will prices, as a result of the feed-back effects of rising prices on money incomes, expectations and real demands, continue to rise, either at a constant or an increasing rate? The three possibilities are illustrated in figure 14.11, where the general level of prices is shown on the vertical axis and time is shown on the horizontal axis. Prior to time t_0, the price level was stable. Suppose that at time t_0 market expenditures increase and economic activity increases to such an extent that there are shortages of certain types of workers, and some industries are working at full capacity. The curves P_1, P_2 and P_3 illustrate the various processes which can occur once prices start to rise. P_1 illustrates the case where, ultimately, a new, higher stable level of prices is reached. P_2 is the case where a process of rising prices is initiated and continues but at a constant rate; P_3 shows the case of prices rising at an accelerating rate—the case of hyper-inflation.

It has already been shown that a rise in the price level may, but need not necessarily, reduce planned expenditures on consumption and investment goods in a given short period. The analysis, however, assumed an identifiable absolute level of full employment output, rather than a zone within which further increases in output are possible. In the preceding section on the role of institutional lags in the determination of money wages, reasons were given why such lags might slow down, but not completely eliminate, the rate of increase of prices. If there are substantial lags, and a significant number of

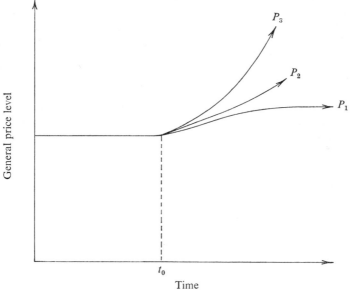

Figure 14.11.

businessmen are price-makers, and there are sizeable groups who cannot protect themselves completely against price rises in the short period, it is possible to postulate plausible conditions which would mean that the actual path of price changes may be P_2 for considerable periods of time. In such an economy the community 'learns to live with' a slow but steady rate of inflation.

The more fortunate groups (which make up the bulk of the community) are able to protect themselves almost immediately either by increasing their product prices (in the case of profit-earners) or by increasing the prices which they get for their services (as in the case of wage-earners). In the short run, the reductions in the real incomes of other groups act as safety valves for the relief of the spending

295

pressure; but over time these groups, or the community (through the government) are likely to take steps to raise the real value of their money incomes. As long as large sectors of the community do not use their powers to influence the prices of their products or services to offset (or more than offset) the expected rise in prices there is no reason why a P_2 situation in which prices rise moderately but steadily should be transformed into a P_3 situation in which prices rise at an accelerating rate. This conclusion does depend, however, on there being substantial lags in the economic system and on the existence of many businessmen who do not charge the full, short-run profit-maximizing price for their products. It also assumes that the money supply is relatively elastic.[1]

In an open economy such as Australia, there is one important group, namely, the primary producers, who cannot protect their real incomes against the effect of a differential rate of increase of internal and external prices. The prices of their products are determined on world markets while their costs are determined primarily by the level of domestic prices and wages.[2] It is believed that farmers' saving is an important determinant of their investment expenditure so that their investment expenditure as well as their consumption demands are closely related to their real incomes. Their total real expenditures

[1] Through the exercise of monetary and fiscal policy, the monetary authorities could reduce the rate of increase in prices, and this would mean that in any short period the changes in the shares of real income arising from the inflationary process would be reduced. However, it is likely that such policies would cause a fall in the short-run level of output, and they may also dampen the long-run rate of economic growth. In this latter event, the growth in the real incomes of the groups which are not adversely affected by increases in the price level will be reduced; and it may be that other groups, such as recipients of social service benefits and salaried groups, who are adversely affected in the short run by an increase in prices, but whose shares in real income are adjusted after a time lag, may also be better off in the long run if the authorities do not attempt to keep the rate of change of prices within narrow bounds.

[2] It was pointed out in the previous footnote that it is possible that the long-run interests of some groups whose real incomes are adversely affected in the short run by inflation, may nevertheless be promoted by a faster rate of price increase if it means a faster rate of economic growth. Exporters are not likely to be such a group; if their real incomes are squeezed too severely they may receive some form of subsidy, and if the inflation gives rise to a balance of payments problem which is corrected by a devaluation (rather than by increased tariff rates or quantitative import controls) the decline in their real incomes will be checked. But in general the interests of exporters, like those of persons living on the income from fixed-interest securities, and those who are living on private superannuation allowances, are best served by a decline in the general level of prices.

demands are likely to be reduced when domestic prices rise faster than external ones. In itself, this will dampen any tendency for a P_2 situation to become a P_3 one.

A second element in the open economy which tends to moderate the rate of increase in prices is the possibility that an excess demand can be met from imported supplies; the competitive effects of imported supplies will also operate to dampen cost inflation. However, these dampening effects imply that it is possible to incur substantial deficits in the balance of trade. Should the import deficit become so great, or endure so long, that it is necessary to correct it by the imposition of quantitative controls, a change in the exchange rate, or a change in tariff rates, these restraining effects will no longer apply.

Control of the rate of inflation requires measures which affect real planned expenditures, and measures to influence the rates of increase of the money rewards of the factors of production. In the final chapter this question is discussed within the wider context of the problem of securing full employment without inflation, balance of payments equilibrium, an equitable distribution of income, and a satisfactory rate of economic growth.

15

ECONOMIC POLICY

1. Introduction

The discussion in previous chapters has been directed mainly towards the provision of tools for the analysis of *how* the economy works; in particular, how the level of economic activity is determined. This, in itself, is a proper subject for study and research. However, an understanding of the economy enables one to go beyond pure analysis and description to a consideration of the ways in which man can control his economic environment. If the manner in which the economy works is known, perhaps the economy can be made to operate in a manner closer to that desired by the community. For some people, the study of economics is an end in itself; but for most, the important thing is increased knowledge which can be used for the purpose of manipulating the economy to contrive particular results. This chapter is concerned with economic policy in the full economy.

It should be stressed that economic policy is only one aspect of government policy, although a very important one. Most government policies have economic aspects, but in many the main objectives are other than purely economic ones, for example, defence, foreign affairs and social welfare. The balancing of objectives is the essence of politics: wealth may have to be sacrificed to defence; economic growth to social equality. The weighting or priority of the various objectives, some of which may conflict, is a political matter, about which the economist *qua* economist has no more expertise than any other man in the street. Thus, although people may attach great importance to the achievement of high production or price stability or some other economic objective, other counterbalancing considerations must always be taken into account. Some people will attach more importance to one objective, others to another; the function of the government in a democracy is to reconcile these and to design a policy which is a kind of consensus.

2. Three major economic objectives

There are many facets of economic policy. Attention will first be paid to three key ones. In all modern mixed economies[1] governments are concerned with the level of employment, the rate of change of the general level of prices and the means whereby international solvency is preserved. In Australia, all the major political parties and the great majority of economists believe that in respect of these three issues, the objectives of economic policy should be:

(1) That the level of economic activity (employment) should be within the full employment zone.

(2) That the general level of prices should be approximately stable.

(3) That the balance of payments should be such that there are no unwanted movements in international reserves; that is, any deficit (surplus) on current payments associated with international transactions should not exceed the acceptable amount of borrowing from (lending to) abroad.

The first two of these objectives are often linked, and their achievement is said to constitute *internal balance*; achievement of the third is said to constitute *external balance*.

It is not difficult to see why governments are greatly concerned with the pursuit of these objectives. If employment lies below the full employment zone, potential production will be lost, and great hardship will be inflicted on those who are out of jobs, and on their families. On the other hand, if there is unsatisfied aggregate demand, inflation will ensue and the second objective will be frustrated.

Price stability is not desired as an end in itself, but because price inflation has an impact on the level and composition of production, the distribution of income and the external trading position. If there is inflation, those with fixed money incomes and those whose money incomes lag behind the rise in prices will suffer losses in their real incomes, while those whose money incomes are derived from buying and selling on a rising market will gain. Economic efficiency is hampered by inflation because rational calculation of the cost and benefits of investment projects is rendered difficult by an unstable standard of value; and speculation is encouraged at the expense of productive endeavour. Furthermore, inflation renders the attainment

---

[1] A *mixed* economy is one in which there is both a private and a public sector and in which the public sector plays a significant part in production and expenditure decisions. The present-day economies of Australia, the United Kingdom and the United States are examples.

of the third objective more difficult because, if domestic prices are rising more rapidly than those in the rest of the world, the balance of trade will move against the home country and international reserves are likely to fall.

A government can choose not to pursue full employment or price stability. However, it is not possible to avoid the issue of the means whereby external solvency is maintained. Foreign exchange must be available to finance imports. In the extreme case in which a country has no foreign reserves and cannot borrow from abroad, imports must be kept below the limit determined by exports proceeds. However, some countries can borrow heavily from overseas almost continuously. In these cases (and Australia is one of them), the government must decide how much borrowing it regards as acceptable. This decision will be influenced by the likely effects on the future balance of payments of the dividend, interest and capital commitments arising from the borrowed funds, and by the degree to which the home country's industries may come under foreign ownership and control through the borrowing of funds from overseas.

3. Three major variables of economic policy

There are three major variables which are relevant to the pursuit of the above objectives.

(1) The level of *planned market expenditure.*

(2) The *absolute level of costs*—in particular, wage rates, profit margins and the prices of imports and exportable[1] goods. These prices are determined on world markets.

(3) The *internal–external price relation*—the relation between the general levels of domestic and oversea prices.

These three variables operate on the level of economic activity, the general level of domestic prices and the balance of payments in a manner which interrelates the three objectives of policy.

It was shown in chapter 4 that changes in the level of market expenditure react directly on the level of economic activity. The higher the level of expenditure, the greater is economic activity, at least up to the full employment zone. As the full employment zone is approached, prices may begin to rise (see chapters 5 and 14); and as market expenditure rises still further, excess demand for domestic

---

[1] Exportable goods are those which are absorbed by the domestic economy but which could be exported; for example, wheat, sugar, steel, cars are goods consumed by Australians, and for which there is also an export market.

goods and services in general will emerge and the symptoms of inflation appear. At the same time rising market expenditure increases the demand for imports and may reduce the supply of exports, thus worsening the balance of trade (see chapter 12). As activity rises towards the upper limit of the full employment zone, a larger and larger fraction of market expenditure will spill over on to imports.

The absolute level of costs may not itself exert much direct influence on the level of economic activity in a closed economy. To the extent it does, its effects are uncertain (see section 3 of chapter 5). However, autonomous shifts in the level of costs, whether as a result of changes in wage awards, or the profit margins set by price-makers, or in oversea prices, will directly affect the price level (see section 2 of chapter 14). The absolute level of domestic costs will affect the relation between internal and external prices, and consequently, in an open economy, will indirectly impinge on both the level of activity and the balance of payments.

The internal–external price relation influences the level of economic activity, because it is an important determinant in the distribution of market expenditure between domestic production and imports (see section 2(b) of chapter 12). It was shown there that the higher the relation, other things being equal, the less competitive will domestic products be compared with oversea ones and the smaller the domestic activity generated from any given amount of market expenditure. The relation is also of critical importance in its effect on the balance of trade. The higher the relation, the less competitive will the home country be. The demand for imports will be greater; the competitive position of the export industries will worsen. Consequently the higher the relation, the less favourable will be the balance of trade.[1]

---

[1] This is subject to the qualifications set out in chapter 12, pp. 252–4, where it was explained that so long as the terms of trade are unchanged and spending is not sensitive to changes in the distribution of income, a change in the relation has unequivocal effects. One particular case where this does not hold occurs where a rise in the world price of imports occurs, and where the domestic demand for imports is highly inelastic; another is where a devaluation of the exchange rate leads to an increase in export production and, because of an inelastic world demand for the exports, world prices decline so that overall export proceeds fall more than import purchases do. Account must also be taken of the cause of any movement in the relation. If the relation rises because *internal* costs have risen, this will be a reflection of a higher domestic price level; but if the relation rises because *external* prices have fallen, this will be reflected in lower domestic costs.

4. Interrelations of the objectives

The preceding discussion has shown that the simultaneous attainment of the three objectives of economic policy is not necessarily possible. For example, as an economy moves towards the full employment zone (from a state of unemployment), prices will tend to rise and the balance of trade will become unfavourable. The uninhibited pursuit of full employment may make price stability and external balance impossible. On the other hand, excessive concentration on price stability may make the achievement of full employment difficult. It will usually be necessary to give way a little on one objective, in order to more nearly achieve another. Thus the policy makers must attach weights to the objectives. It is this weighting which is the essence of the political process. The economic interrelationships between the objectives and the major variables are analysed in this section.

It is convenient initially to concentrate on the first and third objectives and the first and third key variables. It is assumed throughout this chapter that the change in the internal–external price relation occurs without itself directly affecting market expenditure. From the arguments of chapter 12 (see pp. 252–4 and the footnote on p. 301) it follows that this will be the case if the terms of trade are unchanged and if spending is not sensitive to the distribution of real domestic income. Since this chapter is concerned with policy making, only those changes in the internal–external price relation which can be engineered are of relevance; generally, these policy changes do not result in significant changes in the terms of trade.

Given these assumptions, the effects of changes in market expenditure and changes in the internal–external price relation on the level of activity and on the balance of trade can be summarized in the following way:

$$N \uparrow \quad \text{leads to} \quad Y \uparrow, R \downarrow$$
$$N \downarrow \quad \text{leads to} \quad Y \downarrow, R \uparrow$$
$$\text{and}$$
$$P \uparrow \quad \text{leads to} \quad Y \downarrow, R \downarrow$$
$$P \downarrow \quad \text{leads to} \quad Y \uparrow, R \uparrow$$

where N and P stand for market expenditure and the internal–external price relation respectively; Y and R stand for the level of domestic economic activity and the balance of trade respectively; and $\uparrow$ and $\downarrow$ stand for 'an increase in' and 'a decrease in' respectively.

An economy can be in any one of nine situations in relation to the two objectives of full employment and external balance. These nine situations are shown as a matrix in Table 15.1. Activity can be below the full employment zone, within the full employment zone, or there may be unsatisfied excess demand; and the balance of trade may be such that the rate of movement of the country's international indebtedness is unacceptably adverse, is acceptable or is unacceptably favourable.

TABLE 15.1

	Level of economic activity		
	Unacceptable (unemployment)	Acceptable (full employment)	Unacceptable (excess demand)
Unacceptable (excessive increase in net international indebtedness)	1	2	3
State of balance of trade — Acceptable (external balance)	4	5	6
Unacceptable (excessive increase in net international assets)	7	8	9

The change in the net international assets of a country, for a period, comprises the algebraic sum of the increment in its foreign reserves (which may be positive or negative) and the increment in its oversea lending (or borrowing). Where this sum is negative there is an increase in net indebtedness. The factors determining that rate of increase in net international indebtedness which the government considers unacceptable were discussed above (see p. 300). At first sight it may appear paradoxical to speak of an unacceptable rate of increase in a country's net international assets. However, there are two important reasons why a government may wish to moderate the rate of increase of its net international assets. First, the country will be sacrificing the higher current living standard that it could achieve with a higher rate of imports. Secondly, to the extent that the domestic economy has a net export surplus other countries will have net import surpluses; the working of the international trading system may require that the export surplus be reduced.

The ideal situation is no. 5, that is, both the level of activity and the state of the balance of trade are regarded as acceptable. Suppose that an economy is in one of the other situations and that the government aims to move towards the ideal; this will involve operating on market expenditure and the internal–external price relation. First, consider situation no. 1. Here the situation is one of unemployment and an unacceptable deficit in the balance of trade. If market expenditure is expanded ($N\uparrow$) to eliminate the unemployment ($Y\uparrow$), the balance of trade will worsen ($R\downarrow$). Clearly, this is no solution. However, if the internal–external price relation is lowered ($P\downarrow$), not only will unemployment be reduced ($Y\uparrow$), but the balance of payments will also improve ($R\uparrow$). This then would be the correct first policy change. When the internal–external price relation has been lowered enough to produce external balance, the economy may be in either situation no. 4 or situation no. 6, for there can be no guarantee that the reduction of the internal–external price relation, which will produce external balance, will also produce full employment. All that can be assured is that, initially a reduction of the internal–external price relation will operate in *the right direction* in relation to *both* objectives. If the economy turns out to be in situation no. 4, it will be necessary to expand expenditure ($N\uparrow$) to absorb the remaining unemployed, and the internal–external price relation will have to be further reduced to offset the effect of the expansion of market expenditure on the balance of trade. If the economy turns out to be in situation no. 6, it will be necessary to contract expenditure ($N\downarrow$) to eliminate the excess demand, and the internal–external price relation can be raised a little to offset the effect of the contraction of market expenditure on the balance of trade.[1]

Consider situation no. 3. Here the situation is one of demand inflation and an unacceptable deficit in the balance of trade. If market expenditure is contracted ($N\downarrow$), the excess demand will be eliminated and the balance of trade will improve ($R\uparrow$). Thus a policy of contracting expenditure will, in this situation, initially operate favourably in relation to both objectives. Again, the economy, after this initial move, may be in situation no. 4 or no. 6; and the analysis of the preceding paragraph applies in similar fashion.

Consider situation no. 2. Here the required action on both variables is unambiguous. The economy is within the full employment zone, but there is an unacceptable deficit in the balance of

---

[1] If the government had perfect knowledge of the functioning of the economy and of the consequences of policy changes, it could move directly to the ideal situation by making simultaneous changes in market expenditure and the internal–external price relation.

trade. If the balance of trade is rectified by reducing the internal–external price relation, market expenditure will have to be cut to eliminate the consequential excess demand; or if the balance of payments is rectified by reducing market expenditure, the internal–external price relation will have to be decreased to stimulate activity to absorb the consequential unemployment. Whichever way the problem is viewed, it will be necessary to cut market expenditure ($N \downarrow$) and reduce the internal–external price relation ($P \downarrow$).

The other five situations of imbalance may be analysed in a similar manner. To sum up, of the eight non-ideal situations, in four, the appropriate action on both key variables is indicated; but, in the other four, the appropriate action in only one of the key variables is indicated. The argument is illustrated in Table 15.2.

TABLE 15.2

Level of economic activity

		Unacceptable (unemployment)	Acceptable (full employment)	Unacceptable (excess demand)
State of balance of trade	Unacceptable (excessive increase in net international indebtedness)	$P \downarrow$ N?	$P \downarrow$ $N \downarrow$	$N \downarrow$ P?
	Acceptable (external balance)	$N \uparrow$ $P \downarrow$	—	$N \downarrow$ $P \uparrow$
	Unacceptable (excessive increase in net international assets)	$N \uparrow$ P?	$P \uparrow$ $N \uparrow$	$P \uparrow$ N?

The analysis of the preceding paragraphs concentrated on the two objectives of full employment and external balance. If the only cause of inflation was the existence of excess demand, it would not be necessary to pay special attention to the objective of price stability; for by eliminating excess demand, price stability would be assured, and *full employment with price stability* might then be regarded as the *single* objective of internal balance. But this would be a gross over-simplification, and inconsistent with the arguments of chapter 14. It was explained there that as aggregate demand expands and the economy approaches the full employment zone, shortages of particular kinds of labour and materials will cause wages and prices to rise in particular sectors of the economy. It follows that unless the full employment zone is defined as commencing when significant unemployment still exists (perhaps 3 or 4 per cent of the work force), full employment will be accompanied by some price instability; and the smaller the percentage unemployment, the greater the rate of price increases. This means that it may be impossible simultaneously to achieve both the objectives of full employment and absolute price stability. Governments will have to opt for a politically acceptable combination of a small amount of unemployment and a small amount of price instability. Just how small is 'small' is a matter of politics.

The question of price stability is complicated by another important factor. It was shown in chapter 14 that the general level of prices is influenced not only by demand factors and changes in costs *induced* by demand factors, but also by autonomous changes in costs. In practice, perhaps the most important of these autonomous changes are changes in money-wage rates. Increases in money-wage rates are more likely in times of high activity and excess demand, but it is possible for autonomous increases in money-wage costs to occur even though activity is below the full employment zone. This considera-tion is especially relevant in a country like Australia, where the general level of money wages is much influenced by arbitral authorities, whose awards exert a rapid and pervasive influence on the whole wage structure. Even in a situation where there is some slack in the economy, unit wage-costs will rise and prices are likely to follow suit, if wage rates rise more rapidly than the rate of increase of pro-ductivity (gross national product per worker). Autonomous shifts may also occur in profit margins; and domestic costs may be affected by changes in oversea prices working through imports and export-ables. Finally, alterations in the rates of indirect taxation may affect the general level of domestic prices.

5. Weapons of economic policy

(a) Wages policy

While the level of market expenditure and the internal–external price relation are amenable to government action, it is much more difficult for the government to control the absolute level of costs. Indeed, such control would require elaborate and detailed powers of price- and wage-fixing, which would not be acceptable under peace-time conditions. It is true that in Australia, the Commonwealth Arbitration Commission exercises considerable influence over the general level of wages. However, two important qualifications must be noted. First, the Commission is not a branch of the government; its decisions are not part of an integrated economic policy—it is an independent arbitral tribunal.[1] Secondly, the Commission determines only minimum money-wage rates—it is open for employees to demand and for employers to offer over-award payments, and this is the general case. For example, in Australia in the eight years to December 1963, the index of minimum adult male money-wage rates rose by 26 per cent, while the index of average weekly earnings rose by 38 per cent.

(b) Market expenditure

In chapter 11 it was pointed out that a government can exercise a direct and powerful influence on the level of market expenditure. In an economy, like that of Australia or the United Kingdom or the United States, the government's control over spending does not relate to detailed prescriptions of how much particular persons or enterprises should spend on particular items, but the government can influence the broad components of total spending.

Obviously the government can determine its own expenditure; but it can also control in a broad way consumers' expenditure by increasing or reducing personal real disposable income through lowering or raising taxes and raising or lowering cash social service benefits. These two weapons of policy, government expenditure and net taxation, comprise the instruments of *fiscal policy*. Fiscal policy relates not only to the overall amounts of government expenditure and taxation, but also to the composition of the expenditure and the composition and nature of taxation. Many elements of fiscal policy were dealt with in detail in chapter 11.

The government can also influence market expenditure through *monetary policy*. Monetary policy is implemented by the central bank (in Australia, the Reserve Bank of Australia), but it must conform to the government's general economic policy.[2] Monetary policy relates to the quantity and availability of credit and its cost. Since private investment and consumption expenditures, are, in part, financed from borrowed funds, changes in the availability of credit exert important influences on aggregate spending. This matter was discussed in some detail in chapters 6, 7 and 13.

---

[1] On occasions the Commonwealth Government has made submissions to the Commission indicating government economic policy.

[2] In the Australian case, this contrasts with the situation of the Commonwealth Arbitration Commission. Prior to the second World War the central bank in Australia was completely independent of the Commonwealth Treasury.

Two questions arise in connexion with fiscal and monetary policies. How powerful are they in controlling aggregate expenditure? And are they sufficiently flexible to meet the sharp changes that so frequently occur in the economic situation?

Changes in government expenditure on goods and services have a direct and clear impact on market expenditure. The effects of changes in taxation are less certain, because incomes are used for saving as well as for expenditure and taxation. It is conceivable that changes in taxation may have little effect on personal spending. In practice, this may be true of the wealthier sections of the community, whose expenditure may vary little with their disposable incomes. However, in general, increased net taxation will certainly reduce market expenditure (and reduced taxation increase it), although the effect may not be predictable with a high degree of precision. Some of the difficulties in assessing the effects of changes in disposable income on consumption expenditure in the short run were discussed in section 4 of chapter 8.

Taxation is, in principle, a flexible weapon of economic policy, since tax rates can be fairly readily changed. Its flexibility is inhibited by the practice of determining tax rates only at the annual budget. However, this practice is not sacrosanct. Inter-budgetary tax changes do occur; in the United Kingdom the Chancellor of the Exchequer has the power between budgets to vary certain tax rates within set limits. In Australia supplementary budgets have been introduced as emergency measures between annual budgets.

Government expenditure is not nearly as flexible an instrument as might at first sight appear. It is difficult to make large cuts in *recurrent expenditure*, for it finances such services as law and order and education and public health, where continuity of service is essential. It may be equally difficult to make sudden increases in recurrent spending; such increases would involve an increased demand for skilled manpower, the supply of which usually cannot be readily expanded. *Capital expenditure* programmes can be deferred, but deferment frequently involves waste or postponement of services essential for efficient production (for example, as would follow from a reduction in public works programmes for expanding irrigation and power facilities). Public works programmes can also be accelerated, but large new public investment projects require much time for planning and detailed designs. Work on these projects cannot be turned on and off like a tap.

Monetary policy is relatively flexible in the sense that the central bank has the mechanisms (open market dealings and Statutory Reserve Deposit requirements, see section 3(*b*) of chapter 7) by which the liquidity and lending policies of the trading banks can be quickly affected. But its efficacy must be qualified by two important considerations. First, a tightening of monetary conditions may be much more effective in reducing spending than is a relaxation in promoting spending. The promotion of spending requires the existence of willing and credit-worthy borrowers; if economic conditions are depressed, businessmen's expectations may be so pessimistic that the credit-worthy are not interested upon embarking in investment projects. Secondly, the central bank's direct control usually extends over the banking system only. The monetary system includes many non-bank financial institutions—insurance companies, merchant banks, development corporations, hire-purchase finance corporations. By varying the controlled interest rates (the rates offered on government debt and bank interest rates) the monetary authorities can influence the flow of finance to, and the interest rates charged by these non-bank financial institutions (see section 4 of chapter 7). Nevertheless, if bank credit is made scarce by central bank action, the impact on the general availability of credit will be less than the impact on the availability of bank credit, where disappointed bank borrowers can turn elsewhere for their funds.

(c) Internal–external price relation

The government can influence the internal–external price relation by direct means. This relation reflects domestic prices compared with external prices in terms of the currency of the home country. As pointed out in chapter 12, a change in the rate of exchange between the domestic currency and oversea currencies will directly affect the relation. A devaluation of the exchange rate will reduce the relation and an appreciation will increase it; the former makes exportables and imports dearer in the home country in terms of the home country's currency and the latter makes them cheaper. General changes in the tariff would have similar effects on the prices of imports. The determination both of the exchange rate and of the general level of the tariff is usually in the hands of the government. In Australia, international reserves are held by the Reserve Bank, which can fix the exchange rate, subject to consultation with the International Monetary Fund. Although the Commonwealth Government

309

normally follows the advice of the Tariff Board in setting tariff rates for particular items, it can modify the general level of tariff.

To compare the effects of these two measures, consider the case where each is used to produce a fall in the internal–external price relation. Devaluation of the exchange rate would encourage exports by raising the returns to export producers in the home currency in relation to costs; and it would discourage imports by raising their prices in relation to the prices of competing domestic goods. A general rise in the tariff would operate on the import side only. Consequently the choice between the two measures depends partly on an assessment of the domestic supply of exports (will they expand in response to higher rewards and earn more foreign currency?) and the oversea demand for exports (can the oversea market absorb more of the relevant products without an excessive fall in prices?), and partly on the side-effects of the two measures. The most significant of these are the effects on the distribution of income and on the absolute level of internal prices. These are matters of great complexity, but it may be pointed out that in Australia, devaluation will shift the distribution of income in favour of primary and other export producers, whereas a higher tariff will reduce the real value of their gross incomes. Both the devaluation and a higher tariff will raise the cost-of-living. The price of imports will be raised in both cases; and, in addition, devaluation will cause an increase in the price of exportables, particularly foodstuffs, which have an important influence on living costs. The increase in the cost of living, and in the case of devaluation the change in the distribution of income in favour of exporters, will lead to pressure for higher wages. To the extent this pressure is successful, a part of the initial fall in the internal–external price relation will, after a lag, be negated.

The government has available a third weapon, which, although it does not operate directly on the internal–external price relation, has an effect similar to a fall in that relation. It can impose *quantitative restrictions* on imports. These are quotas of the amounts (or values) of various kinds of goods which may be imported. By limiting imports in this way, an unacceptable deficit in the balance of payments can be reduced. At the same time, the reduction of available supplies on the domestic market will stimulate domestic activity. Since the supply of imported goods will be curtailed, it is likely that their prices will rise, so that, after a lag, a fall in the internal–external price relation may occur. Throughout most of the 1950s, the Commonwealth

Government preferred to use quantitative import controls, rather than alternative measures such as devaluation, or an increase in the tariff, to achieve an acceptable external position.

Finally, the relation may be varied by changes in the level of domestic costs. A reduction in the relation would require, for example, a reduction in money-wage rates and/or profit margins. In the real world these do not readily adjust downwards, although they are flexible upwards. As has been pointed out, neither wage rates nor profits are subject to direct influence by government policy, so that this possibility can be ignored for the purpose of this chapter.[1]

The government has then at least three powerful weapons to change the internal–external price relation. But the first of these, a change in the exchange rate, is one which cannot be used with great frequency, nor can its effects be precisely determined. It is a major move, and has wide consequences for a country's standing in the international economy, for its trading relations and for the internal distribution of income. Moreover, if there is a general expectation that a change in the rate is likely, speculation as to the future value of the currency will occur. As a consequence there may be large movements of funds into or out of the country causing substantial fluctuations in the country's international reserves. It follows that a change in the exchange rate cannot be undertaken lightly.[2] A general change in the tariff does not give rise to these consequences to the same extent, but increases in the general level of the tariff may be difficult to reverse and its consequences on the demand for imports are difficult to predict.

These considerations suggest that the exchange rate and the general level of the tariff do not provide flexible weapons of economic policy. Quantitative import restrictions are a much more flexible weapon and their effects on the volume of imports are reasonably certain. However, they have a number of serious side effects. The original quotas must be determined by arbitrary criteria; for example, they may be set in relation to a base year. The quotas tend to freeze trade in fixed channels; they enable particular importers to make monopoly profits; and they encourage domestic production of substitutes which would have been unprofitable under normal market conditions. Moreover, their operation involves an elaborate administrative structure, some-

---

[1] However, see footnote (1) on p. 307.
[2] The Australian exchange rate has been altered independently of the sterling exchange rate, only in the period 1929–31.

what arbitrary in operation and open to abuse; and they create ill-will in the oversea exporting countries.

These malign side effects become more serious the longer quantitative restrictions are in operation. Consequently governments tend to prefer to use this technique mainly as a short-term measure to meet a temporary emergency.

It follows from the argument of preceding paragraphs that, although it may be straightforward for the government to operate on aggregate spending, control of the internal–external price relation is a complex matter. This complexity is increased by the difficulty of diagnosing any particular balance of payments situation. For example, suppose that a large deficit in the current balance of payments occurs because of a fall in export proceeds. Is it a short-lived aberration, which can be financed by temporarily running down reserves and requiring no change in the internal–external price relation? Is it likely to continue for one or two years, in which case temporary quantitative restrictions on imports may suffice? Or, is it a reflection of a fundamental disequilibrium in the relation between domestic and oversea prices requiring exchange devaluation or higher tariffs? There may be no simple or certain answer.

6. Difficulties of economic policy

This discussion on the difficulty of manipulating the internal–external price relation to achieve a particular result has indicated some of the problems which may be involved in the implementation of government economic policy. Further difficulties are discussed below. These difficulties do not mean that governments cannot do a great deal to achieve their objectives. They can and they do. Nor does it mean that it is impossible to achieve one particular objective. For example, the achievement of full employment in isolation from the other objectives is not a difficult task.[1] What is so difficult is the simultaneous achievement of a number of objectives. It would be

[1] Perhaps the only barrier to the achievement of full employment, if other objectives are ignored, is the need for a sufficient supply of complementary factors of production to employ labour fully in any given economy. Australian secondary industries are dependent on imported materials and equipment. If Australia's balance of payments position was so serious that import restrictions had to be imposed of such severity as to cut these essential supplies, unemployment might result. Even in this case, it should be possible to transfer labour, no doubt after some delay, to activities (for example, construction industries) in which few complementary imports are needed. However, the social value of these activities may be low.

misleading to give the impression that governments can control the economy as if it were a relatively simple mechanism like an internal combustion engine or a nuclear reactor; the factors determining the functioning of mechanical devices are known and can be controlled. Although there is a satisfactory conceptual framework for the analysis of the working of the economy, the precise functional relationships between the variables and the exact values of the significant coefficients are not known.

In section 4 above, it was pointed out that a government which was seeking full employment and external balance would aim to be in situation no. 5, in Table 15.1. If the economy were in any other situation the government would take action in an attempt to bring it to no. 5. Even if this could be achieved simply, the government would face the difficulty that the basic conditions of the economy (planned expenditures, export demands, import prices, and so on) are continually changing. The economy would not remain in the ideal situation for long. Economic policy would have to be continuously adjusted.

In the process of adjustment a series of lags occur. Economic diagnosis must rely on statistics describing the behaviour of the economy. These statistics take time to collect and publish, and they take time to analyse. Once made, the diagnosis calls for action. But there may be delays before the decision to act is taken, particularly since political considerations are always involved. The action, once determined, takes time to have effect. Under the most favourable conditions, there may be a lag of, say, six months between the occurrence of the de-stabilizing factor and the impact of the corrective. During this period, the economic situation may have changed materially. It would be fortuitous, if, under these circumstances, policy could achieve all the objectives all the time.

Two other factors are relevant to this discussion of the difficulties of policy making. First, the diagnosis of a particular situation may be difficult because of the uncertainty which attaches to the interpretation of statistical trends. Secondly, the consequences of particular acts of policy are, at best, known only qualitatively; no exact results can be predicted, since the precise quantitative inter-relationships within the economy are unknown.

The difficulties of economic control are enhanced by purely political factors. Most economic actions impose immediate disadvantages for some individuals, even if in the long run the majority

313

of the community will benefit. For example, increased taxation reduces some people's real disposable income; import restrictions cause difficulties to firms requiring imported materials; credit restrictions impair business expansion. Consequently economic policy, particularly when used to restrain the economy, is often politically unpopular. Governments hesitate to take unpopular action. This timidity produces delay; and the action, when taken, may be too late; or initially it may be too slight and harsher action may be required later; or the situation may have changed and the action may then prove perverse.[1]

7. Other economic objectives

The discussion so far has concentrated on the three objectives of full employment, price stability and external balance. There are other important dimensions of economic policy. Two of these—the rate of economic growth and the distribution of income—are discussed in this section.

Economic growth can be measured by the annual rate of growth of the real gross national product. This rate depends on the growth of the work force and on the growth of productivity, that is, production per worker. The former depends on the rate of growth of population, both from natural increase (the excess of births over deaths) and from net migration (the excess of oversea arrivals over departures). The latter depends, among other things, on the growth of technical knowledge, on the improvement of the skill (both technical and managerial) of the work force, and on the growth of the stock of capital equipment. Many governments aim at a high rate of economic growth. This may be partly for defence reasons or for reasons of international prestige. From the point of view of human welfare, a high growth rate relative to population growth enables the citizens of a country to have continually rising standards of living and widening opportunities.

However, at any one point of time, a higher growth rate normally implies a lower current rate of consumption, because a major requirement of growth is a high rate of capital accumulation. In one sense, the decision to accelerate the growth rate involves a redistri-

---

[1] On three occasions in the post-war period, 1952, 1956 and 1960, the Commonwealth Government has taken strong measures to reduce the level of market expenditure. In the two latter cases a plausible argument can be made that the policy actions came too late, and in the event exacerbated a downturn in activity which had not been predicted.

314

bution of the flow of consumer goods in favour of tomorrow's citizens. Whereas the maintenance of the higher growth rate requires a higher ratio of investment to GNP, the increased productive capacity (because of the relatively higher investment) will raise the rate of growth of consumption output; and at some future time the absolute level of consumption output will exceed the level associated with a lower growth rate.

The argument is illustrated by figure 15.1. At time t_1, the potential full employment level of GNP can be divided between capital forma-

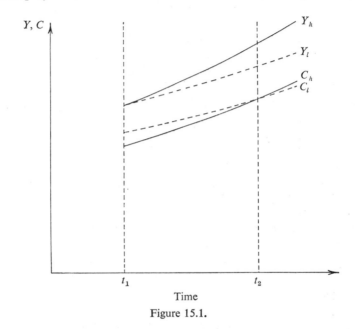

Time

Figure 15.1.

tion and consumption. If a higher ratio of investment to GNP is chosen, the growth of full employment real income, and of consumption output over time will be as indicated by the paths Y_h and C_h. If a lower ratio of investment to GNP is chosen, the corresponding paths will be Y_l and C_l. Beyond time t_2, the absolute levels of the outputs of both consumption and investment goods associated with higher growth rate exceed those associated with the lower growth rate.

Whether the high rate of growth is achieved by increases in the work force or in productivity, a high rate of capital formation is required. If the population is increasing, the capital stock of the economy must be expanded to keep pace. If housing is not increased *pari passu*, the standard of living will fall; if factories are not built and adequate machinery installed, productivity will fall. Similarly, the achievement of a high rate of growth in productivity per worker requires more capital equipment, for a higher ratio of capital to labour renders labour more productive. Consequently rapid growth means heavy investment expenditures, both public investment in roads, transport, power, and schools, and private investment in houses, factories, machinery and stocks. This may be illustrated by a simple example. Suppose that the GNP of an economy is initially $10,000 m., and that the stock of capital is equal to four times the annual GNP. If GNP is to grow at 4 per cent per annum, net investment per annum will have to be $1,600 m. initially ($= 4$ per cent $\times$ $10,000 \times 4$), other things being equal. If GNP is to grow at 8 per cent per annum, net investment will have to be $3,200 m. initially.

If a higher rate of growth is an objective, a higher proportion of production will have to be devoted to investment than would otherwise be the case. To the extent that rapid growth is sought, aggregate demand will be high and the risk of excess demand, rising prices, and balance of payments difficulties will be greater. It will only be possible to achieve rapid growth without seriously endangering the objectives of stable prices and external balance if non-investment expenditure is reduced sufficiently to make room for the capital formation required. This implies a high rate of public and/or private saving. It follows that the successful pursuit of the four objectives: full employment, stable prices, external balance and rapid growth requires the government to operate on a fourth major variable, namely, the rate of saving.

Saving can be encouraged in the private and/or the government sectors. There does not seem to be any simple, generally acceptable and effective method by which the ratio of private saving to private disposable income can be raised.[1] Government saving can be achieved by increasing taxation rates with given levels of government expenditure. The incidence of taxation may be designed to discourage consumption expenditure, say, by sales taxes; and to en-

---

[1] Private saving comprises the saving of the personal and company sectors, and private disposable income is personal disposable income plus retained company income. The effect of changes in the rate of interest on private saving is discussed in section 4 (*a*) of chapter 8.

courage private investment, say, by special taxation provisions to encourage the replacement of obsolete capital equipment. This illustrates that government economic policy may need to be concerned with the composition of aggregate demand as well as with its total level (see section 4 of chapter 11).

The fifth aspect of economic policy to be discussed is the distribution of income. In many Western countries there is a consensus of what constitutes a 'fair' distribution of income. In Australia there is fairly general agreement that extremes of poverty and wealth should be avoided; and the community takes measures to prevent the real disposable incomes of individuals from falling below minimum standards. This objective can be referred to as the desire to achieve an 'equitable' distribution of income. The term *equitable* is interpreted differently in different countries; for example, in New Zealand it appears to mean a much more equal distribution of income than it means in the United States. But the fact remains that governments by their taxing, social welfare and expenditure policies (for example, by progressive income tax, cash social service benefits, free education, subsidized medical and hospital care) attempt to bring about a distribution of real income which differs from that which would emerge from the free play of market forces. This attempt adds another dimension to fiscal policy (see chapter 11, pp. 227-8); and it may clash to some extent with other objectives. For example, heavy progressive taxation may (but, not necessarily, does) affect incentives to work and to invest and, hence, the rate of economic growth.

There are other possible objectives in addition to the five considered in this chapter; but these five play the major roles in the formation of economic policy in a modern mixed economy. The objectives cannot be considered singly; they are closely interrelated and policies cannot be designed to meet them one by one. Economic policy must be conceived as a whole and the impossibility of achieving every objective simultaneously must be recognized. Nevertheless, given a political weighting of the objectives, economic policies can be designed which, with all their imperfections and the imperfections of those who implement them, will steer the economy towards that compromise set of goals which represents the community's conception of human welfare.

LIST OF SUGGESTED READING

CHAPTER I. INTRODUCTION

'John Maynard Keynes', *Current Affairs Bulletin*, 8 October 1951.

Harris, Seymour S. (ed.). *The New Economics. Keynes' Influence on Theory and Public Policy* (New York: Alfred A. Knopf, 1947).

Harrod, R. F. *The Life of John Maynard Keynes* (London: Macmillan, 1951).

Robinson, E. A. G. 'John Maynard Keynes, 1883–1946', *Economic Journal*, vol. LVII, March 1947.

CHAPTERS 2 AND 3. THE NATIONAL ACCOUNTS AND THE INCOME-CREATION PROCESS; THE PRODUCTION–INCOME–EXPENDITURE CIRCUIT AND NATIONAL ACCOUNTING IDENTITIES

Downing, R. I. *National Income and Social Accounts. An Australian Study* (Melbourne: Melbourne University Press, 8th ed., 1964).

Karmel, P. H. *Applied Statistics for Economists* (London: Sir Isaac Pitman, 2nd ed., 1963), chapters XI–XIII.

Report of the Committee of Economic Enquiry, volume II (Commonwealth of Australia, May 1965), Appendices A, D and E.

CHAPTER 4. THE DETERMINATION OF THE EQUILIBRIUM LEVEL OF REAL INCOME

Day, A. C. L. *Outline of Monetary Economics* (Oxford: Oxford University Press, 1957), chapter 5.

Keynes, J. M. *The General Theory of Employment, Interest and Money* (London: Macmillan, 1936).

Lipsey, R. G. *An Introduction to Positive Economics* (London: Weidenfeld and Nicolson, 1963), chapters 30, 31.

Schultze, Charles L. *National Income Analysis* (Foundations of Modern Economics Series; New Jersey: Prentice Hall, 1964), chapter 3.

CHAPTER 5. THE CONCEPT OF FULL EMPLOYMENT

Hancock, K. J. 'Unemployment in Australia', *Australian Quarterly*, vol. XXXIII, September 1961.

Hancock, K. J. 'Unemployment in Australia', University of Adelaide 8th Summer School of Business Administration, 1963.

Solow, Robert M. (Wicksell Lectures, 1964). *The Nature and Sources of Unemployment in the United States* (Almquist and Wiksell, 1964).

CHAPTERS 6 AND 7. MONEY IN THE ECONOMIC PROCESS; THE BANKING SYSTEM AND THE QUANTITY OF MONEY

Arndt, H. W. and Harris, C. P. *The Australian Trading Banks* (Melbourne: F. W. Cheshire Pty Ltd., 3rd ed. 1965).

Coombs, H. C. *The Development of Monetary Policy in Australia* (E. S. and A. Research Lecture, 1954) (University of Queensland Press, 1955).

Day, A. C. L. *Outline of Monetary Economics*, chapters 1 ,2, 4, 9–11.

LIST OF SUGGESTED READING

Davis, R. W. and Wallace, R. H. 'Lessons of the 1960 Bank Credit "Squeeze"', *Australian Economic Papers*, vol. II, June 1963.

Hirst, R. R. and Wallace, R. H. (eds.). *Studies in the Australian Capital Market* (Melbourne: F. W. Cheshire Pty Ltd., 1964).

Wallace, R. H. and Karmel, P. H. 'Credit-creation in a Multi-Bank System', *Australian Economic Papers*, vol. I, September 1962.

CHAPTER 8. THE CONSUMPTION FUNCTION

Ackley, Gardner. *Macroeconomic Theory* (New York: Macmillan, 1961), chapters X–XII.

Cameron, Burgess. 'Hire Purchase and the Stability of Consumption', *Economic Record*, vol. XXXVII, December 1961.

Matthews, R. C. O. *The Trade Cycle* (Cambridge: Cambridge University Press, 1959), chapter VII.

Schultze, Charles L. *National Income Analysis*, chapter 3.

CHAPTER 9. THE DETERMINANTS OF INVESTMENT EXPENDITURE

Day, A. C. L. *Outline of Monetary Economics*, chapter 23.

Matthews, R. C. O. *The Trade Cycle*, chapters II–V.

Schultze, Charles L. *National Income Analysis*, chapter 4.

Walker, Franklin V. *Growth, Employment and the Price Level* (New Jersey: Prentice-Hall, 1964), chapters 10, 11.

Wells, Paul. 'Output and the Demand for Capital in the Short Run', *Southern Economic Journal*, vol. XXXII, October 1965.

CHAPTER 10. THE EFFECT OF CHANGES IN EXPENDITURE PLANS: THE MULTIPLIER CONCEPT

Kahn, R. F. 'The Relation of Home Investment to Unemployment', *Economic Journal*, vol. XLI, June 1931.

Karmel, P. H. 'Giblin and the Multiplier'. In *Giblin—The Scholar and The Man* (Melbourne: F. W. Cheshire Pty Ltd., 1960).

Metzler, Lloyd. 'The Nature and Stability of Inventory Cycles', *Review of Economic Statistics*, vol. XXIII, August 1941.

CHAPTER 11. THE GOVERNMENT SECTOR AND THE DETERMINATION OF REAL INCOME

Eckstein, Otto. *Public Finance* (Foundations of Modern Economics Series; New Jersey: Prentice-Hall, 1964), chapter 7.

Kalecki, M. 'Three Ways to Full Employment', *and*

Schumacher, E. F. 'Public Finance—Its Relation to Full Employment'. In Oxford University Institute of Statistics, *The Economics of Full Employment. Six Studies in Applied Economics* (Oxford: Basil Blackwell, 1944).

CHAPTER 12. THE OPEN ECONOMY

Day, A. C. L. *Outline of Monetary Economics*, chapters 28–31.

Commonwealth Treasury. *The Australian Balance of Payments* (Canberra: Commonwealth Government Printer, February 1966).

LIST OF SUGGESTED READING

CHAPTER 13. THE INTERACTION BETWEEN PLANNED
EXPENDITURES AND FINANCIAL FACTORS

Day, A. C. L. *Outline of Monetary Economics*, chapter 7.

Hansen, Alvin H. *Monetary Theory and Fiscal Policy* (New York: McGraw-Hill, 1949), chapters 4, 5.

CHAPTER 14. INFLATION

Day, A. C. L. *Outline of Monetary Economics*, chapters 19–22.

Farrell, M. J. *Fuller Employment?* (Hobart Paper No. 34; Institute of Economic Affairs, 1965).

Lipsey, R. G. *An Introduction to Positive Economics*, chapter 33.

Lipsey, R. G. 'Is Inflation Explosive?', *The Banker*, October 1961.

Reddaway, W. B. 'Rising Prices for Ever?', *Lloyds Bank Review*, July 1966.

CHAPTER 15. ECONOMIC POLICY

Karmel, P. H. *Economic Policy in Australia—Ends and Means* (G. L. Wood Memorial Lecture) (Melbourne: Melbourne University Press, 1954).

Karmel, P. H. 'A Wages Policy for Australia.' In H. W. Arndt and W. M. Cordon (eds.), *The Australian Economy. A Volume of Readings* (Melbourne: F. W. Cheshire Pty Ltd., 1963).

Lipsey, R. G. *An Introduction to Positive Economics*, chapters 38–41.

Perkins, J. O. N, *Anti-Cyclical Policy in Australia, 1960–1964* (Melbourne: Melbourne University Press, 1965).

Russell, E. A. 'Wages Policy in Australia', *Australian Economic Papers*, vol. IV, June–December 1965.

Swan, T. W. 'Economic Control in a Dependent Economy', *Economic Record*, vol. XXXVI, March 1960.

(Annual) Reserve Bank of Australia, *Report and Financial Statements*.

(Annual) *The Australian Economy* (Commonwealth of Australia).

Statistical Sources:

(Monthly) Reserve Bank of Australia, *Statistical Bulletin*.

(Monthly) *Monthly Review of Business Statistics* (Canberra: Commonwealth Bureau of Census and Statistics).

(Quarterly) *Quarterly Estimates of National Income and Expenditure* (Canberra: Commonwealth Bureau of Census and Statistics).

(Annual) *Australian National Accounts* (Canberra: Commonwealth Bureau of Census and Statistics).

INDEX

actual and planned investment expenditure, 45–6
aggregate consumption function, 51, 112, 120–39
(*see also* consumption function)
aggregate demand and the price level, 268–77
aggregate saving function, 56–7
(*see also* saving function)
aggregate supply and aggregate demand, 42, 47, 199, 225–6, 241–2
Arbitration Commission, 284–6, 306–7
Australian National Accounts, 7, 15 n. 2, 16 n. 1, 18, 23, 29 n., 31, 32, 40, 46 n., 128–9, 196, 198, 200 n. 2
autonomous and induced expenditures
defined, 50
consumption expenditure, 112–13
availability of finance, 79, 108–11, 279
and economic policy, 309
and housing, 140–1
interaction with the level of activity, 259–64
and investment decisions, 155–61
average propensity to consume, 115

balanced budget
inhibiting effect upon fiscal policy, 227–9
multiplier for, 204–6
balance of payments
of Australia, 235
identities, 232–7
balance of trade, 232–7
and changes in income, 245–52
and economic policy, 303–6
and inflation, 300
and internal-external price relation, 301
balance on current account, 32, 232–5

banks, *see* Reserve Bank of Australia, savings banks, trading banks
budget surplus, 32–3
built-in-stabilizers, 214–17

capital
components of, 140
desired stock, 148
real and financial, 12
social, 18
stock of, 29, 161, 293, 314–17
capital inflow, *see* foreign investment
capital market, 77–9, 108–9, 260
imperfectly competitive, 79, 151
rationing in, 155, 159–61
central banking techniques, 98–111
(*see also* Reserve Bank of Australia)
circular flow of production–income–expenditure, 24–33
Commonwealth Employment Service, 65
company income
retained, 155–6
undistributed, 17
company saving
nature of, 28
and excess cash reserves, 265
and investment, 155–8
and the multiplier, 185–92
company taxation, 209
composition fallacy, 185
consumer borrowing, and expenditure, 126–31, 291
consumer expenditure
and consumer borrowing, 126–31
of farmers, 123, 137, 251
hire purchase and, 128–31, 291 n.
induced increments of, 166–8
and investment, 43
planned, 51

and price increases, 289–92
consumer goods
durable and non-durable, 43
purchases of durables, 126–31, 291
(*see also* consumer expenditure)
consumption function
defined, 51–2
and age composition, 123–4
aggregate, 51, 112, 120–39
autonomous shifts and the multiplier, 182–5
break-even point, 115–20
and consumer borrowing, 126–31
and consumption–national income relationship, 201
and contractual saving, 134–5
and income distribution, 120–3, 256–7
individual, 113–17
and interdependence of expenditures, 131–4
non-linear, 171
and normal income, 136–8
and price level, 114, 136–8
and rate of interest, 125
and taxation, 201–3
and wealth, 125
consumption–national income relationship defined, 201

deflationary gap
and deficient demand, 69
and multiplier, 193–4
depreciation
defined, 12, 16
allowances and investment, 28–9
allowances and multiplier, 185–9, 191–2
allowances and taxation, 150 n.
and company saving, 28
and gross and net investment, 28–9

321